Praise for *When Rambo Meets the Red Cross*

"A superb examination of the critically important relationship between civil and military organizations in irregular warfare by an impressive practitioner of and scholar on this subject. Stanislava Mladenova provides a masterful description of how those in uniform, especially civil affairs elements and other special operations forces, interact with their counterparts in civilian organizations, those in governmental and nongovernmental organizations focused on various aspects of nation building at local levels. Importantly, she also lays out how these elements can work together more effectively and achieve synergistic effects in the conduct of their important missions. A very important book on a very important subject."

—**General David Petraeus,** US Army (Ret.), former commander of the Surge in Iraq, US Central Command, and Coalition Forces in Afghanistan; former director of the CIA; coauthor of the *New York Times* bestseller *Conflict: The Evolution of Warfare from 1945 to Ukraine*

"Stanislava P. Mladenova has written an exceptionally insightful and important book on the critical need to integrate the civil-military efforts to stabilize fragile societies. Her valuable experience, thorough research, and creative thinking are clearly evident throughout the book. This is a must-read for military and non-military leaders who will increasingly find themselves faced with these issues in the future."

—**General Anthony C. Zinni,** USMC (Ret.)

"A compelling argument, supported convincingly with data and Dr. Mladenova's extensive personal experience, for a better approach to leveraging the combination of civilian and military efforts in the complex wars that characterize our times. An essential primer for policymakers, donors, and on-the-ground operators from both the military and nongovernmental organizations."

—**General Stanley McChrystal,** US Army (Ret.)

"It's so refreshing to see a book that is focused on the interaction of people, not just of policies, when exploring civil-military interactions in complex environments. What sets this book apart is Mladenova's commitment to exploring the deeper questions. The dichotomy between preserving human dignity and combating terrorism is artfully examined, inviting readers to ponder the true differences between organizations that both believe they are forging a better future for affected populations. This book is a must-read for anyone interested in understanding the intricate dance between military and humanitarian efforts in conflict zones. Thought-provoking in its exploration of fundamental questions, it makes a valuable contribution to the discourse on civil-military relations."

—**Beth Eggleston,** cofounder and director, Humanitarian Advisory Group

"As the current wars in both Ukraine and Gaza demonstrate, close collaboration between military forces and the humanitarian community is vital to accomplishing political objectives. Nowhere is this more pronounced than with Special Operations Forces, who often operate in and among the population. This excellent book is essential to the intellectual discussion that must accompany the decision to employ force in future conflicts. A foundational resource for practitioners and policymakers."

—**General Joseph L. Votel (Ret.),** former US Special Operations Command and Central Command commander

"One of the tragic but real trends of our time is the growing number and severity of conflicts. These conflicts are the epicenter of humanitarian need and a primary cause of ongoing extreme poverty. They are also a place where the international humanitarian community comes into direct contact with international military forces, often coming from the same country. This important book elucidates the nexus in which humanitarian and military forces find themselves and helps practitioners from both sides of the divide consider how they might better cooperate to achieve shared objectives."

—**Raj Kumar,** president, Devex, former humanitarian council chair for the World Economic Forum; member of the Council on Foreign Relations

"As the aid community struggles to promote a nexus approach between humanitarian, peace, and development actors, Mladenova's work superbly traces the quiet, dynamic, and even transformational engagements already underway between these actors in the gray spaces of fragile states. This book is required reading for military and aid practitioners who want to better understand each other's boundaries, mandates, and opportunities for principled and constructive engagement, while holding up the primacy of local voices and communities that too often have been simply instrumentalized in complex mission environments."

—**Jonathan Papoulidis,** vice president, external engagement at Food for the Hungry

"As the fate of fragile states continues to rise in importance across the global security landscape, Mladenova clearly articulates the importance and opportunities for collective understanding and action between military and civilian actors. The world's citizens are frequently in the middle of conflict, and efforts to mitigate civilian harm must be comprehensive and complimentary. This is a must-read for all practitioners, military and civilian, operating in gray spaces."

—Colonel Susan M. Gannon, U.S. Army

"Having worked in many countries around the world, I witnessed firsthand how critical the collaboration—analyzed so expertly here in this volume—between NGOs and the military becomes in addressing complex humanitarian needs, particularly in crisis zones and areas affected by natural disasters. While we need to respect each other's mandates and principles, we are entering a time where increasingly the lines that used to separate us are disappearing. We must find ways to work meaningfully and constructively interact, if not for anything else, at least out of necessity and in the best interests of the communities that we serve."

—Rabih Torbay, president and chief executive officer, Project Hope

"This book is a must-read for anyone who wants to work successfully across civilian and military lines or do truly responsible and meaningful nongovernmental work. To move beyond personality-dependent success, Mladenova's recommendations of institutionalizing a community of practice, measuring relationship durability, and creating practical skills through training and learning are vital. This book should be mandatory reading at the Foreign Service Institute, at the National Defense University, across the US and partner nation war colleges, and in private sector universities for those who want to be effective partners and implementers of programs in fragile states."

—Ambassador Greta C. Holtz (Ret.), president and CEO,
Amideast; director, PRT program in Iraq (2009-10);
senior USG coordinator, Operation Allies Refuge in Doha (2021)

"Dr. Mladenova demonstrates that special operations forces, particularly civil affairs units, as well as humanitarian and development NGO workers, can and do make a vital difference for civilians impacted by violent conflict. They can achieve tactical and strategic effects for stability and peace together in the gray zone. NGOs and military forces should capitalize on this book to develop new practices and doctrine. Scholars and practitioners of peace and security, counterinsurgency, stabilization, and state fragility will benefit from this book."

—Anthony Wanis-St. John, School of International Service,
American University; consultant to the Department of Defense and
the United States Institute of Peace

"Armed conflict zones are areas where local, national, and international complexities are intertwined. In such situations, ensuring the protection of civilians is crucial. Both defense and security actors, as well as nongovernmental organizations, are working towards this goal. Although their approaches may differ, there is a gray area where they can collaborate. Dr. Mladenova's book boldly reflects on the possibility of a partnership between security actors and nongovernmental organizations that play significant roles in conflict zones. Although their roles are perceived as different, they can be complementary and work together towards a common goal."

—**Vianney Bisimwa,** Africa and Middle East director,
Center for Civilians in Conflict

"Dr. Mladenova's extensively documented research makes a significant contribution to addressing contemporary challenges in the field of conflict transformation and peace-building. The potential for overlap between military responses and NGO peace-building interventions poses a risk, where groups targeted for lethal response may be the same ones that NGOs aim to involve in mediation or transform into peace agents. This book underscores the crucial need for communication between civilian and military entities to ensure their collaborative efforts enhance community security in a more cohesive and enduring manner."

—**Laurent Kasindi,** senior program quality specialist,
Search for Common Ground

"This book is essential reading for policymakers, practitioners, and military operators working at the nexus of humanitarian and security crises across the globe today. The author deftly demonstrates that despite cultural differences, NGOs and special forces are well suited to work collaboratively to improve conditions in war-torn countries and fragile regions. With demands for security cooperation and humanitarian assistance increasing as climate acts as a threat multiplier, we all need the type of rigorous analysis Dr. Mladenova provides."

—**Sherri Goodman**, secretary general,
International Military Council on Climate & Security

About the Peace and Security in the 21st Century Series

Until recently, security was defined mostly in geopolitical terms with the assumption that it could only be achieved through at least the threat of military force. Today, however, people from as different backgrounds as planners in the Pentagon and veteran peace activists think in terms of human or global security, where no one is secure unless everyone is secure in all areas of their lives. This means that it is impossible nowadays to separate issues of war and peace, the environment, sustainability, identity, global health, and the like.

The books in the series aim to make sense of this changing world of peace and security by investigating security issues and peace efforts that involve cooperation at several levels. By looking at how security and peace interrelate at various stages of conflict, the series explores new ideas for a fast-changing world and seeks to redefine and rethink what peace and security mean in the first decades of the new century.

Multidisciplinary in approach and authorship, the books cover a variety of topics, focusing on the overarching theme that students, scholars, practitioners, and policymakers have to find new models and theories to account for, diagnose, and respond to the difficulties of a more complex world. Authors are established scholars and practitioners in their fields of expertise.

In addition, it is hoped that the series will contribute to bringing together authors and readers in concrete, applied projects, and thus help create, under the sponsorship of Alliance for Peacebuilding (AfP), a community of practice.

The series is sponsored by the Alliance for Peacebuilding, http://www.allianceforpeacebuilding.org/ and edited by Charles Hauss, Government Liaison.

Oct. 24, 2024
Devex World

To Michael,

with best wishes,

When Rambo Meets the Red Cross

Civil-Military Engagement in Fragile States

Stanislava P. Mladenova

ROWMAN & LITTLEFIELD
Lanham • Boulder • New York • London

Published by Rowman & Littlefield
An imprint of The Rowman & Littlefield Publishing Group, Inc.
4501 Forbes Boulevard, Suite 200, Lanham, Maryland 20706
www.rowman.com

86-90 Paul Street, London EC2A 4NE

British Library Cataloguing in Publication Information Available

Library of Congress Cataloging-in-Publication Data

Names: Mladenova, Stanislava P., 1980– author.
Title: When Rambo meets the Red Cross : civil-military engagement in fragile states / Stanislava P. Mladenova.
Description: Lanham, Maryland : Rowman & Littlefield, [2024] | Series: Peace and security in the 21st century | Includes bibliographical references and index.
Identifiers: LCCN 2024000088 (print) | LCCN 2024000089 (ebook) | ISBN 9781538187715 (cloth : acid-free paper) | ISBN 9781538187722 (paperback : acid-free paper) | ISBN 9781538187739 (ebook)
Subjects: LCSH: Civil-military relations—Developing countries. | Non-governmental organizations—Developing countries. | Political stability—Developing countries. | Legitimacy of governments—Developing countries. | Nation-building—Developing countries. | Developing countries—Politics and government.
Classification: LCC JF195 .M585 2024 (print) | LCC JF195 (ebook) | DDC 322/.5091724—dc23/eng/20240206
LC record available at https://lccn.loc.gov/2024000088
LC ebook record available at https://lccn.loc.gov/2024000089

♾️™ The paper used in this publication meets the minimum requirements of American National Standard for Information Sciences—Permanence of Paper for Printed Library Materials, ANSI/NISO Z39.48-1992.

Contents

List of Figures and Tables

FIGURES

TABLES

Foreword

Few of us who have lived through the realities of war would underestimate its demands and complexities. The term "Small Wars," as many conflicts are often called, is misleading, as they are often terribly destructive to the communities caught in them. Additionally, these are typically wars provoked by economic instability and depredations against human dignity in all its forms. General Krulak famously described them as the "three-block" war—places not at war, but neither at peace. As we in the United States reposition ourselves for the so-called Great Power Competition (GPC) and support our allies in large-scale conflicts in Ukraine, we are also challenged by the new technological frontiers of conflict, fraught with geopolitical implications. But perhaps the most pertinent and substantial challenges we face today are those of the human condition in fragile spaces. It is in these spaces that two-thirds of the world's poor will be living by 2030. It is also in these spaces where populations will increasingly suffer from a range of vulnerabilities including environmental disasters, extreme poverty, inequality, and insecurity. And it is also from these spaces where we will nearly inevitably see the emergence of persistent insurgency and revolutionary warfare.

As American foreign policy balances hard and soft power in fragile states, we continue our search for appropriate forms of civil-military engagement. What I learned as a Commander in Iraq and Afghanistan and as Special Presidential Envoy for the Global Coalition against Islamic State of Iraq and the Levant is that the lines that once separated security forces from developmental and humanitarian actors are usually blurred and are, indeed, fading. Navigating this relationship should be one of our top priorities. In trying to answer how civilian and military entities interact in fragile states, Stanislava Mladenova shows us how the tangle of bureaucratic, organizational, and behavioral constraints, as well as the corporate cultures and mandates of militaries and nongovernmental organizations (NGOs), can obstruct their collective ability to work together and to generate essential synergy. This should not be a breaking point, but an opportunity and a higher calling for both militaries and development actors to find a way forward together.

Stanislava Mladenova has made it her mission to explain how these actors, often laboring through strained relations, *can* put their differences aside. She demonstrates how the most valuable interactions in the fog of war are led not by a search for answers but by the ability to listen and ask questions. Fragile spaces—where the military does not control the terrain and where NGOs and official donors are often the main providers of basic services for populations—are fertile ground for an effective relationship between security and nongovernmental actors to thrive. By examining the functional makeup of these entities, Mladenova unfolds and reveals the advantages of civil-military cooperation in fragile states and identifies the potential benefits for stability and humanitarian effectiveness alike. The result is a sobering analysis of how, despite the messiness of conflict where much can go wrong, there is much that these actors bring to the table and to each other. Mladenova draws upon extensive knowledge of the subject, as well as her own experiences. She was a key member of my staff in Afghanistan and played an important role in assisting NATO ISAF in dealing with these difficult realities. This book should be required reading at staff and war colleges. I'm afraid as Western professional military educational institutions become, increasingly, "blinded by the light" of GPC, we're taking our eyes off the realities of the perennial causes of human strife, and their resulting conflicts that have no direct relationship to GPC but which persist as the most likely sources of instability and unrest in the world today. Stanislava Mladenova has done us all good service with this book.

John R. Allen
General, U.S. Marine Corps (Ret.)
Mount Vernon, Virginia

Preface

As a NATO Political Advisor in Kabul, Afghanistan, between 2012 and 2014, I was responsible for the human rights and humanitarian portfolios for the NATO Senior Civilian Representative Office, where I oversaw UNSCR 1612—the recruitment of child soldiers into the armed forces. There had been reports that the Afghan Local Police (ALP) were recruiting children under eighteen—the legal age for when children are to be recruited into the armed forces. One morning I received a call from my UN counterpart that a certain large International Non-Governmental Organization (INGO) was coming to do a field assessment on the situation, asking me to set up a meeting. I quickly turned to a colleague who was a U.S. Special Operations Forces (SOF) soldier. At that time, SOF were the implementers of Village Stability Operations (VSO), which sought to bring security, governance, and development to key remote districts in Afghanistan. Among its many lethal tasks, SOF had been working to help the ALP set up a human resources system for the force. Compared to other organizations, whose main offices were in Kabul, or whose footprint was smaller, SOF had the most visibility over whether underage recruitment was occurring—a daunting undertaking, as so many Afghans did not know their real age.

One day later, huddled inside a makeshift office built of shipping containers at Camp Eggers, this meeting did not kick off with friendly small talk and handshakes. My INGO colleagues were hesitant, driven by the default setting that their mission was different from the military's, and speaking with them would be a violation of their principles. For SOF, the success of the VSOs and the casualties that Afghans as the partner force were taking were their primary concern, and the strategic guidance of Security Council Resolutions was the lesser of their concerns.

We sat down, and fifteen minutes into the meeting, we were able to break the ice. The SOF representative talked about their efforts to recruit and retain members of the ALP, and the general challenges of professionalizing the force. The INGO spoke about the challenges of adhering to international law in these contexts and highlighted some of the human rights violations that others were tracking. They were also surprised at all of the efforts the military was investing in, and their deep understanding of the terrain, be it physical or human.

One hour later, no magic moment had occurred between these parties. But what did occur was a deliberate and diligent explanation of their mission and the challenges in meeting it, many of which were shared—fitting a governance model to local structures or trying to professionalize an organization in just a few years, when in reality it would take at least a generation. The meeting ended with an exchange of cards, and a promise to keep in touch and let each other know what each was seeing and learning.

After twenty-three months of deployment as an international civilian, and as the convener of this meeting, I continued to struggle with the neat boxes inside of which these organizations separated—one working to preserve human dignity, and the other seeking to hunt down terrorists. Was this the black-and-white reality of war? In their attempt to preserve human dignity and strengthen security, what were the *real* differences between these organizations, *both* of which thought they were establishing a better future for the Afghan people? It was these questions, which fascinated me in my early career, which I have continued to ponder. It is also the self-described "knuckle draggers" and field operators on both sides, who continue to fascinate me. They interact with local communities and have the power to shape the narrative around *how* we as outsiders are perceived by these same communities, more than the Ambassadors or Commanders who issue our orders.

It is these ground operators of field workers and tacticians who are central protagonists in the infinite laboratory of the civil-military relationship at the local level. They inspired me to write this book, which does not focus on a single country or mission. Instead, it draws on expertise gathered from military and NGO personnel who have served in the past or are currently serving in a variety of countries, and from populations in semi-permissive settings—mostly, but not exclusively, where SOF are conducting training missions. I hope that in trying to give some answers, I have mostly convinced my colleagues to ask more questions.

Acknowledgments

I wrote this book after fifteen years as a practitioner. I had spent years analyzing and giving guidance on strategic decisions. Yet, my most fascinating and frustrating encounters happened when I interacted with tacticians. I thank all of them—my colleagues in the military, humanitarian, and development communities—who shared their stories and experiences. Many of them have become my friends and mentors. To the members of the local communities, thank you for inviting me into your lives. This book started as a blank page, and you helped me write its story. All of the identities of those who took the time to share their experiences have been omitted, and what they told me remains anonymous. Notwithstanding their contributions, any errors or interpretations remain my sole responsibility.

This book was borne out of my years of working in the field, and out of my passion for continuously trying to find ways for common ground between civilian and military cultures. It was this fascination with the intellectual and human journey of this topic that brought me to my doctoral research out of which this book was borne. I would like to thank my advisors and reviewers—David Betz, Amanda Chisholm, Anthony Wanis St. John, Kristian Gustafson, and Vinicius de Carvalho. To Raj Desai, Naysan Rafati, Assad Raza, Zack Bazzi, and Susan Gannon—you encouraged me to ask contrarian questions and patiently helped me get this book to its completion, while also helping me connect with the community. I owe all of you a huge debt of gratitude. I am especially grateful to Beth Eggleston and Ambassador Philip Kosnett for giving me helpful feedback to improve the content and clarity of this work.

I dedicate this book to my parents, who taught me to respect those who make it their life's work to teach others. To my colleagues and mentors in this field, who make a difference every day, even if many of us do not always get it right, despite our good intentions. You continue to teach me every day. And finally, to the people of the world, who suffer from conflict and insecurity, and who seek a better future. They have much to teach us all.

List of Acronyms

AFRICOM	United States Africa Command
AFSOC	Air Force Special Operations Command
ALP	Afghan Local Police
ASCOPE	Areas, Structures, Capabilities, Organizations, People, and Events
ATP	Army Techniques Publication
CA	Civil Affairs
CAFE	Civil Affairs Framework of Engagement
CAO	Civil Affairs Operations
CAOS	Civil Affairs Operating System
CARE	Cooperative for Assistance and Relief Everywhere
CENTCOM	United States Central Command
CERP	Commander's Emergency Response Program
CFT	Cross-Functional Team
CIMIC	Civil-Military Cooperation
CMO	Civil-Military Operations
CMOC	Civil-Military Operations Center
CMSE	Civil-Military Support Element
COIN	Counterinsurgency
CT	Counterterrorism
DFID	Department for International Development
DOD	Department of Defense (U.S.)
DOS	Department of State (DoS)
DSCA	Defense Security Cooperation Agency
E	Enlisted (a reference to non-commissioned officer)
ECOWAS	Economic Community of West African States
EU	European Union

EUCOM	United States European Command
FA	Foreign Assistance
FARC	Fuerzas Armadas Revolucionarias de Colombia
FHA	Foreign Humanitarian Assistance
FID	Foreign Internal Defense
FM	Field Manual
GAO	Government Accountability Office
GCC	Geographic Combatant Command
GIZ	Gesellschaft für Internationale Zusammenarbeit
GSMSG	Global Surgical and Medical Support Group
GWOT	Global War on Terror
HA	Humanitarian Assistance
HAC	Humanitarian Affairs Centers
HN	Host Nation
HTS	Human Terrain System
ICAF	Interagency Conflict Assessment Framework
ICRC	International Committee of the Red Cross
IDP	Internally Displaced Persons
IFRC	International Federation of Red Cross
INDO-PACOM	Indo-Pacific Command
INGO	International Non-Governmental Organization
ISAF	International Security Assistance Force
LAF	Lebanese Armed Forces
MAT	Ministerial Advisory Teams
ME	Monitoring and Evaluation
MEDCAP	Medical Civic Action Program
MITAM	Mission Tracking Matrix
MOOTW	Military Operations Other Than War
MSF	Medicines Sans Frontiers
NATO	North Atlantic Treaty Organization
NCO	Non-Commissioned Officer
NGO	Non-Governmental Organization
ODA	Operational Detachment Alpha
OECD	Organization for Economic Co-operation and Development
OHASIS	Overseas Humanitarian Assistance and Shared Information System
OHDACA	Overseas Humanitarian, Disaster, and Civic Aid
OSD	Office of the Secretary of Defense
OSOCC	On-site Operations Coordination Centers
OTI	Office of Transition Initiative
OXFAM	Oxford Committee for Famine Relief

PMESII	Political, Military, Economic, Social, Information, and Infrastructure
PMSC	Private Military Security Company
PO	Psychological Operations
PRT	Provincial Reconstruction Team
QIP	Quick Impact Project
R2P	Responsibility to Protect
SF	Special Forces
SFA	Security Force Assistance
SoA	Spirit of America
SOF	Special Operations Forces
SOIC	Stability Operations Intelligence Centers
SOUTHCOM	United States Southern Command
SWEAT-MSO	Sewage, Water, Electricity, Academics, Trash, Medical, Safety and Other considerations
TCAF	Tactical Conflict Assessment Framework
TSOC	Taskforce Special Operations Command
UNDP	United Nations Development Fund
UNHCR	United Nations High Commission for Refugees
UNICEF	United Nations Children's Fund
UNOCHA	United Nations Office for the Coordination of Humanitarian Affairs
USAID	United States Agency for International Development
USG	United States Government
USMC	United States Marine Corps
VSO	Village Stability Operations

Chapter 1

Introduction

Approximately 1.5 billion people live in fragile states and countries experiencing low-intensity conflict.[1] The Organization for Economic Co-operation and Development (OECD) projects that, by 2030, that number will increase to 2.3 billion, including 60 percent of the world's extreme poor.[2] A variety of factors are increasing cross-regional fragility, including climate change, resource dependence, commodity shocks, communalism, and natural disasters, all of which contribute to economic vulnerability, human rights abuse, and political instability. As a result, this fragile "gray space" is riven by weak governance, vicious cycles of poverty, persistent instability, state fragility, and low-intensity conflict—just short of full-scale war. In these spaces, the roles of development, humanitarian, and U.S. military actors often intersect. In this space, the U.S. military has straddled the line between serving as a robust, conventional armed combative force and fulfilling the role of a non-traditional development and humanitarian actor. In doing so, it crosses paths with multilateral, governmental, and non-governmental actors whose conventional role *is* the provision of humanitarian and development assistance.

Our current understanding of the intersection between security and development stems from three occurrences:

First, in addition to its hard power, the U.S. military often finds itself fulfilling the role of a development and humanitarian actor. With the Global War on Terrorism (GWOT) from 2001 and the ensuing major wars in Iraq and Afghanistan, the U.S. military took part in designing and implementing some of the largest development and humanitarian assistance projects in recent history, in a complex tapestry where development assistance and combat operations intertwine. While the wars are over now, Special Operations Forces (SOF) Civil Affairs (CA) units continue to lead or support the implementation of hundreds of small-scale development and humanitarian

1

projects—building schools and clinics, and providing emergency and disaster relief services in over one-hundred countries in any given year. As a result, the military continues to take on the role of a quasi-development and humanitarian actor. It does so on a global level, even if on a small scale, as part of meeting its security objectives, and across every mandate—peacekeeping, disaster response, complex emergencies, training other militaries, counterterrorism, counternarcotics, and counterinsurgency in operations across every continent. Highly trained and skilled, they can be security providers, intelligence gatherers, medics, combatants, mentors, and teachers of other militaries.

Second, in terms of humanitarian assistance, similarly, traditional development actors such as aid agencies and Non-Governmental Organizations (NGOs) also navigate a wide spectrum of the civilian environment. In their programming, they no longer exclusively address short-term humanitarian needs in crisis settings or develop social and economic systems in peaceful ones. In the past two decades, they have entered fragile spaces once principally restricted to security actors and humanitarian actors with strict short-term mandates. These development organizations have scaled up their presence in places which were once not sufficiently stable for normal development programming to occur. In doing so, they are having to navigate both new fragile settings in which they are operating, as well as interests of their shareholders or funders, alongside the needs of local communities. As the providers of humanitarian and development assistance, donors, including bilateral and multilateral development organizations, international and local NGOs, are increasingly supporting governments or operating in every space that SOF can or already does.

Third, conflict has almost completely lost its linearity. As a result, the tidy sequence of when security actors stabilize an environment, while humanitarian agencies meet immediate needs, so that development actors can follow up with long-term social and institutional programming, has almost completely diminished. In this non-linear context, security, humanitarian, and development actors are overlapping, prolonging, and diversifying their engagements in fragile spaces. Because these spaces are just short of war, the military is not deploying its conventional power in them, and development and humanitarian actors, while becoming less constrained, enter them only under certain conditions. As a result, the nature of the civil and military actors' interaction is also changing.

SIX MISSING PIECES

There are several gaps in our knowledge about civil-military engagement that need to be explored.

First, our knowledge about the military carrying out development and humanitarian activities is derived mostly from the work of military scholars. Where such scholars discuss the military's role as a development actor, it is about conventional forces' engagement in development work, not special operations. Progressive scholars and practitioners, such as Sarkesian, Nagl, Mattis, and H. R. McMaster, recognize the civilian dimensions of the military's engagement in spaces which are ambiguous, and subject to a constant shift between security and insecurity, but again, most of their analysis is through the lens of security.[3] Contrarily, the traditionalist approach to thinking about the military outside of its core business aligns with Huntington's and Gentile's views that the military's main job is to meet security objectives, not replace the work of the non-security actors, such as what we saw in the big wars of the last twenty years. Galula and Kilcullen do a masterful job of providing an understanding of how the civic environment is a primary component in counterinsurgency warfare.[4] At the same time, analysis by development scholars such as Sachs and Moyo is about how development actors can be more effective, not about how their engagement with militaries in fragile settings is to be improved.[5] Collier suggests that there is a role for both military and development actors, as a way to break up a cycle of fragility and poverty.[6] But again, this is mostly through the lens of development.

Second, the red line marking the separation between where development and security actors operate is diminishing, but the scholarly debate has not addressed what happens to the civil-military relationship in this new landscape. Rosa Brooks[7] writes about the disappearing boundaries of war, while Duffield describes a constant shift of stability and instability as a permanent fixture in the international arena.[8] How this applies in practice is clearly reflected in the U.S. strategy to prevent conflict and promote stability, where fragile states are referred to as conflict-affected, with fragility resulting from "a combination of ineffective and unaccountable governance."[9] This materializes in what General Krulak described as the three-block war, where a soldier would be involved in a series of relationships with hostile, neutral, and friendly forces, and where a soldier can be involved in high-intensity combat, low-intensity peacekeeping, and humanitarian assistance.[10] It is in these spaces where soldiers must exercise restraint, where stability operations are often conducted, and where Taw warns that a large footprint military is not appropriate.[11]

Third, our knowledge of how civilian and military actors interact focuses on large and regionally focused operations, and less on the functional analysis of smaller-scale engagements which happen globally, or the interactions of the actors involved. Alex De Waal explores Darfur's humanitarian crisis, giving insight into the misalignment of priorities and expectations between the locals and humanitarians.[12] Mackinley investigates institutional differences in complex emergency contexts from the Balkan conflicts of the 1990s to Afghanistan, arguing that the linkages between coordinating structures change in each new type of conflict.[13] Ankersen examines civil and military interactions in peace operations in Bosnia, Kosovo, and Afghanistan through the prism of the Canadian response.[14] In her analysis of "Strange Bedfellows," Donna Winslow diligently describes the composition of the conventional military and NGO actors, assessing them as complete opposites due to their culture and organizational makeup.[15] Yet, these contributions leave us wondering what the civil-military relationship looks like across a full array of low-intensity conflict spaces and with a smaller footprint. What does the role of interaction between SOF CAs and NGOs look like, and how might this look from a functional standpoint of these organizations' structural inner workings? What drives their success or failure?

Fourth, in the last twenty years SOF's operations which, at their genesis, were designed to work with and among civilians have become increasingly lethal. This has resulted in little attention being given to their ability to deal with non-military actors, namely NGOs. This gap has not gone unrecognized, as in the last twenty years, military scholars have been raising flags about SOF's ability to deploy its soft power, questioning whether its lethality in fragile settings is to its detriment. Simultaneously, since the end of the Cold War and since 9/11, the military's engagements have encompassed a range of operational activities—from "the most benign peacetime military engagement with foreign militaries, to high-end war-fighting."[16] This huge spectrum touches upon all the contexts in which SOF can be or is involved, including complex emergencies, counterinsurgency, counternarcotics, peacekeeping operations, and Foreign Internal Defense (FID) programs. All and any of these mandates cut across the globe with operations in Afghanistan, Iraq, Lebanon, Colombia, the Philippines, Kenya, Somalia, or Kosovo, to mention a few.

Fifth, we have limited knowledge of how the civil-military relationship is changing for non-security development actors in the new context of fragile spaces, which until just a generation ago was off-limits to them. The trigger for this has been the New Deal for Engagement in fragile states,[17] allowing international organizations and NGOs to move away from the once-limited project implementation to "weak states." As a result, development actors are in many of the same spaces that military actors are. I hope to shed light on what scholars have recognized to be a real cost for NGOs operating in insecure areas, leading development actors to consider "new thinking and revamped approaches to civil-military relations."[18]

Sixth, we have limited insight as to how populations perceive the military and NGOs are engaging them, or how effective they appear to be. Both of these actors have it as their mission to decrease state fragility, albeit by different means. The actions, behaviors, and interactions of security and non-security actors are constantly—directly or indirectly—impacting populations. Montgomery McFate provides a thoughtful anthropological lens to help the military's interaction with populations, but again that is mostly focused on security.[19] Hilhorst, Christoplos, and Van der Haar examine how populations can shape development programming from within local communities, not how this is done when civil and military engagement are at play.[20] Anderson, Brown, and Jean consult over 6,000 people worldwide, seeking to find out their views about development and humanitarian assistance done by development actors, not the military.[21] Furthermore, our knowledge about fragile spaces is mostly written by Western thinkers, with little representation of the voices of scholars, or populations from non-Western contexts.

THE AIM OF THIS BOOK

To navigate the gray space, both civic and military actors are forced to adapt to the changing landscape of conflict and fragility. In this space, the military cannot solely rely on traditional hard power. Meanwhile, NGOs must navigate fragile spaces which are neither experiencing large-scale humanitarian crises, nor are fully and immediately ready for, or responsive to, traditional development programming.

The central question, then, is: Can SOF and NGOs be effective partners in low-intensity conflict?

In answering this, a series of more specific questions is posed: (i) Can U.S. SOF be development and humanitarian actors in tandem with their role as hard power and reconnaissance players? (ii) Can NGOs simultaneously meet the needs of local communities while also staying accountable to those who fund them? (iii) Considering the different demands of their leaderships, how do the interactions between small SOF and NGO teams contrast against the modi operandi of the larger organizations to which they belong? (iv) What are the functional, structural, and behavioral constraints and opportunities for these actors' interactions? (v) Do populations feel that NGOs and the military listen to their concerns? And, (vi) When the military and NGOs engage with populations, how do either of these actors incorporate community needs into their missions?

To help answer these questions, I draw on operations or missions that are currently occurring or have occurred under the umbrella of the GWOT in the past two decades. I do not focus on a single country or mission. Instead, I examine the functional behavior of these actors through a collection of engagements across a mix of missions, and with partners in Afghanistan, Burkina Faso, Tajikistan, Latvia, Lebanon, Kenya, Kosovo, Mali, Jordan, Colombia, Ukraine,[22] the Philippines, Bosnia, Somalia, Syria, Chad, and Niger, to mention a few. Some but not all of these countries are currently

Chapter 1

suffering from active insurgencies or even humanitarian crises. Some of these places are suffering from prolonged and higher intensity conflict, while others are experiencing lower intensity conflicts and are constantly shifting between stability and instability. What they all have in common is that they all are recipients of some form of U.S. security equipment, training, capacity building, development, or humanitarian assistance. This assistance organically draws on the pillars of security, development, and humanitarian aid. While I touch upon the dynamics of development, diplomacy, and defense, also known as the 3Ds, the focus of this analysis is not the United States Government (USG) interagency. Rather, I seek to shed light on SOF CA's interaction with the civilian environment outside the walls of the U.S. Embassy. Conversely, I examine how these interactions are perceived by civilian actors, namely NGOs, INGOs, and local populations.

In solving the puzzle of whether SOF and NGOs can be effective partners, I examine current civil-military relationships that occur across the five Geographic Combatant Commands (GCCs). To do this, I speak with more than seventy military and local and international NGO personnel who have recently served in the past or are currently serving in a variety of countries. I draw on firsthand interviews and other scholars' contributions on the perceptions of populations in semi-permissive settings—mostly, but not exclusively where SOF are conducting training missions. I also seek to include the perspectives of the knowledge from disciplines that come to life in the field—military, development, and humanitarianism. When speaking about the actors, spaces, and actions of the civil-military relationship, I use several key terms.

Gray space. Be it irregular warfare, low-intensity conflict, insurgency, or stability operations, this type of intervention has had many names. In this space, the military may simultaneously support with logistics, engage with civic actors, and conduct humanitarian activities, while also serving as a lethal asset. The gray space is not associated with large-scale reconstruction and rebuilding efforts, following conventional war, in which large sums of money are invested. There may not always be humanitarian crises, a Responsibility to Protect (R2P) mandate to protect large masses of civilians from harm, or a peacekeeping operation. It can occur where no war was declared or even fully comes to fruition. Instead, the gray space contains a series of sources of insecurity. Those might be climate change, resource scarcity, and communal conflicts, all factors which are continuing to increase the number of people living in fragile or conflict-affected countries. Consequently, the gray space borrows elements from various doctrines, and yet it belongs solely to none. It is a living organism of movement between military, civilian, political, and economic factors. As Robert Muggah states, "the phenomenon of fragility is more easily described than defined."[23] The analysis draws a clear distinction between the two types of military engagements—high-intensity conflict, where the military is fully in charge and owns the physical terrain,[24] and low-intensity conflict, where the military is not in control, but is present.

The military. SOF, and specifically SOF CA units are one of the main protagonists of this analysis. Yet, my use of the term is a loose one and interchangeable at times. When I refer to the *military*, what I mean is the U.S. military institution as a whole—both special and conventional forces, active duty, and reservist military forces. A subset of this term refers to the wide usage of the specific community with whom I engage: SOF CA. When referring to SOF, this analysis refers to SOF teams composed of Green Berets, CA units, and Psychological Operations (PO)[25] units—all entities operating in publicly known overt engagements and missions, not in covert operations. As such, this analysis mostly refers to them as SOF, SOF CA, SOF SF, or simply CA or SF. These are simply SOF. The focus of this study is predominantly on SOF CA units, which work among populations as part of SOF overt missions, which are available in the public information domain, or missions that were described by interviewees as having been carried out in public spaces, and are known by actors outside of the military.

Non-governmental organizations. The definition of an NGO in this analysis is a not-for-profit civil society entity that is directly or indirectly engaged in the provision of a public good or service in a community. This can include but not be limited to advocacy or program implementation. NGOs in the context of the functional examination I provide may or may not be implementing partners of donor agencies. They may have direct or indirect interaction and engagement with any branch of the U.S. military or host nation military. NGOs can be international and be based in Western capitals, or they may be local branches under the auspices of a larger international umbrella, or grassroots organizations. To demonstrate the vast sector that comprises the humanitarian and development communities, this analysis takes a holistic approach to these entities *within* the interworking of their structures. It draws on all of these categories of organizations, predominantly focusing on their funding and organizational makeup, with less differentiation of them as local or international.[26]

I argue that while these actors may have historically played disparate roles, in fragile and conflict-affected settings these actors' relationship changes, and they can be effective partners. This argument contrasts with the conventionally understood civil-military dynamic, whereby civil and military actors are distinctly different and uphold differing objectives and principles. This is because both actors seek to address sources of insecurity, and when examined more closely they do it in similar ways and by using similar tools, despite their different institutional objectives. Their structures, processes, cultures, and organizational habits are not completely different. As ground operators, they have much more in common than first meets the eye. This is because, in the gray space, these actors' structural differences tend to dissolve as they adapt their organizations' practices, processes, and structures in ways that are increasingly similar to one another. The gray space can also, at times, encourage these entities to share information, as well as consult on project design, implementation, and post-project monitoring and evaluation. Inevitably, these forces lead to mimetic behaviors, blurring traditional distinctions between the military and civilian actors in fragile environments.

My governing hypothesis, therefore, is: SOF CA and NGOs are more likely to form a productive and effective civil-military relationship and converge if conditions in the gray space, such as permissiveness of the physical terrain and needs of local communities, can overcome broader organizational stasis. This is facilitated by individual personalities who are responsible for civil and military engagements and who can innovate, improvise, and adapt to the constantly shifting conditions of the gray space. As each of these sets of actors mobilizes itself in these areas, they increasingly come across one another. As they interact—by design or by accident—these actors naturally converge or diverge due to a series of factors that push them toward one another or pull them further apart.

TOGETHER BUT APART

This analysis argues that in navigating the fragile gray space the relationship between civil and military actors transcends the peace and conflict landscape, as well as the role of the military and NGOs as hard and soft power actors. Instead, civil-military engagement in fragile spaces is transformed, as shown in figure 1.1. Civil and military actors are pressured to adapt, becoming more similar. This occurs through institutional "isomorphism" where these entities adapt each other's structures and behaviors.[27] These influencers come in the form of both push factors from the outside, such as the civic environment, and pull factors by the needs which both of these entities experience as ground operators.

On Institutional Convergence

Push factors are external to the interworkings of civil and military actors as organizations. They are naturally occurring and reactive dynamics of the reality on the ground. Push factors could be financial incentives imposed by higher command for the military or by donors for NGOs. They could also be public perceptions by external actors, which may sway in a more positive direction when these institutions are seen as cooperating, for example, when populations perceive a greater sense of security when the military is present and seeks to work with NGOs, or when the military's presence is viewed as heightening security concerns.

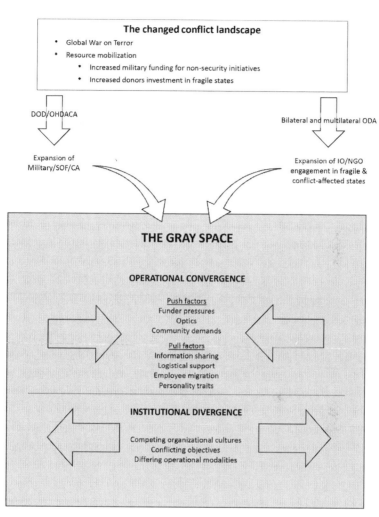

Figure 1.1 Military-NGO Interaction in the Gray Space. *Source*: Author.

Three push factors are responsible for potential increased cooperation in gray spaces. First, both NGOs and the military can be pressured by funding constraints to engage in joint programming, though often in ad hoc ways. This can take different forms, as SOF have at their disposal small amounts of money, contrary to what was the case with the big conflicts in Iraq and Afghanistan with the Commander's Emergency Response Program (CERP). Nevertheless, funding, particularly from public sources, that aims to address some of the human and socioeconomic sources of fragility often requires humanitarian and security actors to coordinate roles. Second, the perception of common purpose, implementation, and support for development and humanitarian activities in communities affected by conflict is valuable to both military and civilian organizations, hence creating additional converging pressures. Third, as both military and civilian entities each seek to respond to the population's basic needs and demands, it is often the case that local communities demand or require coordination, explicitly or implicitly.

By contrast, *pull factors* refer to those forces that encourage NGOs and the military to seek each other out for specific coordinating roles, mostly limited to their internal adaptation to the gray space. These include but are not limited to: NGOs providing information to military units on an as-needed basis, military units providing security or logistical support to NGO staff, and in some cases, NGOs actively recruiting staff with military experience.

Regarding pull factors: (1) When it comes to information sharing, both civil and military actors are pulled naturally toward one another by the need for information in order to carry out their programming. For the military, information is necessary in order to better understand, and as a result, navigate the civic environment through the prism of security. For NGOs, information around security is of the essence for their ability to safely carry out their work. (2) The military can provide logistical support, which is not readily available to NGOs. As a result, these actors pull closer together and form an almost interdependent relationship. (3) The skills of military members are highly useful for NGOs who navigate conflict settings. As a result, retired military are frequently hired by NGOs to carry out work in more dangerous settings. (4) Personalities—on both the military and NGO sides, it is the people, who ultimately drive the relationship of these institutions.

On Institutional Divergence

Despite converging, civil and military entities are still pushed apart due to a series of ground realities that they must navigate. First, their cultures are different, even if in some instances SOF and NGOs can be similar in their small size, agility, and adaptability. Second, the military and NGOs have conflicting objectives, even if they are both ultimately seeking to stabilize an area through security or resilience of institutions. Third, they diverge in their deployment cycles—changing in and out of the country, but also through their institutional makeup—Department of Defense (DOD) is large, heavily and publicly funded, and NGOs are disparate and funded with a mix of public and private money.

WHAT'S TO COME

My aim is to tackle less the policy of *why* the military gets involved outside its core business, or *what* has led NGOs to expand in size, scope, and complexity. My intent is to demonstrate *how* the military and NGOs deploy their available toolkits when engaging with one another and with populations. In doing so, I hope to show junior operators the importance of their multidimensional mindset, the role of NGOs for the people inside the spaces where they are operating, and the complex world of development and humanitarian assistance. I also hope to give them a tool to help them embody the Strategic Corporal, which General Krulak once described. For NGOs, I hope to give them a glimpse into the military and convince them of the complex role that military operators are constantly having to navigate. To do this, I organize this analysis in six chapters:

Chapter 2: The Non-Humanitarians

Can SOF be humanitarians? Considered the military's warrior diplomats, SOF's work in the last twenty years has become increasingly focused on highly lethal missions, distancing itself from its soft power. While humanitarian assistance is one of SOF's core tasks, and they have superior skills to connect with local populations, understand the civilian environment, and work with civic actors, SOF are unable to be humanitarians, despite having everything at their disposal to be so. The small-scale projects they implement serve security cooperation objectives, not human needs. Where human needs are met, this is a by-product of security engagements, not deliberate programming. Such benefits cause a natural convergence between SOF and civic actors in the low-intensity conflict space, despite their focus on security first. However, SOF's self-focused approach as an organization causes it to simultaneously diverge away from the same civic actors.

Chapter 3: The Entrepreneurs

Are NGOs altruistic or entrepreneurial in meeting the needs of their beneficiaries? NGOs have fundamentally changed the development and humanitarian landscapes, as they have increased in size, complexity, and areas of operation. NGOs are not simply short-term program implementers in humanitarian crises or medium-term development actors in peaceful contexts. Instead, they navigate this spectrum. As a result, they have diversified in how they fund their work through both public and private money, making them accountable to different entities and in different ways. NGOs operating in conflict zones have become more adept at project management under conditions of instability and threats of violence. Evidence suggests that some NGOs are savvy entrepreneurs, who are increasingly mimicking the structural and behavioral attributes of military actors. There also seems to be an organically formed and tight-knit network of NGO professionals, who are former military, and who enrich, strengthen, and ultimately lead SOF and NGOs to converge in the spaces where they operate.

Chapter 4: Brothers from Another Mother

Are SOF and NGOs organizationally compatible but institutionally restrained? Contrary to what is generally understood as DOD being overfunded, but official and private foreign assistance being small by comparison, at the project level, DOD spending on small-scale projects in the gray space is comparable and sometimes dwarfed by its NGO counterparts. Contrary to the hierarchical versus decentralized dichotomy, I find that these organizations—small SOF CA teams and small NGO footprints on the ground—are similar in terms of how they budget, organize, and sometimes deploy. I seek to demonstrate this by examining these organizations for their diversity, autonomy, generalist versus specialist expertise, transparency, organizational independence, and scale. While they are still governed by different sets of rules, SOF CA and NGO teams are transforming and converging in attributes, function, routine, and personnel.

Chapter 5: Ground Operators: Between a Rock and a Soft Place

How do NGOs' and SOF's organizational and personal attributes drive the relationship between civil and military actors? Categorized as what I call the loyalists, the bridge-builders, and the converted, I demonstrate that each group possesses a set of specific behavioral traits. Unlike the case in disaster response and complex emergency contexts, where coordination occurs under temporary, heavily proscribed coordination structures, coordination and consultation in the gray space tend to be extemporaneous, primarily driven by the personalities of individuals in the three groups, and to a large degree independent of institutional mandate. Despite their diverging incentives, different mandates, values, or objectives, NGOs and SOF reach a cooperative equilibrium in the ground operating space where these individual traits are able to overcome structural constraints.

Chapter 6: The Center of Gravity

How are SOF and NGOs perceived by intended beneficiaries in the gray space? I explore the generally accepted divergence in these actors' relationship—how NGOs are more connected to and able to understand the needs of local communities than the military whose primary job is around security. Yet, despite SOF's ability to be soft power actors, in the eyes of the local populace, SOF's image is *softened* when they appear to be working alongside or coordinating with NGOs. Second, SOF's coordination with NGOs as a way to understand the local environment and deconflict its projects, leads it to produce more positive development and humanitarian outcomes for local communities. Third, what forms locals' perceptions is the utility of the assistance provided by outside actors, rather than *who*—NGOs or the military—is providing it. Fourth, when it comes to both of these actors, it is the interpersonal skills, respect for the local culture, listening to local grievances, and understanding of the local context which drive the NGO and SOF actors to be perceived positively or negatively inside of local communities.

CONCLUSION

I conclude by demonstrating that SOF and NGOs *can* be effective partners, and the newfound traits of the space which they are navigating provide impetus and momentum for them to do so. The overall supposition that the military is hard power, and NGOs are soft power, is false. The military very much has an increasing role and purpose outside its core business, and NGOs have much to teach it in the process. This analysis shows that the military, just like NGOs, has everything at its disposal to "soften up." What prevents them from doing so is the lack of other organizational factors more common among development actors. On their end, NGOs, too, have everything at their disposal to "harden up," and depending on conditions on the ground, choose to do so. With the softening of the military's hard power and the hybridization of the NGOs' soft power in the less threatening gray space, there is ample opportunity to synergize, coordinate, inform, and consult.

NOTES

1. Gisselquist, "Aid and Institution-Building," 6–21.
2. Organization for Economic Co-operation and Development, *States of Fragility, 2018*, 6.
3. Huntington, "New Contingencies," 38–43; Gentile, "A (Slightly) Better War," 57–64; Gentile, "The U.S. Army Must Remain Prepared for Battle."
4. Galula, *Counterinsurgency Warfare*; Kilcullen, *The Accidental Guerilla*.
5. Sachs, *The End of Poverty*; Moyo, *Dead Aid*.
6. Collier, *The Bottom Billion*.
7. Brooks, *How Everything Became War*.
8. Duffield, *Global Governance and the New Wars*.
9. U.S. Department of State, *United States Strategy to Prevent Conflict and Promote Stability*.
10. Krulak, "The Strategic Corporal."
11. Taw, "Stability and Support Operations," 387–407.
12. De Waal, *Famine That Kills*.

13. John Mackinlay, "Co-operating in the Conflict Zone," NATO, 2002.

14. Ankersen, *The Politics of Civil-Military Cooperation*.

15. Winslow, "Strange Bedfellows," 35–55.

16. West, Canfor-Dumas, Bell, and Combs, "Understand to Prevent," 129.

17. Nussbaum, Zorbas, and Koros, "A New Deal for Engagement in Fragile States," 559–87.

18. Brainard, Chollet, and LaFleur, "Chapter 1—The Tangled Web," 23.

19. McFate, "Anthropology and Counterinsurgency."

20. Hilhorst, Christoplos, Van, and Haar, "Reconstruction 'From Below'," 1107–24.

21. Anderson, Brown, and Jean. *Time to Listen,* 91.

22. The writing of this analysis is prior to the February 24, 2022 invasion of Ukraine by Russia—an event that is being described as a large-scale, conventional conflict.

23. Muggah, "Chapter Two: Stabilising Fragile States," 34.

24. In this definition, terrain could refer to any physical element, including ground, air, and water.

25. As enablers for SOF, PO influences the dissemination of information. Many operations do not fall neatly into psychological operations or civil affairs.

26. Another differentiation is how NGOs are public and privately funded. This is discussed at length in Chapter 3.

27. DiMaggio and Powell, "The Iron Cage Revisited," 147–60.

Chapter 2

The Non-Humanitarians

CAN SOF BE HUMANITARIANS?

> You get your D-Day by taking your men into battle, not by building a well.[1]

This chapter argues that Foreign Internal Defense (FID), as a training mission, under whose auspices Special Operations Forces (SOF) conduct small-scale humanitarian and development missions, is poorly suited to achieve favorable humanitarian or developmental outcomes, even if it has everything at its disposal to achieve them. Later chapters explore how even despite SOF not positioning themselves as humanitarian and development actors, the projects they deploy have some unintended but positive consequences for the population. Ultimately, this chapter argues that this is because FID is fundamentally subordinate to and constrained by security-oriented objectives. Consequently, the progress of FID operations inevitably becomes hindered by excessive complexity, some contradictory incentives, conflicting lines of accountability, and an inability to receive input from affected communities. It is these factors that, as discussed in later chapters, cause the institutional divergence between SOF and civic actors.

SOF are not humanitarians, and they do not possess the large-scale logistical capabilities or footprint of conventional forces. While humanitarianism and civic engagement are one of SOF's twelve core tasks, SOF's projects are rarely initiated based on the needs of the population but rather on the demand for meeting military objectives. The point at which the needs are met is a by-product of these engagements, not a primary goal of the mission. For these reasons, evidence supports that the claimed humanitarian and development nature and value of the projects deployed by SOF CA are frequent targets of NGO and donor criticism. Although CA units use a variety of tools to assess the environment in which they operate by consulting between and with these entities, SOF's projects are not designed with development and humanitarian needs in mind. Currently, no scientific measuring exists of SOF's humanitarian and development efforts, neither in planning nor follow-up. In the gray space, CA as part of SOF conducts civil reconnaissance by forming relationships with civic actors—such as village and municipal representatives, local public officials, and civil society. Nevertheless, these relationships are not established for the social and economic benefits they would serve in development project management, such as coordinating community-driven development efforts, procurement, implementation, and monitoring of services. Instead, they are established primarily for the purpose of securing military advantages.

GREEN WARRIORS

Historically, SOF's primary job has been as a trainer and enabler of local forces. Formed in 1952 from psychological warfare forces and self-described as "adaptive problem solvers," SOF is the premier partnership force responsible for U.S. efforts in training other militaries. They operate in unconventional warfare, FID, Security Force Assistance (SFA), counterinsurgency, counterterrorism, direct action, counter-proliferation, and special reconnaissance. During the Cold War era, SOF trained anti-Soviet guerrillas, and after 9/11 they were the first ones to infiltrate Afghanistan from the North as the military's "horse soldiers." The typical Green Beret who carries out overt operations of SOF, General Votel stated in his testimony to Congress, is "older than counterparts in the conventional forces, has attended multiple advanced tactical schools, and has received specialized cultural and language training."[2] Known for their ability to navigate complex political and military environments, SOF are known as the quiet professionals who train, teach and mentor, and shadow traditional diplomacy. Of the 70,000 SOF,[3] approximately 30,000 are Special Forces (SF). One third of SF are deployed at any one point in time.[4] Every morning, SOF wake up in at least seventy countries, at least thirty of which are known operations.[5]

SOF get deployed only in special circumstances, often through a United States Government (USG) interagency arrangement which includes an invitation by the host nation (HN) government, and through the Department of State (DOS) in the host country. Requests are evaluated through the guidance and assessment of the Geographic Combatant Command (GCC) and in coordination with the HN. Once an assessment has been conducted, a decision is made on whether a general or a specialized force should be deployed. It is based on this assessment that the extent of SOF's footprint is decided, whether it be training a local force, conducting a civic engagement, or setting conditions for transition. While the request for SOF's engagement, during most circumstances, comes from within the HN government, such invitations are primarily for SOF's hard power capability, not the development activities they perform, which are the main theme of this analysis. Yet, these hard power engagements are accompanied by a series of development and humanitarian activities, which become an integral part of SOF's work.

As a smaller unconventional force compared to large and bulky conventional forces, SOF are flexible and nimble, easy to stand up, and easy to shut down, making them the preeminent force of choice in spaces of "political, economic, informational, and military competition more fervent in nature than normal steady-state diplomacy, yet short of conventional war."[6] Responsible for tackling some of the most lethal missions, respondents to this study expressed that what distinguishes SOF from all other forces is their ability to understand the cultural context in which they are operating, to build rapport with interlocutors, and to have the ability to understand the distress and grievances of others. As one respondent shared, "SOF prides itself on being operational artists—expressing empathy, knowing when to go soft and when to go hard."[7] SOF combine a multitude of skills and human qualities by "coming from all walks of life and personalities—those who came from the streets and know how to hustle, and those who can kill their interlocutor with kindness," according to one military respondent.[8] It is this ability that General Robert Scales, who also served in Vietnam, coined as essential to engaging with local populations.[9]

Yet, despite their outstanding soft skills, SOF's identity is now in a crisis.[10] Since 9/11 and throughout the two decades of the Global War on Terrorism (GWOT), the personality, motivations, and size of SOF have changed. SOF grew from nearly 30,000 in 1999 to almost 70,000 today.[11] Such has been the growing demand for SF during the last two decades of the GWOT that the recruitment of rank has gone from an E (Enlisted) 5 requirement for recruits who are in their mid to late twenties, to an E3, and 20 years old. The force, which had been small and nimble, has now become more lethal and larger. As such, this is not an enabling quality but rather an obstruction in operating in the gray space. SOF's lethality has gotten it further away from its genesis, where it could work with civic actors and in low-intensity conflict.

But this new generation of soldiers is not attracted to working with and through partners. These young soldiers are mostly drawn to the most lethal components of the job, where some argue their lethality has also lowered the threshold for using force. "When we recruit," one SF officer shared, "we are overrepresenting direct action and underrepresenting the partnership piece."[12] This has changed SOF's ability to fulfill FID missions, which are mostly about being a quiet professional behind the scenes. "The most successful missions with partners are not about violence," one military respondent noted, "but about teaching and training the local partner who is in the lead."[13] Edward C. Croot further supports this in his study, which found that 34 percent of SF are not committed to a partnership approach.[14]

The mass production of a precise lethal force has caused SOF to turn away from its warrior-diplomat ethos. By 2006, it became mostly synonymous with kicking down doors and capturing enemy combatants.[15] Williamson Murray explains this is an example of "generational change that occurs in military organizations as the collective experiences of the senior officer corps evolve with the passage of time. Such a change has been occurring in the American military over the past decade as the Vietnam War generation has reached retirement."[16] In referring to this changed military culture, a participant during a forum on how SOF have evolved stated that before 9/11 there used to be a lot of investment in language and culture,[17] but the military-centric approach in Iraq and Afghanistan of "close quarters battle, such as raids,"[18] has created a tribe obsessed with chasing down terrorists, and is attracting a different type of recruit for SOF.[19] In this changed military culture, "everyone is an 'operator,'"[20] with action-hungry soldiers posting photos on social media of themselves jumping out of helicopters. As a result—as opposed to making the gray space more conducive to civic and military actors working together, which is discussed at length throughout later chapters, and is at the core of what I hope to convey—SOF's lethality has caused these actors to diverge.

Today, the majority of SF is forty years old and younger, and most of them remember the recent big wars in Iraq and Afghanistan. They have transformed into a force where "the universal desire to be a gunslinger has overshadowed other aspects of Special Forces."[21] In a force that once prided itself on its linguistic and cultural skills, today only one-third of SF believes that language skills are necessary to have, and 62 percent are not maintaining their knowledge of it regularly.[22] The ability to interact with civic entities, non-state actors, and populations has also been alienated in SF's toolbox—a topic later addressed in this analysis. As one retired SF Officer shared, "I had commanders that told me: 'hey, we speak two languages here—5.56 and 7.62,' those being the caliber of our weapons."[23] As mentioned before, the desire to focus on the lethal has caused SOF something else. SOF's lethality has undermined their ability to work with civic actors, causing a divergence from these actors, as is discussed in later chapters.

Ironically, while SOF and the military at large are becoming more lethal on one side, they have also become more risk-averse,[24] mostly in reaction to the fact that American casualties never sit well with the U.S. public and are to be avoided by commanders at all means. "It's all about risk mitigation," one military respondent said, "nobody wants to see KIA [killed in action] statistics. It is this risk aversion which drives many of the decisions of commanding officers."[25] The same interviewee reflected on the decision to pull out from Niger after a SOF team was ambushed in 2018, "tell me what did it cost us to keep a few people in Niger after the attack happened? Sometimes we pull the lever too hard and lose sense of the big picture."[26] This abrupt ending of relationships further exacerbates SOF's lack of permanence—an inhibitor to its ability to form relationships with other actors—a challenge which I discuss later.

Foreign Internal Defense

SOF can and do operate across a variety of missions. Despite their high lethality, there is also an argument for SOF being well suited for peacekeeping, for example.[27] But SOF's bread and butter is training other militaries. In providing support to and reinforcing partner nations' own security capabilities, U.S. security assistance is generally divided into two categories—SFA and FID. There is still some question as to the exact difference between the two, but generally, FID is tactical, while SFA is strategic and operational.[28] It is the tactical level, which is the predominant focus of this analysis. FID is a way for SOF to provide training, equipment, and advice to foreign military, police, or other groups, to counter internal threats from narcotics, terrorism, or insurgencies. But FID is much more than this. The U.S. Army manual on engaging with other military and non-military entities in support of humanitarian operations defines FID as:

> Agencies of a government in any of the action programs taken by another government or other designated organization to free and protect its society from subversion, lawlessness, and insurgency. FID is an umbrella concept that covers a broad range of activities. Its primary intent is always to help the legitimate host government address internal threats and their underlying causes. Commensurate with U.S. policy goals, the focus of all U.S. FID efforts is to support the HN [host nation] program of internal defense and development. FID is not restricted to times of conflict. It also can take place in the form of training exercises and other activities that show U.S. resolve to and for the region.[29]

Taking into account the increasingly lethal nature of SOF and the mass production of the force in the last two decades, the flexibility provided to this force is both a blessing and a curse. Originally developed in 1976 as a "euphemism for 'support for counterinsurgency,'"[30] FID is unique and agile. It includes the *full spectrum*—from the building of infrastructure and economic and military capabilities to combat operations. As part of FID, and any other security cooperation arrangement between the U.S. military and the HN military, is a series of Military Civic Action activities. Across the Geographic Commands each year, approximately 120 countries receive assistance in several areas of humanitarian assistance, through the Overseas Humanitarian, Disaster, and Civic Aid (OHDACA) budget line,[31] which will be discussed at length later. OHDACA is the primary budget authority through which the Department of Defense (DOD) provides: (1) disaster risk reduction and preparedness; (2) health-related efforts; (3) basic education; (4) water, sanitation, and shelter (basic infrastructure); and (5) Humanitarian Mine Action (HMA).[32] These projects are mostly consulted with the United States Agency for International Development (USAID), local ministries, and sometimes NGOs.[33]

These projects are usually in a package as a larger capacity and institution-building program. They can also involve multiple agencies, such as the Federal Bureau of Investigation, the Department of Agriculture, the Department of Interior, and so on, as part of the interagency. It is SOF's conducting of these activities that causes it to operationally converge with civic actors whose primary role *is* to carry out these activities.

Because of its multitude of facets, FID is inherently cross-functional and complex, entailing "diplomatic, informational, military, and economic instruments of national power."[34] While FID is carried out by the military, it is overseen by the DOS as part of a larger security cooperation package. DOS coordinates FID activities, but they are ultimately approved by the overseeing commander as part of a larger campaign plan. In a given country, FID is most often a program, but if security escalates and the HN military is unable to respond, FID can turn into an operation under special U.S. government funding authorities. As a result, FID can happen during peacetime and war, where "in 2008 SOF were engaged in the execution of FID in both combat and peacetime environments in over 40 countries."[35]

With the agility of these missions and SOF's changing nature, once they are in the country and the field, SOF hold a *carte blanche* as to how, where, and with whom they engage, within the confines of their mandate, and agreement with the HN partner. Later chapters explore how SOF's ability to transform themselves based on the operational environment, which includes the full spectrum of conflict and contexts, carries across their mandates, but not always positively. The analysis discusses how SOF's autonomy puts the burden on the individual, not the organization, providing ample opportunity for both productive but challenging relationships between both civilian and military actors.

Partners FIDelis—SOF and the Host Nation Military

The HN military with which SOF engage is not the primary focus of this analysis, but it is SOF's primary interlocutor in carrying out FID missions. In addition to the multiple and complex relationships which SOF has with other entities, the SOF-HN partner relationship carries its own dynamic, as SOF face many challenges in training HN militaries. According to one respondent, "it's not just the populations that we [US SOF] may not understand. It's the people we are training too."[36] The hard power training provided to the HN is at the nucleus of the interaction, as SOF are constrained to their role as a trainer, but there are many more and complex layers to the SOF-HN military relationship.

Chapter 6 discusses the civilian population as the center of gravity of any mission. While development projects are not the primary reason for which SOF are invited to a country, they provide an opportunity for SOF to form a growing positive relationship with local populations and the HN military. Part of training the HN military could be to help them develop their CA branch, a key military element for improving the relationship between the HN military and the local population. By conducting Civil-Military Operations (CMO),[37] part of a FID mission may be teaching the HN military how to provide medical assistance not only to its own soldiers, but also to its citizens. As one U.S. military respondent said, "You can tell a lot about the country's military from how much they believe the population to be central to their mission and to how developed of a branch the civil affairs component is."[38] As a result, when trying to impact a positive relationship with the local population and HN partner, it is key that the right people are placed in CA specialties, or the opposite can occur, where the lack of skill by the military in engaging with the local populations can have an adverse effect.[39]

To achieve a positive impact, influence can take many forms. In Burkina Faso, SOF's training is focused "on community engagement between the Burkinabe military and civilians," with emphasis on gaining civilians' trust and countering Improvised Explosive Devices (IEDs).[40] Within the Colombian military, which has been trained by U.S. SOF for decades, the branch of the Colombian military's CA—Accion Integral has become a professionalized branch of the armed services. U.S. SOF CA teams from the 98th CA battalion in Colombia do little to implement community civic assistance efforts or to engage with NGOs. The lead is taken entirely by Acción Integral as SOF's main interlocutor. There are exceptions where U.S. SOF CA engages in repainting schools and handing out backpacks. As one U.S. CA officer noted, "Projects don't have to be big. Sometimes buying paint to beautify a school is just as sufficient as building a school."[41]

There are other instances where the HN military oversees security and DOD finances projects.[42] In such cases, SOF are working alongside the HN military, and if not a direct doer of the task at hand, the U.S. have direct visibility. U.S. SOF CA in Colombia engages as a way to simply "provide medicine, for example, and provide the money, but it does not run any program," one military respondent shared.[43] When attending an event, during a Medical Civic Action Program (MEDCAP) exercise that covered specialties from gynecology to optometry to family medicine, one U.S. CA soldier expressed the high degree of professionalism with which a local NGO, in coordination with the Colombian military, conducted the event. As a participant in the MEDCAP, the local NGO, with security from the Colombian military, provided all the work, and the U.S. CA Officer was simply invited as a guest: "Here is your seat, ma'am," the military respondent said,[44] referring to how little they had to do, as it was all professionally handled by the HN military. In Lebanon, SOF helped stand up the Lebanese Civil-Military Cooperation (CIMIC) directorate, whose job is solely focused on dealing with the population.[45] The Lebanese Armed Forces (LAF) is in competition with Hezbollah for influence over the populace, but "as long as the perception is that LAF is helping, even if it's with US money, it's all that matters," a military respondent shared.[46] Therefore, "it's extremely important that the HN military puts the people as the center of gravity, and it is something that DOD is adamant about."[47] As one military respondent noted, "The secret to SOF's success is a good host nation partner."[48]

The HN partner force's recognition of, and investment in its relationship with the population is not a given. In theory, the HN should always be in the lead,[49] but often they are not. This is not an entirely uncomfortable reality for SOF, whose natural inclination is to be in the driver's seat, and which reality SOF welcome. Where the HN partners are not in the lead, U.S. SOF are eager for the opportunity to create their own reputation among the populace. Where the partner force is not focused on engaging with their own people, SOF do it alone, despite risking that it might achieve the opposite effect of helping the force be self-sufficient and put the United States, as opposed to the HN, into the business of winning hearts and minds. One military respondent noted, "We are in a bit of a Catch 22. Not all relationships are developed like the one we have in Colombia. We are the new kid on the block, and we have to prove ourselves to populations, too."[50] This creates an almost competition for the affection of the populace, and a sobering reality. But even with SOF conducting these activities in place of the HN military, there is no guarantee that the desired outcome of positive perception by the population toward the HN military would be achieved. As one military respondent noted, "There is no way to sustain our interest with the nation if the nation cannot sustain it [themselves] with their own people," and "yet we want the partner force to be in charge."[51]

One of the most active areas for CA engagement by U.S. SOF has been in the area of health, and there has also been a recognized shift to medical stability operations (MSO).[52] The United Nations Development Programme (UNDP) *Human Development Report* has identified the lack of health services as a security issue, especially human security.[53] In assessing needs in West Africa, one U.S. SOF medic respondent spoke about how medical assistance is a low-hanging fruit of getting "in" with the population, and how:

> Medical stuff is easy. Short-term vaccines, life, and limb are not difficult to manage. Unless it's terminal. Nobody is going to say no to medication. Everybody wants to live. Human needs don't change. Whether it be meeting short-term needs with vaccines or giving out nets to protect against malaria mosquitos, or tablets for water purification.[54]

It is these medical activities, which SOF carry out, as part of their missions, which cause them to converge with NGOs, which also provide medical services in the gray space.

Some occurrences are less calculated, and gaining the affection of the population happens simply in the course of taking action when it is needed. One U.S. SOF medic recounted an experience during their deployment in West Africa where a pregnant woman was in a car crash: "Everybody saw her. We treated her. And everyone saw *us*."[55] In another instance, a HN soldier had been injured. The medic recounted how they used blood from within the U.S. unit's own blood bank reserve for the transfusion, "now we were blood brothers. What can be more powerful?"[56] In another instance, after performing cataract surgery on an elderly woman in the Philippines, an SF soldier noted, "when she woke up and opened her eyes, the first person she saw was a US medic. That's pretty powerful!"[57]

In Burkina Faso, an attack had occurred several years ago on the HN military, and U.S. assets were used to evacuate the soldiers to safety. One SOF respondent shared their memory about their deployment in Burkina Faso: "When we returned to Fada, the soldiers and villagers were incredibly happy and embracing. It's not something you can measure, but you just know it."[58] Another military respondent provided a contrary opinion, "whether people like us or not is always a mixed bag."[59] The HN military are not just soldiers; they are also citizens of the communities they protect and recipients of assistance provided by outside actors. They form opinions, take sides, "mediate, and act,"[60] making the interaction between HN and U.S. SOF even more complex.

Besides the motivation factor to gain affection from the population toward the military, there is a deeper chord that the process of training other militaries strikes. Respondents overwhelmingly spoke about the emotional sentiment that the HN military relationship carries. When they train together, SOF and the HN partner develop a camaraderie that is difficult to match. As one military respondent put it, "there is a certain brotherly bond which forms when training with the host nation partner. If you are fighting together, you bond well together."[61] During FID missions, there is a certain connection that occurs in sharing an arduous environment. One military respondent noted, "We would live on the bases with the soldiers. We use the same bathrooms and shower. We sleep in the same tents. They are there with us in the trenches."[62] The forming of this logical and organic connection does not imply equality, however. It is a partnership with boundaries. Because of SOF's engagements in politically complex environments, there is also a known risk and distrust between these groups. "Never tell your partner everything they need to know because one day you might have to come back and potentially kill them,"[63] one former SF soldier shared. The fragility of trust is real, as demonstrated by insider attacks such as the ones in 2011 and 2014, where the HN soldiers turned on and killed their training partner in what is supposed to be "an environment of trust and confidence."[64] One such case was the killing of General Greene in Afghanistan in 2014.

CIVIL AFFAIRS

General Gordon Sullivan once referred to CA as "one of the most misunderstood Army missions and—to some who see it as 'unwarriorlike'—the most criticized."[65] They are master networkers, working among the populace. They conduct civil reconnaissance, but unlike intelligence operators, this is not their only and primary function. Encompassing 39 battalions and 840 Civil Affairs Teams (CATs) of four to five members each, CATs work in up to 120 countries a year to assist and build capacity in disaster risk reduction, health, education, basic infrastructure, and HMA.[66] Comprised of active duty, reservists, and sometimes the National Guard, CATs work in justice and security, reconciliation, humanitarian assistance and governance, economic stabilization, and infrastructure.[67] The teams are based at the theater or country level. CA touches at the tactical, operational, and strategic levels. They do so through four distinct units—Civil Military Support Element (CMSE), the Regional Civil Military Support Element, the Theater Civil Military Support Element, and the Trans-regional civil-military engagement element.[68]

Civil affairs teams may be present in many of the places where the United States has an Embassy. Their role can be driven by many factors, and particularly the larger security cooperation agreement which exists between the U.S. and the HN government. In such contexts CA may be present because the U.S.-HN relationship necessitates it, or because the HN does not oppose it. These teams' missions are cross-cutting between development, humanitarian and civic assistance programs, and security assistance programs, with the primary function being as an instrument of engagement with the populace.

At least three field manuals define the work of CA concretely,[69] yet CA's role can deviate from these, depending on the intention of the commanding officer. CA engages in providing Foreign Humanitarian Assistance (FHA), and Foreign Assistance (FA). FHA and FA are different, in that FHA responds to a direct humanitarian need and is limited in time as its purpose is "to alleviate the suffering" for vulnerable populations.[70] FHA may be part of many types of activities, each with its own trait, "stability operations, foreign assistance, peace operations, noncombatant evacuation operations, civil-military operations, mass atrocity response operations, international chemical, biological, radiological, and nuclear response."[71] On the other hand, FA could include the full gamut from foreign military sales for FID missions to goods and medical assistance that "may be provided through development assistance, SA (Security Assistance), or humanitarian and civic assistance."[72] Ultimately, depending on the commander's objectives, CA's work may emphasize one or multiple of these objectives.

There are many examples of prominent, effective CA engagements. The CMO manual covers the full gamut of CA's work across a variety of contexts, where commanders establish relationships with all entities—NGOs, civic authorities, and the civilian populace, in friendly, neutral, or hostile environments.[73]

Operation Just Cause in Panama saw CA help restore the police and government ministries. In the mid-1990s in Northern Iraq, as part of the U.S. Marine Corps engagement, CA set up Obstetrician-Gynecologists (OBGYN) clinics, and in Somalia, they established a Police Force.[74] In the late 1990s, CA advised the Haitian government on "justice, finance and banking, commerce, education, foreign affairs, agriculture, health, public works, interior and others."[75] Starting in the mid-1990s with Operation Joint Forge in Bosnia and Operation Joint Guardian in Kosovo, CA simultaneously provided humanitarian assistance and support to Ministerial Advisory Teams (MATs) for nearly a decade. These activities are in tandem with the logistical mastery that the military exhibits. One of the biggest examples of the military's logistics capability is the 2010 Haiti earthquake, where the Air Force Special Operations Command (AFSOC) 1 SOW "arrived 26 hours after the earthquake and reestablished flight operations 28 minutes after reaching the scene."[76] Following the commencement of Operation Allies Welcome from Afghanistan in 2021, marines and sailors from the 2nd Combat Logistics Battalion built a small city out of tents in Quantico, Virginia, for "1,000 people in less than 36 hours."[77] During the wars of the 1990s, and particularly in the Balkans, much of CA focused on post-conflict reconstruction and engagement.[78] But contrary to the logistical support provided in disaster contexts, the role of CA in places ridden by continual conflict is less straightforward. As a group of researchers described, the more violent the context, "the more likely humanitarian activities will occur with the CA units," and conversely, "the more stable a nation is, the more likely CA units will assist in its protection to preserve the current humanitarian assets."[79] From the thirty-nine fragile countries identified in the World Bank's fragility list, there have been overt CA missions that deployed to nearly half of them.[80] Moreover, the majority of these countries have a low military footprint and military presence.[81] It is this cross-cutting—between what the military identifies as low-intensity conflict, and what development actors define as fragility, which causes these entities' objectives to converge.

Today, CA's engagement has become much more proactive and more socially scientific, as these teams seek to identify the gaps in the gray space which serve as potential sources of instability. CA's function is vital "in areas of the world that are recently recovering from the effects of past armed conflict, or where armed conflict remains a possibility."[82] This view places CA's ability to conduct stability operations on equal footing with offensive and defensive warfare.[83] As discussed earlier, unlike large conventional forces' logistical capabilities which place the military as *crisis responders* and draw them into emergencies to respond to the symptoms of conflict, CA as part of SOF are *sources of instability seekers,* with the mission to identify root causes of potential violence, such as scarcity of basic services or lack of governance, to name a few.

Unlike in disaster response where civilians are in charge, and conventional warfighting where the military is in charge, the gray space is less straightforward. Despite the lack of large-scale disruptions in the fluid gray space, basic services may still be scarce, and there may not be a local government authority in charge of providing them, be it military or civilian.[84] In their hybrid roles as part soldiers and part social scientists, CA teams seek to predict and address the sources of insecurity, often caused by this lack of basic conditions. This makes CA's job even more complicated and constrained. How can CA operate effectively in a situation where millions of displaced people have fled to places such as Lebanon, Turkey, and Jordan from the border with Syria, in the Beqaa Valley, next to the Lebanese border? "Syrian refugees are squatting on people's farms. This is a source of insecurity," one military respondent shared in speaking about their experience in Lebanon.[85]

The absence of sanitary conditions and lack of available toilets at a school can have a huge communal impact on security. "The parents didn't want to send their children to school, since the kids had to wait two hours to go to the bathroom. So they keep them home. They go roaming the streets, instead, getting up to no good. This is a source of insecurity," a military respondent shared.[86] The logic of how security shapes decisions about everyday life is shared by development data, which has found that children who are living in fragile settings are "nearly three times as likely to be out of primary school," compared to children in a developed country.[87]

Doctrine says that "the focus of CA is to engage the civil component of the operational environment by assessing, monitoring, protecting, reinforcing, establishing, and transitioning—both actively and passively—political, economic, and information (social and cultural) institutions and capabilities."[88] As such, SOF recognize that security is not to be seen only through the prism of a physical threat, and that "instability is not always directly correlated to the existence of an insurgency in a local region."[89] Alternatively, a purely humanitarian effort, which occurs in contexts where security is not an issue, may not necessarily remain *only* in the humanitarian space. Humanitarian disasters can quickly turn into unstable and crime-ridden ones.[90]

What is challenging for SOF is their ability to understand the civilian environment and consequences of their response to sources of insecurity. As one SOF CA respondent described:

> Where it goes wrong is when we do not fully understand security. We would go to an area where ISIS runs the show. The government is too weak to defend themselves. So it's just a hotbed. ISIS is the actual government in the host nation. So, we set up a clinic in the Beqaa Valley, which is less secure and might serve the population. But the same clinic also services the enemy. The idea is to counter ISIS, not to provide them with medical care.[91]

These small-scale sources of potential instability undoubtedly add to a collection of large-scale strategic decision-making and the timing of it—"If Boko Haram came in the week before to offer basic services to the village, where we are trying to influence, we need to do one up on them," one military SOF CA respondent notes.[92] This is not uncommon. Maria Kingsley wrote about how the "FARC used some of the revenue it earned from illicit drug taxation to carry out infrastructure projects in local communities."[93] In the early 2000s, Hezbollah-backed humanitarian NGOs provided 45 percent of the water needs of Beirut's southern suburbs.[94] Democratic governments, dictatorial regimes, and terrorist groups have all sought to ensure the needs of their people by providing services or meeting basic needs. All recognize the importance of winning over the population, and all are vying for this position.

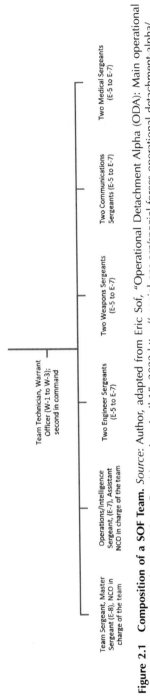

Figure 2.1 Composition of a SOF Team. *Source*: Author, adapted from Eric Sof, "Operational Detachment Alpha (ODA): Main operational element of Army Special Forces," Spec Ops Magazine, April 15, 2022 https://special-ops.org/special-forces-operational-detachment-alpha/.

Team Leader, Captain (O-3); Commander

Team Technician, Warrant Officer (W-1 to W-3); second in command

Team Sergeant, Master Sergeant (E-8), NCO in charge of the team

Operations/Intelligence Sergeant, (E-7), Assistant NCO in charge of the team

Two Engineer Sergeants (E-5 to E-7)

Two Weapons Sergeants (E-5 to E-7)

Two Communications Sergeants (E-5 to E-7)

Two Medical Sergeants (E-5 to E-7)

Trading Places

Lastly, there is yet another complication to SOF's engagement with civilian actors. CA teams are not the only ones that engage with the populace to collect information. How active or reactive SOF or CA are depends on the context in which they are operating and the composition of SOF and CA (figures 2.1 and 2.2). In a less permissive environment, SOF SF have a very solid role and have most of the interaction with the population. On the flip side, SOF CA is very active in a permissive environment and may be the only and primary interlocutor for populations. Such is the nature of the gray space that "depending on the day, and the area, the space can change overnight, and so can the need,"[95] leading the level of permissiveness and threat to constantly shift.

Ultimately, just like hard power, CA, and sometimes SF, is a tool in the military's toolbox. Their purpose is just the opposite of destroying or disrupting. Their job is to seek out, initiate, and maintain relationships, not to end them. The technological advancement of capability and weaponry is designed for battle or to lethally target. CA's main purpose is to "sustain and exploit security and control over areas, populations, and resources,"[96] to support the military's efforts. It is the chameleon nature of their role, which creates complexity in their relationship with civic actors.

THE 95TH CIVIL AFFAIRS BRIGADE

Referred to as the Birkenstocks of the military, the 95th Civil Affairs Brigade (Airborne)[97] out of Fort Liberty is the enabling active duty soft arm of SOF and the military at large. They work to acquire knowledge through various networks and organizations on the ground. Every day, between 200 and 300

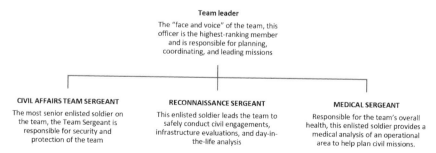

Figure 2.2   Composition of a Civil Affairs Team. *Source*: Author, adapted from Eric Sof, "Operational Detachment Alpha (ODA): Main operational element of Army Special Forces," Spec Ops Magazine, April 15, 2022 https://special-ops.org/special-forces-operational-detachment-alpha/.

personnel from the 95th Brigade are deployed in over twenty-five countries.[98] Across all the military and services, the 95th Brigade "are the most knowledge- able about NGOs," as admitted by one long-time NGO operator.[99] The informa- tion which CA gather is used by military leaders "to influence the population without lethal measures."[100] Yet, even the non-lethal measures that the military uses are questionable by both those within the military and outside of it. Many of the military respondents for this study expressed concerns about mislabeling of the military's engagement with humanitarian and development projects[101] referred to in table 2.1. Several respondents reiterated that despite their label- ing and advertising them as such, the projects which the military carries out are not truly humanitarian because there is no humanitarian need to be met. As one development professional puts it, "It's using a training mission to do health diplomacy."[102] As a result, the focus and center of these activities is the training within FID contexts, as a primary objective, and maintaining relation- ships with civic actors, for the purpose of meeting security needs, as a second- ary objective. To gain access, soldiers from the 95th can conduct a series of activities. For example, they may set up an "antenna for communications back to headquarters during the first of a two-day combined medical and dental civil assistance project."[103] In 2009 in rural Benin, soldiers administered veterinary services for the cattle of communities, as part of a military exercise with the Benin military.[104] This might seem unusual, but is a regular military practice,

Table 2.1   Activities/Services Provided by SOF CA for Communities

Goods and Services

- Build schools (Guatemala)
- Provide Personal Protective Equipment (PPE) for COVID (Burkina Faso)
- Refurbishment of schools (Bulgaria)
- Distribution of school backpacks (Colombia)
- Vaccination of cattle (Niger)
- Supply of fire retardant (Lebanon)
- Supply winter jackets to children (Tajikistan)
- Supply/ship a firetruck (Lebanon)
- Build bathrooms (Lebanon)
- Provide clean water (Tanzania)
- Repair fire stations (Latvia)
- Conduct Medical Civic Action Programs (MEDCAP) (Colombia)
- Provide sanitary supplies (Lebanon and Jordan)
- Distribute hygiene kits to schools (Lebanon and Jordan)
- Distribute masks, gloves, hand sanitizer, and medical information (Lebanon and Jordan)
- Fix of water supply (the Philippines)
- Provide medicine to rural health centers (the Philippines)
- Implement flood prevention programs (Bosnia)

Source: Author, based on interviews, images and storyboards from Defense Visual Information Distribution Service.

where "veterinary Corps officers and enlisted animal technicians have been part of SOF since at least World War II."[105]

Access and placement is not *only* for conflict settings. In NATO countries, such as Bulgaria, the U.S. military conducts small-scale community projects specifically for security cooperation activities,[106] funded by OHDACA. This is done as a way to build goodwill among friends and allies. In analyzing the strategic value of the relationship with the partner, military staff/leadership is asked to what extent the partner nation gives access to airspace, ports, and facilities, not to what extent programs benefit populations. This is less in line with OHDACA's other purpose:

> To relieve or reduce endemic conditions such as human suffering, disease, hunger, privation, and the adverse effects of unexploded explosive ordnance (UXO), particularly in regions where humanitarian needs may pose major challenges to stability, prosperity, and respect for universal human values.[107]

As mentioned earlier, in strictly logistical contexts, where civic actors are in charge, the military's practical assistance—for example, in distributing portable kitchens and blankets—is welcomed. It is what the 95th do with the information which they acquire that is problematic for development actors. Following 9/11, with the heavy focus on CT, CA's role in reconnaissance has dominated over any other soft power role they may play. Yet, the tasks of collecting information in the operating space to gain valuable access while simultaneously helping populations with basic needs, "are not mutually exclusive,"[108] according to one military officer. While NGOs have qualms about this, in later chapters, it is discussed how in the gray space populations are less concerned about who provides a basic service or assistance and more about whether or not it is provided. What becomes more challenging to understand is how this shapes CA's relationship with NGOs, a topic this analysis explores at length in chapters 4 and 5.

CIVIL RECONNAISSANCE

One of CA's main tasks is civil information management (CIM) in the open and unclassified space. It engages in a process of collecting, analyzing, and warehousing civil information in all its aspects—"geospatial, relational, and temporal."[109] Reconnaissance, in the classic counterinsurgency context, seeks:

> To collect civil information in order to engage the civilian population with precision; provide an overall enhanced understanding of the human terrain; impede the enemies ability to operate freely among the population and use it as cover

and concealment for operations; reduce the risk of undesired secondary and tertiary effects of military operations; and capitalize on opportunities to gain the trust and confidence of the civilian population.[110]

This civil reconnaissance role is not limited to counterinsurgency contexts; its scope and the means to achieve objectives vary depending on the situation. This is part of the problem and confusion for outsiders. Many of the military and NGO players intermingle, regardless of the mandate, be it in counterinsurgency, natural disaster, complex emergency, or peacekeeping operations contexts.[111] These are different mandates, but as one military respondent noted, even within the various branches of the military, "depending on people's experiences within the military, they have a different view of what civil affairs does."[112] In one instance they could be providing humanitarian assistance and implementing development projects—and on the other—CA could be interrogating prisoners.[113] The latter is a far cry from humanitarian activities, and the divide between hard and soft power is less clear in the gray space, where there is not always an outwardly active insurgency. But interviewees within both the NGO and military communities expressed concerns regarding the military using its role as a reconnaissance actor interchangeably in other contexts. Overall, the reason why CA's function does not sit easily with development actors and NGO interlocutors is, as one NGO professional shared, "the fact that they want this access, and that they wear civilian clothing, when they try to meet with communities who mistakenly think that they work *with* us or *for* us. This is what we all hate."[114] This is also what creates confusion on the ground and within the communities in which the military operates. One NGO respondent, supported by others, was very critical of the military noting how "they show up to parties dressed in civilian clothing, and you can't let it escape you that the 95th's goal is to collect information."[115] This is of no surprise, as there is recognition of treating the gray space with an "adversary fixation and near exclusive reliance on classified sources."[116] However, "despite this, the 95th know more about NGOs than most people in the military."[117] This can be not only dangerous and counterproductive in CA's relationship with civic actors but also difficult to overcome in the more benign low-intensity conflict and low-threat, fragile environments.

On their end too, the military respondents gave little explanation of how, in these differing mandates, their behavior and response as a matter of course drastically change between information collectors, or agents of humanitarian and development activities. As mentioned earlier, depending on one's experience with CA, there are differing perceptions of what CA do, and how they should behave according to the context, even within CA themselves, and the U.S. military at large. Conversely, even in instances where CA projects are done with humanitarian and development purposes in mind, the craft of the

95th is such that in any case, regardless of their objectives, these soldiers are perceived as intelligence collectors. In their own manual, they warn that:

> There is a great hazard in persons collecting civil information being perceived as covert intelligence assets. Every effort must be made by soldiers to avoid this perception. The strength of this information is that it is collected through interaction with the population.[118]

In either case, whether they intend to only serve in a reconnaissance role, or not, and whether they do this successfully or unsuccessfully, the 95th's reputation with NGOs is subject to suspicion.

THE NON-HUMANITARIANS' TOOLS

Let us assume for a moment that CA are *not* exclusively a reconnaissance collector, and that there *are* humanitarian and development benefits to the activities mentioned in table 2.1. What tools do SOF CA possess to do this?

When it comes to development and humanitarian actors assessing local needs, these entities assess the availability of basic services, such as water, hygiene, and education in order to respond appropriately. On the military side, the civic projects which CA carry out *do* serve a double purpose—to conduct reconnaissance for access and placement, and maintain, keep, and use the information gathered from entities with whom they interact. The humanitarian and development purpose of these projects is a second-order effect. But this does not mean that the military cannot be effective as humanitarian and development actors, as clearly they deploy similar activities to those of humanitarian and development organizations, even if on a minuscule level. In communicating with local communities, and taking into account consultations between the military and civic actors, what tools that CA deploy are designed with this civic purpose in mind?

When the military's main job is humanitarian, not security or reconnaissance, CA units deploy a humanitarian assistance response by performing SWEAT-MSO analysis—sewage, water, electricity, academics, trash, medical, safety, and other considerations—to identify what their lines of effort will be. These assessments are done across all contexts and doctrines, be it during times of peace or conflict. CA also deploys a series of other tools. Specifically, these are Political, Military, Economic, Social, Information, and Infrastructure (PMESII) and Areas, Structures, Capabilities, Organization, People, Events (ASCOPE) matrices. These tools assist in identifying societal systems and the communities' impact on the military's own mission. ASCOPE and PMESII are designed to give a holistic insight into how the various economic and social pillars will aid or hinder the success of the military's mission. Used together, these matrices enmesh—ASCOPE is vertical, and PMESII-PT is horizontal, as they each draw on civic considerations (ASCOPE), and operational variables (PMESII). As planners outline their course of action (COA), they take into consideration "second-order effects and subsequent tertiary effects for each course of action."[119] But practitioners have argued, and many respondents too, that what these tools do not help determine, is how any COA by the military will have an impact on the economic and social conditions of a community. These mechanisms do not "mobilize the theoretical traditions of anthropology, sociology, and other relevant social science disciplines."[120] Instead, they are more suitable for intelligence gathering, not the anthropological and social contexts of missions.[121]

Others have called PMESII and ASCOPE tools appropriate for targeting enemies, as they do not assess human needs.[122] As one military respondent puts it, "The same process we use to drop a bomb, we use to target a project."[123] Ultimately, there is little in the military's planning tools that examine the second-order effects—positive or negative—on communities. The focus of these tools is on how the civic environment will impact military success, not how the military will impact the civic environment. Some have argued that these tools are not effective, as "PMESII and other linear, reductive, threat focused tools show the what without the so what,"[124] meaning that little afterthought is given to how these tools help think through courses of action or impact the operational environment. Others have noted that these tools are not sufficient to demonstrate the cause and effect of local factors, namely how dependencies occur in local contexts.[125] This is problematic, as these tools fail "to influence the behavior of a foreign population or defeat a foreign adversary,"[126] which commanders seek. Also, despite SOF seeking out sources of insecurity, these tools are not always sufficient to predict them.

There are some tools to help SOF identify sources of instability in local contexts. SOF look at the scarcity of basic needs through "a number of approaches for measuring key statistics and qualitative success within a locality or region. This includes CAFE (Civil Affairs Framework for Engagement) and CAOS (Civil Affairs Operating System)."[127] These frameworks are used to establish the physical area and focus of CA's activities. This is done at the macro level, where a series of municipal areas are identified to examine under-governed spaces and which looks through the lens of "terrorist and illicit activities" and "violent extremist groups."[128] At the micro analysis level, CATs seek to engage with the populace and "leadership patterns that affect stability in a region," or whether everyday activities, such as "the economic activity occurring amongst farmers can negatively affect a local region."[129] Perhaps the closest to an assessment of the civilian environment is the utilization of Area Studies, typical for all SOF. But these are focused on power relationships within a community, not the needs of the population.[130] Also, there is no "single" or institutionalized format for an area study.[131]

Ultimately, when initial assessments are conducted in the gray space, they are not done with the recipients in mind, but with the implementor's own benefits. This is one of the diverging factors between NGOs and SOF in the gray space. Where assessments occur, it is *not* by a mandate from the organization, but an activity which is left up to the SOF operator's own initiative. Let us explore.

Assessing Local Needs

Because of their tactical culture, SOF's autonomy shifts power from the organization to the individual. This leaves much of the consideration for populations' needs and working with NGOs up to the individual SOF operator, not the institution. Because doctrine speaks only to "what to do and what the aims are, but not how to do it,"[132] much of the ingenuity of how to assess and address the issues affecting the population falls on the individual. Measuring impact does as well. In Colombia, one respondent said:

> We got backpacks for the kids at a school, with stickers of the police number to call in an emergency. It was more of a project to help influence the population to feel empowered to report on criminal activities. To trust the security. We measured success by how many more reports and calls the police were getting from that particular community.[133]

When it comes to implementing projects for the military, teams would "go in a country and break it up into thirds, from most permissive to least permissive. This is how we pick where we work,"[134] according to one military respondent. "In Burkina Faso, this was the West side—Bobo Dioulasso—the most stable area. Generally, we would show up to provide medical care and execute a survey on the way out."[135] In Afghanistan and Iraq, tools such as the Tactical Conflict Assessment Framework (TCAF) were utilized by the Army, Marines, and USAID. TCAF gave agency to locals and sought to gain *their* perceptions of stability in communities through questionnaires.[136] It sought to include the full gamut of "analysis, design, and monitoring/evaluation."[137] The purpose of these survey efforts was to assess stability, but they quickly fell out of favor because they put the locals at risk, as there was too much mingling between locals and outsiders. Also, it was not the fact that the military was deploying monitoring and evaluation tools for development activities—a model more common among donors and NGOs. It was the fact that having people in uniform distribute assistance that triggered the wrong optics for the insurgency which were watching Allies' every move.

In the gray space, where the military does not own the physical terrain like it did in Iraq and Afghanistan, things are more restricted. In these instances, if SOF CA were to operate beyond the walls of the Embassy, they would need HN approval. This would likely occur through the military-to-military relationship which SOF have with the HN security forces they are training or with a security cooperation agreement between the U.S and HN government through the Embassy. In Iraq and Afghanistan, host nation sovereignty did not play a primary role, as it does in many of the countries examined as part of this analysis—Niger, Lebanon, Kenya, to mention a few. In these instances, it is neither the Combatant Commander, nor the Embassy, who ultimately decide what SOF CA, USAID, or any other branch of the U.S. Government will do, but it is the HN partner. This might be the MOD, on security cooperation initiatives, or any non-security ministry.[138]

CA may be tasked with accessing an area that would not otherwise be visited by other branches of State and USAID, likely for security reasons. In these cases, on-the-ground surveys of needs may be conducted, or CA may proactively initiate a program. As one respondent noted, "The person that is on the ground, they have the best sense of what is actually required—they are coming up with these ideas."[139] Or, it might be the Ambassador in the country who decides on what to employ. However, it is ultimately up to the GCC to approve it, beyond the country team, as these are ultimately DOD approval and budget authorities and money (see figure 2.3).

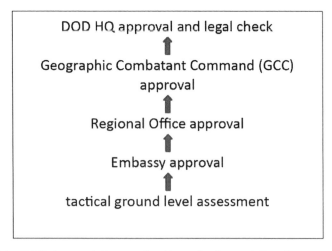

Figure 2.3   DOD Approval Process for Humanitarian and Development Activities.
Source: Author.

The process for how all of this occurs is not too scientific, either, as one military respondent noted that "ultimately, it's up to me, as the Captain to sell it."[140] This shows that indeed projects are driven from the bottom up, namely from lower ranks to higher ranks, at least as far as initiating them is concerned. But even with the self-initiated approach by individuals, there is little evidence that such assessments persuade commanders to prioritize population needs. Conversely, there are instances in which populations have the trust and relationship established with U.S. soldiers, and proactively reach out to them with their needs. In one example, a military respondent spoke of how during their deployment in Fada, Burkina Faso, farmers were getting hit with IEDs. The military reached out to one of their close NGO collaborators, who then provided the locals with metal detectors that enabled them to detect any explosives on the ground.

There is another complication to the implementation of these projects. There is little understanding of how information capturing turns into knowledge, project design, and assessment. In short, the process of assessment, design, implementation, and follow-up monitoring is ad hoc at best.

One of the alternative ways for the military to conduct assessments is to engage with NGOs, which, as non-lethal security actors, whose main task is to focus on the social and economic, are more able to plug in with local communities, and as a result have a better sense of the needs on the ground. As far as the military reaching out to leverage NGOs, one medic described the steps taken, "We go in and see what the [medical] NGOs are missing, and we find a way to provide it for them."[141] This is a natural touchpoint between NGOs and the military, and it should not be surprising. When it comes to shared areas for engagement between the military and NGOs, those of "governance and health are the most common."[142] Among the hundreds of projects carried out by CA in other countries, the majority are related to medical and dental services. Others are focused on disaster prevention. As one interviewee shared, local communities in Lebanon had suffered wildfires, destroying much of the land for olive oil production, and a major source of income for local farmers. In addition to shipping in some equipment after consulting with the local mayor, SOF CA also worked with a local NGO, teaching them skills on how to prevent fires by placing fire retardant. As one respondent mentioned, "We can't task the NGO, but we consulted and informed them, and they did the work."[143] Contrastingly, there are other instances where "even when we do try," they continued:

MSF [Medicines Sans Frontiers] will not work with us [the military], so we end up talking to those who are willing to talk to us. It's just the reality that there are some who will never work with us in order to maintain a neutral stance.[144]

A humanitarian professional confirmed some NGOs' adamant approach to stay away from the military completely, "MSF will never come to the meetings with the military. People have given up on inviting them."[145] Others have had consistent experiences where MSF "are almost puritanical in their adherence to impartiality and thus shun working with military units."[146] Other NGOs, however, such as Spirit of America (SoA), which is discussed at length in chapter 3, serve as enablers and work hand in hand with the U.S. military. Yet, just like with MSF, "very small NGOs representing churches and other philanthropic organizations . . . those want nothing to do with the military. Yet, at the strategic level, these organizations are not as adverse to coordinating."[147]

When it comes to assessing local needs in the gray space, CA officers are at times left to determine for themselves how to proceed. There are instances in which assessments are conducted, and they are ad-hoc at best. "Yes, we do surveys," one CA officer noted, "but there is no systematic way to do it. The areas we choose are based on strategic importance first, then needs are identified once we are in the community."[148] One respondent echoed that "there are no official assessment tools for these projects,"[149] while another bluntly stated, "what we do is not based on the need. It's based on what our budget will allow us to do."[150] Even in cases where projects might be a single event, one participant noted:

> If we are going to give out backpacks, let's do it at the beginning of the school year, not when OHDACA is approved. If we are going to try to do medical programs for malaria or flu, then we need to align our efforts for malaria and flu season.[151]

In some instances, projects have nothing to do with need, but are based on the individual military member's interest. One CA soldier spoke about their personal initiative and experience of driving the proposed project: "My wife was a teacher, so when I was on deployment, because I knew a lot about education, it was a good idea to do something educational."[152]

This justification, together with mostly selecting places that are strategically important, is often how decisions are made about which projects to pursue and where. In Lebanon, a survey was taken in the community and asked what they wished to see more of from the LAF. The community expressed how they struggled with electricity, as so many in the community steal it from the grid, and as a result, leave another large number of people in the same community without it. In speaking about the steps that the military can take to address grievances, one military respondent described the process:

> We decide it's something we can do for them. NGOs might have the ability or be more suitable to deliver these things to the community, but they can't

always go to where the help is needed. NGOs put a lot of money into stuff, but they never get to see the effects. They don't have true assessments of what the people actually need. We as the military have a much better ability to do this, particularly in non-permissive environments.[153]

But this was not shared by all military respondents. Even though respondents generally gave examples of where they were equipped to adequately assess local needs—in Colombia, the Philippines, and Burkina Faso, to mention a few, thoughtful assessment, design, implementation, and follow-up is ad-hoc at best. One military respondent noted how:

The US in general does a bad job at listening to people. We provide funding for projects, but we don't see the money's function come to fruition at the tactical level. A big part of SOF is to go out to make the assessments to see if the local communities are seeing these changes. In one instance, the US gave money to Lebanon to build a base near Tripoli. We set up a clinic, which was to be open to the public. The deal between the Libyan Army, our partner force and the Mayor, was that they would be given access, and they would treat the public. But this didn't happen, and unfortunately, because of the high level of turnover, there is no way to see projects through.[154]

There is no question that there is evidence of some attempt by SOF CA to deploy mechanisms for assessing local needs, whether those be institutionalized or initiated by the individual. It becomes clear, however, that the military's position on how to engage with the populace and its needs is based on SOF's need to understand how the civilian environment will impact its mission, not on how its mission will impact the civilian environment. There are specific questions as part of the military's tools that seek to account for the impact on the military's activities.[155] But when it comes to assessing local needs, and incorporating them as part of project design, or even accounting for the second-order effects, one military respondent said, "nobody cares about the local population. The budget cycle for doing projects for the population is adjusted to the deployment cycle, not to the needs of the people, or to the most vulnerable."[156] And ultimately, planning guidance manuals state, plain and simple, that "sometimes civil considerations are not the commander's top priority."[157]

Yet, when stripped off of their lethal capability, and examined under the prism of development and security actors, SOF have *everything* at their fingertips to be successful actors who attend to community needs in the gray space. This *should* be the case, considering that FHA is one of SOF's twelve core objectives. This includes access, tools, training, resources, intellectual, and individual competency. The *lethal* having trumped the *non-lethal* is much of what has led SOF into the conundrum of NGOs not willing to engage with them—a notion discussed in later chapters and an overall criticism that SOF, regardless of their soft power, have simply become door kickers and lethal killers. It is the over-obsession to assess and view the operating environment through the prism of physical security objectives, knowing full well that conflict is a symptom of social and economic vulnerabilities, that makes SOF non-humanitarian. It is also their obsession with meeting their own needs first and not fully taking into account the second-order effects of their lethal actions on the population, which makes them non-humanitarian. This self-serving approach is one of the factors that cause SOF to diverge from NGOs and development actors in the gray space. Where SOF's assessment of local needs, and engagement with NGOs occurs, it is ad-hoc at best. In the instances that SOF *are* successful in their humanitarian and development activities, it is because of individual operators' initiatives, not because of mandate or guidance.

CONCLUSION

SOF and CA teams are to the gray space what conventional power is to high-intensity conflict. Considering their skills, facets, omnipresence, and cross-cutting nature, can SOF teams be humanitarians, and effective humanitarians at that?

The U.S. military is all about logistics and operations. One of SOF's twelve core activities is humanitarian assistance. They possess the mechanisms and structures to be a sufficiently robust actor in this space, not only because of logistical capability, but mostly because of their sophisticated training and ability to engage with and understand populations. The fragile settings in which they train other HN militaries through FID missions are ripe with sources of insecurity, but these settings are also a constant convergent factor between SOF and civic actors such as NGOs. This convergence is not because of an institutionally agreed closeness of the organizations. It is because of the characteristics of the gray space—maneuverable, permissive, sufficiently void of basic needs, and a need for outside intervention by both military and development actors. In those contexts, SOF can provide basic services as a way to prevent conflict but diverge away from NGOs because of their opposing objectives. SOF have become much more lethal, getting away from their multifaceted character. Where they assist local populations, they use instruments that are inherently self-serving in their design.

Ultimately, SOF's role in fragile settings in training other militaries is not a well-suited context for SOF to be humanitarians. This is also the case for SOF's role vis-à-vis other actors, namely the HN military. This military-to-military relationship complicates things further, as in its role SOF should be followers and mentors of the HN military, which is in the lead. This role may be difficult to achieve due to the competitive nature of SOF operators. In all their interactions, relationships, engagements, and expected outcomes, SOF is fundamentally subordinate to security-oriented objectives. This is even if the humanitarian and development projects they carry out are a mechanism to eradicate sources of insecurity. It is not solely SOF's lack of impartiality and neutrality, qualities often associated with NGOs, which make them non-humanitarian. It is also not SOF's hard power exertion, which is often seen as a complicating factor in complex emergencies where the military must not only be warriors but also humanitarian providers. In these complex contexts, the military's role is to manage "warring factions, ensuring that international law is complied with and providing civil and humanitarian assistance in co-operation with NGOs,"[158] therefore making it a useful partner. In fragile settings which are not ridden by high-intensity conflict, where SOF provide training for other militaries, they are hindered by excessive complexity, some contradictory incentives, conflicting lines of accountability, and a lack of valuing and integrating communities' input into their program design. Where SOF seek to launch their tools as a way to gain better access to the civil environment, it is with their own interest in mind, not the interest of the civic organizations or populations, causing a divergence between SOF and civic actors. Yet, they can be useful interlocutors to both the HN and civic actors, causing operational convergence between all these actors. They can also be effective in humanitarian and development efforts, even if not as humanitarian or development actors. Their effectiveness is less deliberate, and more a by-product of their efforts to meet security objectives. Meeting security objectives first, as an effort of their core business, aligns with Huntington's and Gentile's views that the military's main job is to meet security objectives, not replace the work of civic actors. Contrarily, the evidence also shows that the military is not only a hard power capability. Its ability to combine hard and soft power, as progressives, Sarkesian, and Scales argued, is also a large part of what the military does. In threading the gray space, SOF's ability to have a role as part social scientist, part security actor, and part humanitarian, is not a surprise but an inevitability.

NOTES

1. R 61—Senior NCO Military Respondent, April 16, 2021.
2. U.S. Congress, House Armed Services Committee, *Statement of Joseph L. Votel.*
3. The command has approximately 70,000 personnel assigned to its headquarters, its service components, and sub-unified commands. This includes the 70,000 personnel assigned to the

USSOCOM's headquarters, including military and civilian personnel. See US Library of Congress, Congressional Research Service, Defense Primer and U.S. Special Operations Forces (SOF): Background for Congress, Feickert, RS21048.

4. This number is approximate. For example, in 2016, over 7,500 SOF were deployed in over 90 countries.(see U.S. Congress, House Armed Services Committee, Statement of Joseph L. Votel.) Operations include combat and non-combat missions. In 2017, 8,000 SOF were deployed globally in 80 countries, and in 2016, SOF missions occurred in 70% of the world's countries. In 2007-08 SOF forces had deployed to 60 countries around the world, by 2011, this number had doubled (see Turse, "American Special Ops Forces Have Deployed to 70 Percent of the World's Countries.")

5. Turse, "American Special Ops Forces Have Deployed to 70 Percent of the World's Countries"; "Civil Affairs Association Roundtable 2022."

6. Votel, Cleveland, Connett, and Irwin, "Unconventional Warfare in the Gray Zone," 102.

7. R 15—Senior NCO Military Respondent, February 17, 2021.

8. *Ibid.*

9. Scales, "Clausewitz," 26.

10. Croot, "There Is an Identity Crisis in Special Forces."

11. U.S. Government Accountability Office, *Special Operations Forces: Opportunities Exist to Improve Transparency.*

Cancian, "US Military Forces in FY 2021."

12. Brennan, Marks, and Croot, "The Turmoil of Identity Crisis."

13. R 35—Senior Military Officer Respondent, March 11, 2021.

14. Croot, "There is an Identity Crisis in Special Forces," 33.

15. Bachmann, "Kick Down the Door," 564–85.

16. Murray, "Does Military Culture Matter?," 30.

17. Online Forum on Special Operations Forces Conference 2021, Yale University, March 3, 2021.

18. Norwood, "Russian Hybrid."

19. Ansbacher and Schleifer, "The Three Ages," 32–45.

20. Norwood, "Russian Hybrid."

21. *Ibid.*

22. Croot, "There Is an Identity Crisis," 27.

23. Brennan et al., "The Turmoil."

24. Lythgoe, "Our Risk-Averse Army."

25. R 18—Civil Affairs Officer, February 18, 2021.

26. R 15.

27. Breede, "Special (Peace) Operations," 221–40.

28. Matelski, "Developing Security Force Assistance."

29. United States Department of the Army, *Multi-Service Techniques for Civil Affairs Support to Foreign Humanitarian Assistance,* 2–3.

30. Curtis E. LeMay, "Center for Doctrine and Development Education," *Introduction to Foreign Internal Defense,* 2.

31. Department of Defense Security Cooperation Agency, Overseas.

32. Department of Defense Security Cooperation Agency, *Overseas Humanitarian, Disaster, and Civic Aid (OHDACA).*

33. The consultation with USAID does not apply to those countries where there is no SOF CA or USAID presence, either because of the level of development or because the relationship between the U.S. and host government does not allow for it.

34. United States Air Force, *Irregular Warfare,* 6.

35. Matelski, "Developing Security Force Assistance," 5.

36. R 54—NCO Military Respondent, April 11, 2021.

37. Civil-military operations (CMO) are a unique angle of FID where CMOs are used across all the phases of conflict prevention, reconstruction, and combat operations.

38. R 13—Civil Affairs Officer, February 16, 2021.

39. R 15.

40. Mednick, "In Burkina Faso."

41. R 18.

42. This is specifically the case for Colombia, where Accion Integral is in the lead for civic engagement and the CA Battalion only provides the funding.

43. R 18.

44. R 13.

45. It is important to differentiate between CIMIC and U.S. Civil Affairs. CIMIC may have disparate definitions according to the country where it is occurring. Among NATO Allies, CIMIC may be more or less driven by the civilian or security apparatus, or both. The NATO definition of CIMIC is "a military joint function that integrates the understanding of the civil factors of the operating environment and that enables, facilitates and conducts civil-military interaction to support the accomplishment of missions and military strategic objectives in peacetime, crises and conflict." Reference as per MC 0411: NATO Policy on Civil-Military Cooperation (CIMIC) and Civil-Military Interaction (CMI)— https://www.cimic-coe.org/branches/cic/nato-cimic/

46. R 15.

47. *Ibid.*

48. R 35.

49. There are exceptions to this rule. In projects which the military conducts as part of security cooperation, where CA reservist units are involved in engaging with the population, the host nation military may not be necessarily receiving training. There are instances in which U.S. CA is simply working to win goodwill with populations as a way to gain local support for U.S. missions. See Grad-ishar, "Civil Affairs Teams."

50. R 16—Senior NCO Military, February 18, 2021.

51. R 18.

52. Donovan II, "Medical Stability Operations."

53. UNDP, Human Development Report as referenced in Aldis, "Health security."

54. R 16.

55. *Ibid.*

56. *Ibid.*

57. R 7—Senior SF Officer (retired), February 9, 2021.

58. R 16.

59. R 39—Senior Civil Affairs Officer, March 17, 2021.

60. Dijkzeul and Wakenge, "Doing Good," 1140.

61. R 16.

62. R 19—Military SF Officer February 19, 2021.

63. Brennan et al., "The Turmoil."

64. Tan, "Report."

65. Bingham, Rubini, and Cleary, "US Army Civil Affairs," v.

66. Department of Defense Security Cooperation Agency, *Overseas.*

67. U.S. Department of the Army, *Civil Affairs General Concepts.*

68. Department of Defense Security Cooperation Agency, *Overseas.*

69. Hinds, Ott, Regan, Pena, and Schott, "Civil Affairs Veterinary," 7.

70. U.S. Department of the Army, *Civil Affairs General Concepts,* 27.

71. *Ibid.,* 28.

72. *Ibid.,* 25.

73. U.S. Department of Defense, *Civil-Military Operations.*

74. Armed Forces Staff College, "Anthony Zinni: Operations Other Than War."

75. Brewer, "US Army Civil Affairs," 4.

76. Cecchine, Morgan, Wermuth, Jackson, Schaefer, and Stafford, "The U.S. Military Response to the 2010 Haiti Earthquake," 34.

77. Jenkins, "Operation Allies Welcome."

78. Bingham et al., "US Army."

79. Hinds et al., "Civil Affairs Veterinary," 7.

80. World Bank, "FY22 List of Fragile and Conflict-affected Situations," and Defense Visual Information Distribution Service - https://www.dvidshub.net.

81. States or regions in which civil affairs may be engaged, but whose engagement is not available in the unclassified space, have not been accounted for in this study. Considering the criteria for deploying CA teams, it is safe to conclude that civil affairs have engaged in almost all of the countries on the World Bank's Fragility list.

82. Whalley, Vendrzyk, and Calfas, *Improving US Army Civil Affairs Assessment*, 614.

83. Sisk, "House Divided," 1.

84. Authorities could be government or the military. In places like Colombia, for example, the Colombian military provides basic services for the population. Basic services can also be provided by NGOs, or other security actors.

85. R 15.

86. *Ibid.*

87. World Bank, "World Development Report 2011," 62.

88. U.S. Department of the Army, *Civil Affairs Tactics, Techniques, and Procedures*, 1.

89. Hinds et al., "Civil Affairs Veterinary," 12.

90. Bremer and Cawthorne, "Haiti."

91. R 15.

92. *Ibid.*

93. Kingsley, "Ungoverned Space?," 1023.

94. Flanigan, "Nonprofit Service," 509.

95. R 19.

96. U.S. Department of the Army, *Civil Affairs Planning*, 1–2.

97. The 95th is comprised of the 91st Battalion for AFRICOM, 92nd Battalion for EUCOM, 96th Battalion for CENTCOM, the 97th Battalion for INDOPACOM, 98th Civil Affairs Battalion for SOUTHCOM, and the hybrid of general purpose force and special operations force duty—the 83rd civil affairs battalion.

98. "Civil Affairs Association Roundtable 2022."

99. R 40—NGO/Development Sector Respondent, March 23, 2021.

100. Lamb and Munsing, "Secret Weapon," 33.

101. R 61 and R 39.

102. R 40.

103. Defense Visual Information Distribution Service, "MEDFLAG—Medical Assistance Project by USAFRICOM."

104. *Ibid.*, "Beninese People."

105. Vogelsang, "Special Operations Forces Veterinary Personnel," 69.

106. U.S. Embassy Sofia, "Renovation."

107. Defense Security Cooperation Agency, "Chapter 12."

108. R 35.

109. Burke, "Civil Reconnaissance," 1 and 5.

110. *Ibid.*, 2.

111. International and multilateral coordination efforts are not the focus of this analysis. There is a multitude of actors who are engaged in these contexts. In the civ-mil craft, one of the most recognizable actors is United Nations Office for the Coordination of Humanitarian Affairs, the body which leads coordination for humanitarian response worldwide, where various other agencies may take the lead on specific issues, such as protection, water, sanitation, and so on. This coordination may occur in partnership with the host nation government, as well as international actors, where the host nation government does not have the capacity to respond to large-scale natural disasters and complex emergencies. Unlike SOF CA units' interaction with civilian actors, which may entail reconnaissance,

and access and placement, UNOCHA's work is not for meeting security objectives, bit is focused on humanitarian efforts.

112. R 75—Senior Military Officer Respondent, August 12, 2021.

113. Brinkerhoff, "Waging the War and Winning the Peace," 40.

114. R 29—NGO Respondent, March 4, 2021.

115. R 40.

116. Hanhauser IV, "Comprehensive Civil Information," 1.

117. R 40.

118. Burke, "Civil," 4.

119. U.S. Department of the Army, "Civil Affairs Planning," 3–11.

120. Whalley et al., *Improving,* 614.

121. Enstad, *Warriors or Peacekeepers?*.

122. McCauley, "Failing with Single-Point Solutions."

123. R 44—Civil Affairs Officer, March 30, 2021.

124. Pike, "Beyond PMESII."

125. *Ibid.*

126. *Ibid.*

127. Hinds et al., "Civil Affairs Veterinary," 3.

128. *Ibid.*, 11.

129. *Ibid.*

130. Whalley et al., *Improving.*

131. U.S. Department of the Army, *Civil Affairs Operations*, Appendix G.

132. Egnell, "Civil-Military Aspects of Effectiveness in Peace," 20.

133. R 18.

134. R 15.

135. R 16.

136. Wilson and Conway, "The Tactical Conflict Assessment Framework," 10–15.

137. Hinds et al., "Civil Affairs Veterinary," 10.

138. If SOF CA were to operate beyond the walls of the Embassy, they would need host nation approval, even if they are not consulted on every project.

139. R 17—Military Officer (Retired) February 18, 2021.

140. R 18.

141. R 16.

142. Brass, et al., "NGOs and International Development," 137.

143. R 16.

144. *Ibid.*

145. UNSW Canberra, "Operating."

146. Scheidt, "NGOs in the Operational Theater," 7.

147. R 30—Senior NCO Military Respondent, March 8, 2021.

148. R 45—CA Officer—March 30, 2021.

149. R 3—Senior Military Officer, January 22, 2021.

150. R 35.

151. R 61.

152. R 54.

153. R 15.

154. *Ibid.*

155. United States Marine Corps, "PMESII and ASCOPE Matrices Templates."

156. R 61.

157. U.S. Department of the Army, "Civil Affairs Planning," 3–6.

158. Pettit and Beresford, "Emergency Relief Logistics," 319.

Chapter 3

The Entrepreneurs

ARE NGOS ALTRUISTIC OR ENTREPRENEURIAL IN MEETING THE NEEDS OF THEIR BENEFICIARIES?

> Anyone could be an NGO. These places are so ungoverned and messed up, I could show up in the field, call myself an NGO, and nobody would know the difference.[1]

Much of the development discourse focuses on the effectiveness of aid in the places where NGOs are operating. The debate is mostly directed toward seeking answers as to whether NGOs weaken local governments as they replace them, whether aid prolongs or mitigates conflict, and what drives NGOs' allocations across places, projects, and people. But there are many more complex and simultaneous forces pushing the debate into less explored territory. With the increase in bilateral and multilateral donor funding for fragile state assistance, and an expansion in the number of NGOs, these entities are increasingly operating in the gray space, tackling problems created by instability, conflict, and weak governance. As such, their operational engagements are increasingly eliminating the boundaries between themselves and the military. Their evolved organizational attributes lead them into a series of operational convergences with the military. But NGOs are experiencing something much more fundamental than this.

In operating in conflict zones, NGOs are replicating some of the structures and behaviors of military actors. This occurs through two separate but related processes. First, by directly recruiting retired military personnel into their organizations, NGOs are bringing certain practices and operating procedures into their organizational culture, as a form of "mimetic" isomorphism. With former military personnel bringing their experience and skills into the leadership roles of the NGO humanitarian and development space, they now oversee this work in unstable environments and potentially facilitate more productive civil-military relationships. As such, employee migration from military to NGO is not only an operational convergence between the two organizations but it also seems an organic and logical transition for the professionals working in conflict settings.

Second, NGOs themselves have evolved, becoming savvy charitable operators, contracting many of the same hard-power skills and assets held by the military, through the acquisition of private security services. This gives them more flexibility to operate on the ground. Also, depending on how they are funded, NGOs may have different accountability requirements. Funding arrangements also give NGOs much more flexibility in how, when, where, and with whom they operate. In examining a series of international, privately and publicly funded NGOs, and their functional makeup, the analysis presents insight on two fronts. First, the analysis provides an overview of the vast landscape of organizational, financial, accountability, and relationship mechanisms that exist within these entities. Then, the analysis also explains what is pushing them to become more similar to military actors.

Ultimately, NGOs' organizational complexity, and the nebulous gray spaces in which they are operating, offer both constraints and opportunities. The evolution or hybridization of NGOs has led them to establish a well-connected network of knowledgeable and experienced individuals in the gray space. This hybridization is placing NGOs on the cutting edge of conflict management and response, placing them closer to the military's operations.

NON-GOVERNMENTAL ORGANIZATIONS

Just like the military's multitude of functions, specialties, and branches, NGO operations can also be vast in scale, specialization, and outreach, spanning a complex mix of humanitarianism, development, and advocacy. When speaking of NGOs, a host of "non-governmental, private, civil-society and not-for-profit organizations" encapsulate this diverse and loosely used term for an organization.[2] From small village groups to publicly supported national or international organizations, to large-funded global mega-foundations, to small groups of volunteers, these organizations include a variety of "religious, humanitarian, social, and professional organizations."[3] While some humanitarian actors are NGOs, not all NGOs are humanitarian actors. As a sector, NGOs' involvement spans the development of economies and markets and promotes good governance, gender equality, and even religion.

In explaining the terms in chapter 1, an NGO was defined as a not-for-profit organization that may or may not be an implementing partner of donor agencies and have direct or indirect interaction and engagement with any branch of the U.S. military or host nation (HN) military. As previously mentioned, NGOs are diverse, categorized along the broad themes of publicly or privately funded, local or multinational, but in this analysis, they are examined less within their categories and more through the lens of their complexity and interaction with the military and communities. It is this complexity, and the fact that any of them—regardless of structure, specialty, or funding—can interact with military actors, which adds to the debate around the civil-military relationship. The focus of the analysis here examines *how* NGOs, whether they are local, regional, or international, interact with military actors, and what inside of their makeup drives and empirical or challenging relationship with military actors.

During World War II, there were about 3,000 international NGOs; the civil conflicts of the 1990s brought this number to over 13,000. Also in the 1990s, NGOs ran nearly a third of clinical healthcare in Cameroon, Ghana, Malawi, Uganda, and Zambia.[4] By 2006, the number of NGOs had reached 38,000. With the wars in Iraq and Afghanistan, this increased to over 50,000, with private, non-governmental, and philanthropic organizations joining the mix.[5] The direct impact on the ground in local communities is significant. By 2005, "90% of villages were home to at least one NGO" in Bangladesh.[6] Globally, about 4,500 humanitarian NGOs are working in the field. Out of these, 4 out of 5 are local NGOs.[7] The Mormon Church carried out "1,031 projects in 151 countries and territories" in 2020.[8] The Mormon Church's ecclesiastical and NGO leadership is the same.[9] For the Catholic Church, these arms are separated. Catholic Relief Services, for example, do not proselytize to acquire more members.[10] The missions of these NGOs vary as much as their number. As Antonio Donini describes the situation in Afghanistan, "some NGOs have been around for years and years. Some turned up last year. Some deal with leprosy and some deal with hairdressing . . . some exist in one person's briefcase, some have established offices."[11] In sum, putting NGOs under one umbrella would not be a fair description of this complex sector.

Private and Practical

Unlike the military, most NGOs are not funded by a secure stream of approved public money coming from government taxpayers. In recent years, certain NGOs have had a wide range of funding sources, which include government donors, but also a series of religious charities, philanthropic fundraising efforts, as well as individual, private, and corporate donors. Most invest significantly in maintaining a team of fundraising staff.

More than 60 percent of international and humanitarian development aid to NGOs in 2005 were funded with private money.[12] Between 1990 and 2014, NGOs' humanitarian spending increased from $2 billion to nearly $20 billion.[13] More than 90 percent of Medicines Sans Frontiers (MSF) money comes from individuals, not governments.[14] One example of this increase in private funding is within United States Agency for International Development's (USAID) implementing partners, where "during fiscal year 2016, for example, the nearly 600 NGOs that are United States Agency for International Development (USAID) partners received $23.8 billion in support from private sources, compared to less than $3 billion from the USAID."[15] By using diverse funding streams, the International Rescue Committee (IRC) has tripled its budget in the last several years.[16] Many NGOs, such as World Vision, Oxfam, Save the Children, MSF, and so on, all now claim budgets larger than many UN agencies.[17] These large sums of money give international NGOs the ability to also dominate certain parts of the sector with their size. For example, World Vision has more staff than international organizations, such as the World Food Program.[18] World Vision also implements more than 80 percent of the UN's work.[19] There is still a question about what drives private money to outweigh public funding to such an extent, but some have suggested that it could be attributed to the promotion of an organization's mission via media,[20] or humanitarian fundraising campaigns.[21] In such instances, the organization would show the dramatic images of malnourished children in Ethiopia or destroyed infrastructure in Syria. NGOs are also funded through smaller donations from individuals, which make up a large part of the revenue for large international NGOs. In 2017, Catholic Relief Services received approximately 40% of its revenues from private donations and 60% from public sources.[22]

While expansive in funding, the privatization of aid has achieved another advantage but also created challenges. Private funding can be largely unrestricted—unlike public funding distributed by governments. Organizations can raise private money and choose how to spend it without the heavy burden of bureaucratic requirements and waste. As a result, much of the data on NGO aid allocation only covers projects that receive public co-financing because those NGOs are required to comply with this level of transparency. Many big international NGOs do not take money for one specific area to work in—for instance, in only a certain area of health or a certain area of education. However, in Afghanistan, Save the Children took 34 million dollars over five years as it primarily invested in a single province.[23] Chapter 6 further addresses how even when funding is not specified for a single issue or a single place, it still can do great harm to the communities where it is disbursed.

NGOS AND DONORS' RELATIONSHIP
STATUS: IT'S COMPLICATED

When money does come from public entities, and not through private means, it creates other complications.

First, bilateral and multilateral donors have increasingly relied on NGOs for programmatic purposes, especially in fragile states, as will be discussed later. Nearly 95 percent of USAID's work is conducted through implementing partners, namely NGOs. USAID, and a range of bilateral and multilateral aid agencies, similarly, have incorporated NGOs into their programmable aid projects and with other bilateral donors such as the British Department for International Development (DFID), Germany's Gesellschaft für Internationale Zusammenarbeit (GIZ), the Japan International Cooperation Agency (JICA), or the EU institutions, which together comprise the largest donors to fragile contexts.[24] Large amounts of public money also go directly to governments—a relationship that is not the focus for this study. In such cases bilateral donors rely on aid that can require recipients to make use of NGOs based in donor countries by bringing those recipients into the project, and linking the project to a specific sector or required reform as identified by donors to be a priority. As discussed in chapter 1, much of this is being mitigated, especially in fragile contexts, through the New Deal, where countries are given a voice at the table. The opposite also exists, where donors simply provide the funding, but expect NGOs to come up with the ideas.

Second, when it comes to NGOs implementing projects for public donors, the picture is yet more complex. Donors use a mix of local and international NGOs to implement their work. Each carries its own dynamic. Multilateral donors, such as the World Bank or the Asian Development Bank (ADB), are much more likely to include local NGOs as partners, as there is a serious premium on funding local NGOs as part of project design. But to reach that point, often large multilateral donors partner up with large international NGOs first, who in turn partner with local NGOs. In this case, those subcontracting the work take their financial cut along the way, even if they are not carrying out the actual project implementation.[25] In short, as NGOs have diversified their funding, factors such as interests, accountability mechanisms, and requirements of how and when to implement project stages—further complicate this sector and the gray space.

Third, there has been wide recognition in program implementation about the importance of locally driven solutions in development. This drives the need to employ local staff. This is good news, as the sourcing, expertise, and capacity of human capital have traditionally taken a top-down approach, and have been centrally designed from outside the geographic area of operations. More local staff is a way to build capacity, ensure safety, and increase credibility in the eyes of local communities. More local staff also make better business sense in terms of operating expenses, as they require fewer fringe benefits—as opposed to expatriates who may need housing and other incentives. Local staff operate under the radar in a way that expatriate staff, who require security and are entitled to special privileges and immunities, could not. This is particularly true in fragile settings where local staff possess the sensitivity and awareness of local dynamics. They are more adept at project management in difficult conditions, dealing with warring parties, and managing tensions. Local staff also provide a presence within a community, which internationals could never have. But locals' salaries and compensation are far less than those of internationals. One NGO respondent noted that while local NGO staff are from and work in the local community, compared to their counterpart NGO staff from developed countries, "they do the riskiest work with the least amount of pay and with the least risk mitigation."[26] These large, international NGO employers potentially create a wider net of economic disparity in these regions. NGOs can inflate salaries, creating competition with national ministries in what is already limited local capacity, lack of opportunity, and brain drain in fragile states. As a result, local government agencies' salaries are unable to compete with those of NGOs.[27] The positive outcome of all of this is that higher salaries by NGOs *do* drive up the quality of life for local employees, but they also drive up the cost of living for everyone else where the staff reside. As a result, local institutions, which do not receive international funding, cannot compete, resulting in an inequity across sectors, potential earnings, and economic brackets.

Fourth, this inequity also exists along human resource models used for NGOs in Congo, such as rewarding for good performance, which are not widely accepted policies for personnel management in the workplace.[28] Ultimately, it is difficult to make a case for or against these practices. There is an element of a "Catch-22" with respect to NGO presence in fragile states. On the one hand, it is possible that extant economic gaps within communities can be made even deeper in cases where NGO activities divert precious resources from the few government institutions which *do* exist. On the other hand, if NGOs were to be completely absent, the availability of basic services might degrade even further.

Fifth, linkages to international NGOs are also unequal, in that "countries with ties to international NGOs and donor organizations tend to have more local NGOs."[29] Small and local NGOs possess invaluable, close-knit relationships and cultural knowledge within the communities where they live and serve. Sometimes these local actors are simply a group of women who may be engaged with anything from running a feeding program for undernourished children to providing medical training for the local military.[30] Large NGOs' local staff is central to making invaluable connections within the community,

enabling outside organizations to work in a foreign environment and language. Local NGO workers are members of the community where assistance
is received and part of "a web of indigenous officials and resources."[31] As a
result, they are better suited to carry out the work than their well-connected
and better-branded global NGO counterparts, such as MSF, Red Cross, Red
Crescent, World Vision, Save the Children, CARE, and Oxfam, who have
greater access due to their strong relationships with donors. But these small
and local entities are outsiders to the UN and global donor system, and do not
always possess the political prowess or communications budget to compete
for grants. They also "do not benefit from the same attention and funding as
their more worldly brethren."[32] Where the relationship can work is where
local conglomerates of international NGOs "help connect local NGOs into
broader networks that can confer money, legitimacy, motivation, and many
other valuable resources."[33]

One solution to bridging this gap has been through working with local
branches of international NGOs. But local branches of international NGOs
have:

> Become adept at complying with the fiscal monitoring and evaluation require-
> ments which international donors impose on their grantees and contractors.
> These local institutions may do excellent work, but their dominance in the local
> markets means that smaller community-based organizations may not be noticed
> by the donors.[34]

Sixth, an all-outsourced approach to local NGOs or implementing partners
creates another unfortunate dynamic:

> Local organizations often feel that they are "used" by international donors to
> deliver goods but that they have little influence on how to allocate resources
> or decide what is actually done. Even when local NGOs are seen to function
> effectively, some people feel that they are just one more layer in the delivery
> system that requires funding to operate—meaning that fewer resources actually
> reach intended beneficiaries.[35]

This is not surprising. As donors hold the purse strings, they often dictate
the agenda. As a result, NGOs bow "to donor-specified terms and conditions,
and suffer [ing] the indignity of donor-led evaluations" and are forced to take
on any contract to pay the bills.[36] As a result, NGOs, and especially local
ones, find themselves in an incredibly difficult balancing act; they continue
to assess local needs, create programs to meet those needs, and write grant
proposals to gain enough money to keep their shops running. As mentioned
above, an NGO that has a pre-established relationship with a donor can often

win funding over an NGO that is equally qualified to do the job. As a result, this leaves those who do not benefit from such a relationship constantly competing for donors' attention, not for the attention of beneficiaries. According to one NGO respondent:

> In Africa, it was all about child and maternal health. You might be an NGO that does sanitation. They have to weave in child and maternal health. They are not experts, it's not part of their mandate, but they are willing to shape shift, even if they have nothing to add because they have no income. So, it's a competition game, and the ability for an NGO to influence the government and donors is a huge win.[37]

In assessing disaster-prone areas in Bangladesh, "the consortium which commissioned the study wanted to prove that girls were more at risk than boys because addressing gender inequality was where the money was."[38] Such has been predominantly the case for HIV/AIDS, where for NGOs in Africa the focus has been on "activity central to the world polity"[39] over local needs.

Chapter 2 established that Special Operations Forces are not well suited to be development and humanitarian actors because of a variety of mission-driven objectives. How are NGOs better suited to do this?

NGOs, much like the military, are not always able to align their work with the needs cycle. Taking into account that organizations can be frequently strapped for cash, "life does not work on a donor project cycle; clinics and schools cannot close because the critical fax has not arrived from Rugby, Zeist, or Norwalk Connecticut. Crops must be planted on time, not later."[40] While Smillie's reference is from a couple of decades ago, it is still the case that some NGOs use money already received from one donor to pay for the project of another donor. Therefore, they pre-finance portions of one project before receiving donor approval, in order to keep the work moving. NGOs *have to* do this, as they manage their available resources with the need to deliver, and the need to stay afloat.

Moreover, NGOs' dependency on donors has pushed them "to mimic the structures and behavior of their northern counterparts."[41] With their increase in number, size, and scope over the last fifty years, NGOs are increasingly being held to higher professional standards by donor governments and international organizations, "as a means of developing greater precision in goals, objectives, inputs, outputs and 'objectively verifiable indicators' of achievement."[42] Working toward program results is not always aligned with working toward organizational efficiency—a contrast driven by a variety of factors. According to Smillie, "achieving results in projects is one thing, but institutional performance is often a very different matter."[43] This shaping of how intra-organizationally NGOs are to operate and behave inside of their own organizations, is especially prevalent when it comes to northern donors' expectations vis-à-vis organizations from the Global South. One Jamaican local NGO manager notes how "Northern donors 'have an enormous amount of power. They can shape the lives of the organizations they support, not simply because they fund them, but also because of the processes and disciplines they require the organizations to become involved in."[44] This is not so clearcut. If more money is increasingly being given to local NGOs to carry out programming, visibility and accountability not only become more difficult, but even more paramount.

NGOs have also acquired more "technocratic approaches to complex developmental challenges,"[45] while at the same time they have become "more vertical and less horizontal."[46] Along with NGOs developing their organizational structures, there have come into being a variety of strengthened accountability measures for how these entities carry out their work. Requirements from donors have led NGOs, from both the Global South and North, to establish management processes, budgetary oversight, performance indicators, and audits. Such improved business processes allow these organizations to demonstrate a strong commitment to management, oversight, and efficiency to executive boards and members. However, an increased local partnership between donor governments and large International Non-Governmental Organizations (INGOs) creates another challenge. There is a need to please the policy needs of the donor as a means to get funding. This creates a series of second-order effects, making NGOs turn to "rent-seeking or nonprincipled motivations," and operate as a business.[47] Helmut Anheier argues that unlike a business "nonprofit organizations are mission-driven rather than profit-driven," and are not "non-profit-making" but rather "non-profit-distributing."[48] But this is not quite the case. With the need to compete for funding, NGOs have begun operating their organizations like a business. Being run like a business is a way for NGOs to improve their intra-organizational management. As non-state actors, even if they fail to meet the needs of populations where the government cannot, NGOs are acting less like a government, whom they often replace, and more like a business, where they "have become more transactional, more business-like, and are seen as such by the general public."[49]

Some have argued that "while a business seeks rapid turnover of products, an aid agency seeks rapid turnover of projects."[50] Several international NGOs "have recruited corporate representatives to their boards of directors or hired people from the private sector to lead their organizations."[51] These days, donors and NGOs talk about value for money, results-based management, and deliverables. CEOs and boards of directors of aid agencies discuss their "return on investment" and the "branding" of their organization's work to distinguish it from others. With donor support, consortia of aid agencies have developed standards for "professionalism" in the aid industry.[52] But efficiency in resources is not necessarily a negative. Many more are the benefits of running organizations with more stringent oversight, transparency, and efficiency—all contributing factors to the professionalization of these entities, which sometimes have a mixed reputation. The contrary view to this is that among the various authorities which partake in the running of NGOs—internal managers of NGOs, trustee boards, donors, and volunteers—each has an expectation of how the organization is to behave, and how its performance is to be evaluated against a set of expectations. Therefore, with all of this complexity and conflicting interests, how are these entities still able to respond to the needs of their recipients? Let us explore.

Monitoring, Evaluation, Impact

> The positive effects of even a much-needed road or water supply system provided through aid can be either reinforced or undermined by the processes of aid.[53]

How do NGOs address the needs of their beneficiaries, and respond to the needs of donors? Later chapters discuss how the consultation with and receiving feedback from recipients of assistance occurs. However, the process of selecting projects and ensuring their appropriateness and success in an area has its own cycle and is driven by the donor and the potential for receiving funding, not necessarily by the needs of the populace. Generally broken up between needs and feasibility assessments, evidence-based policy work requires monitoring and evaluation (ME) of programs funded by donors. But development has become an industry in and of itself and has created an entire generation of ME specialists who are trained in rigorous methods and strategies for assessing programs. Chapter 2 discussed the small-scale Overseas Humanitarian, Disaster, and Civic Aid projects deployed by the military, and how the military does not maintain visibility over them. This is not because it cannot, but because it is not in its objectives to follow up on their effectiveness. Yet, in a different way, donors are also removed from the spaces where NGOs carry out the programs and projects donors have funded. As donors have increasingly channeled funding through NGOs, they have sought to understand the effectiveness of the programming they are funding, imposing greater accountability and transparency measures through ME.

ME is a science in itself. At the most elementary level, it requires qualitative reporting, compliance, and information on costs and expenditures against programs, all of which can be further supported by auditing. On the delivery front, ME could consist of assessments of how an NGO implements its work, with an NGO providing a series of objectives, deliverables, and feedback from recipients, all set against a framework that was produced before the start of a project. Or so it works in theory. ME specialists are employed to track the success and effectiveness of donor-funded programs. But some have argued that ME is inherently flawed as they are designed by the donor agency as "control and justification mechanisms."[54] There is little baseline data, making evaluations vulnerable to influence by the evaluator, and ME is often employed as an evaluation of the NGO, not the project it is carrying out. Expectations for evaluations are often ambiguous, and fulfillment of them is sometimes based on "outputs for detail, and on sketchy evidence of achievement in relation to broader project goals."[55] There is no straightforward explanation for why that is, but it can be mostly attributed to scale and funding. It used to be that few NGOs had a self-contained evaluation arm, but that has changed now, as evaluation is the way to show program results and get funding. Large and international NGOs can engage consultants and research specialists, but smaller organizations have fewer such resources. Some NGOs have implemented metrics per the requirements from external donors and governments. Others have developed their own instruments. Scholars have even found that "NGOs with university-educated staff also may have a greater aptitude for monitoring and evaluation than nonprofits that rely less on formally trained employees."[56]

Where evaluations do happen, there has been a question as to the extent to which results from ME are fed into the program design.[57] As one NGO respondent argued:

> Every NGO has to do a needs assessment. To access money for the needs assessment, they have to determine what the project is going to be. Often the assessment may come after a project has already started implementation. It's a vicious cycle.[58]

In referring to a health center built in East South Sudan, one respondent spoke of how a needs assessment was done after the health center was built, and "any of the results which did not fit in with what was built were discarded."[59] The cause and effect of either NGOs or military programming is difficult to predict, and even if they were not, in the real world "predicting results is not the same as achieving results," in what is "the 'empty behaviour' of oversimplification and false quantification" of outcomes.[60] NGO programming has been put under question, where some have argued its heavy reliance on "a tenuous causal chain."[61] For example, both security and development analysts point to the fact that unemployment is the primary motive for joining rebel movements or gangs, and that injustice and poverty are viewed as the primary drivers of violent conflict by people living in FCAS.[62,63] It is easy to see why on the side of the military there is an assumption that in acquiring a job, young males will feel a sense of worth, convincing them not to turn to the insurgency. Similarly, there is an assumption that giving women economic empowerment in unstable areas of the developing world will decrease the violence against them: "Providing rape victims with sewing machines (or chickens, or the means to set up a beauty salon) will help these women gain financial independence, which will in turn give them greater political voice, and will thus help end sexual violence."[64] Even if well intended, sometimes the prioritization of these projects is not well-thought-out. One NGO respondent shared how funding was directed to fix one problem, when another was inherently more urgent to address:

I had been assigned to assess the vulnerabilities for child mortality rate caused by drowning due to flooding in a Bangladeshi community. I went into a community with a very open approach asking the people about their needs and experience. There was a flood line above a child's head, so it was striking. But people were very honest and open and they said 'we know when the floods are coming, they are regular.' So these people changed location or changed the cycle of the school year. Some people froze to death, as it got to 1 or 2 degrees Celsius. So basically all they needed was warm clothes. But this was not part of what the assessment was looking to prove. Up to 20 kids a year were dying from the cold, but only 3 from drowning. But we need to focus on drowning. So I said look there is money to support if there is drowning.[65]

The respondent shared another similar story:

There was a theory that during a flood, girls are more vulnerable to sexual assault because they can't access private latrines, or even pads for their periods. This was not true. It was the same amount. Girls just stayed closer to home, so in fact there was less risk because they were not in a school far away. But this did not support the data that was already established.[66]

All these firsthand accounts suggest that a lot of the time there is no existing robust assessment mechanism for understanding communities' true needs, which would mean driving project initiation and needs assessment from the ground up.

Several interviewees, on both the military and NGO fronts, shared that there is an assumption that local communities will use what is provided to them anyway, regardless of whether their needs are fully met. Even when assessments are done:

Those interviewed are handpicked by "us," [Westerners] and they are highly versed with speaking and operating around NGOs. People are not dumb. As soon as a foreigner shows up, they tell you how desperate they are. People would switch religions based on whatever church is giving out the most money. At a more macro level, places such as Kenya and Botswana, and middle-income countries, know how to play the game. But other places, such as South Sudan and Ethiopia are often overlooked. It's all political strategy, and communities are political entities.[67]

Whatever assessment occurs, one NGO respondent argues, "ultimately these people know better, and they would never bite the hand that feeds them. Whatever content is gathered from local communities is highly anecdotal."[68] Other studies too have found that whatever information is drawn from the local community is not always reliable. In an instance in Burkina Faso:

> Confronted with the hegemonic "project" of the donor, the local population, for fear of losing the aid offer, prefer to remain silent about their practices and aspirations. This is because these practices and aspirations are perceived to be so far away from those of the donor that they are better not disclosed. Such is the vicious circle of development cooperation: the fear of avowing the discrepancy between the two views because it could lead to the discontinuation of the aid relationship.[69]

In turn, this "has the effect of strengthening the donor's confidence in the validity of the participatory approach."[70] A head of an INGO at the Thai-Burma border noted that "there are times that INGOs do not provide what people need. For some NGOs, the projects are designed top-down. They should listen to the people from the communities."[71] What is drawn from the views of recipients, and NGO professionals is that there is a disconnect between what information is given, who receives it, and how it is interpreted. Chapter 6 discusses the challenges involved with NGOs' accountability toward populations they seek to benefit. Namely, there is evidence that some NGOs can prioritize the needs of donors before the needs of beneficiaries.[72]

Clearly, in the donor-led ME approach, upward accountability to donors for deliverables often trumps substantive change toward communities and longevity of any positive impact. Furthermore, the evaluation focuses "primarily on short-term 'functional' accountability responses at the expense of longer-term 'strategic' processes necessary for lasting social and political change."[73] In the last twenty years, as more aid, more NGOs, more ideas, and more maneuverability by these actors have occurred, so has a shift in how closely connected, but also how hierarchical they have become. Donini writes:

> Gone are the days of the erratic telex, the occasional fax and the expensive and therefore very brief satellite telephone conversations between aid workers in the field and their managers at headquarters; now multiple daily emails and teleconferencing are the norm. However, at the receiving end, aid agencies do more or less the same things, the same type of community-based relief and small-scale rehabilitation projects as before.[74]

As one NGO respondent noted, "we as the implementor justify our existence with the amount of reports we need to send to the donor."[75] A study of listening to local populations across countries that received assistance finds that "in all types of programs, aid agencies submit proposals and write reports claiming achievement of grand goals on fixed and regular schedules in brief prescribed periods."[76]

Lastly, NGOs' ability to plan is hampered. Often the program's design and implementation phases are difficult to keep apart, segmented and consecutive, as program activities have to be adapted to the continually changing conditions on the ground. This is because "it has become more difficult to apply standard appraisal criteria because implementation is frequently not under an NGO's direct control."[77] In later chapters, the NGO and the military are compared as processes and structures. But when it comes to planning, the military experiences challenges much in the same way as NGOs, as it seeks to plan based on limited outlook and incomplete information. As one military respondent questioned,

> How does a short-term plan of reacting to another Ebola outbreak occur, when and if there is another terrorist attack? What does our long-term plan for what Africa should look like in 40 years compare to dealing with next year's projected drought or famine?"[78]

Such questions, should and must be addressed by realities on the ground for both of these organizations, which are constantly being considered in reformulating plans, where ground truth information "does not always feed into a strategic vision."[79] One aid donor agency respondent noted, "the strategic objective overrides the need objective,"[80] posing the question of whether projects are conducted with the intention to improve communities, or just to "check the box."

Biased and Unneutral, or Too Political and Poor?

In examining the relationship between NGOs and the military in Provincial Reconstruction Teams (PRTs) in Afghanistan, Donini asks, "Can an NGO conduct local situation analyses for a Coalition or ISAF Provincial Reconstruction Team (PRT) in a contested area and still expect to be seen as impartial or humanitarian?"[81]

Donini's question is about impartiality and neutrality in the high-intensity conflict and political fracturing in Afghanistan.

In Afghanistan, in all its degrees of high- and low-intensity conflict-ridden spaces, NGOs found themselves working alongside the military in unusually dangerous settings. Organizations such as MSF that have been omnipresent for decades lost many of its staff and ultimately evacuated from Afghanistan.[82] MSF blamed the military who, "blurred the lines between humanitarians and military organizations by deliberately giving the impression that humanitarian aid was in support of its military and political objectives."[83] While the gray space has fewer of the characteristics of high-intensity conflict and the clear need for separation of military and civilians, Donini's question is equally applicable to the gray space in which the military and NGOs are still perceived as opposite in values. There is a general belief that some NGOs are better placed than the military to carry out their programming in a neutral and impartial way. Such attributes are unique and necessary in organizations where their efforts are deemed to "establish relationships between adversarial communities, foster mutual confidence, and provide peaceful mechanisms for dispute resolution."[84]

Many NGOs have been known to claim subscription to the values of impartiality and neutrality from parties in conflict, as per the International Federation of Red Cross code of conduct.[85] But the image of NGOs as solidarity organizations is one that only a few uphold. NGOs who take a "rights-based approach" are choosing not to be neutral in an active way. Also, as mentioned earlier, in many cases NGOs are known to direct their attention and focus on themes and projects based on their ability to raise money, especially when it comes to benefiting from the institutional currency of public donors—a topic discussed earlier in this chapter. But even in their impartiality, they are always backed by funding from someone—it could be a political party or organization an ally, or a terrorist group,[86] or an individual, at the onset, both in conflict settings and from within the donor country. This is similar to what scholars have long argued to be the indefensible and "crumbling perceptions of impartiality."[87] Except for some humanitarian NGOs, most NGOs are neither impartial nor neutral, if not at the onset of their programming, then as a consequence of it. This is either in their relationship with recipients, whom they seek to benefit, local political structures or warring parties, which they must navigate, or donors whom they have to convince and whose values they must promote. This is equally difficult in all programming contexts. Taylor Seybolt argues that "active involvement in complex emergencies cannot be strategically neutral."[88] He reinforces that even "In natural disasters, as when a cyclone hits Bangladesh, Hindus should get as much attention as Muslims, country dwellers as much attention as city dwellers."[89]

In short, it would be naive to assume that assistance does not have political consequences, a notion, which Karen Guttierri further supports by positing that the sheer fact of being an outsider represents a political position.[90] In later chapters, this analysis argues that the military's mere presence, and their behavior as development actors in local communities, by default make them development actors in the eyes of the populace. Seybolt suggests that simply recognizing that NGOs' presence can have political consequences can help keep misperceptions about their neutrality and impartiality in check. In short, *how* and *if* NGOs can maintain neutrality and impartiality is the wrong question to ask. As NGOs increasingly inhabit the gray space, they become savvy in navigating and adapting to it.

So does the lack of neutrality and impartiality by NGOs cause them to converge with SOF?

In the world of Foreign Internal Defense (FID), engagement by SOF with the HN military, and by extension NGOs, cannot be neutral. This leads NGOs and SOF to converge in their non-impartiality and non-neutrality. What becomes clear is that all three of these groups—communities, military, and NGO actors—are all to a lesser or greater extent political entities. Communities are by definition actors within the larger societal landscape of the HN. SOF, due to their hard power, are almost always used to reinforce a political agenda. And NGOs, as the implementors of donors, can almost never be apolitical, as they are agents of foreign policy, and policy almost always takes a side.

NGOS IN THE GRAY SPACE

If ever there is doubt as to whether there is a direct connection between conflict and NGOs, one is reminded that some of the world's best known international organizations, such as the Red Cross, the International Rescue Committee, and Save the Children were established between or as a result of the two World Wars. Amnesty International was founded in 1961. Human Rights Watch in 1978. Transparency International in 1993. Oxfam was started to address the Greek Famine of 1943. MSF and Concern were both formed following Nigeria's Biafra War (1967–1970) and the Bangladesh Bhola cyclone (1970). NGOs often fill one or more roles of governments, especially in fragile states, where governments are not able to provide basic social services such as health, education, sanitation, and so on, to their people.

NGOs have not crept into the role of security actors in the same way the military has moved on to take more *civilianized* roles in development and humanitarianism.[91] NGOs, however, do not merely operate in stabilized and permissive environments. They are equally experienced in both low- and high-intensity conflicts and can operate in such areas because of their low visibility. Since NGOs have been operating in various degrees of conflict for several decades, their operational engagements are increasingly erasing boundaries between where they and the military operate. The problem of NGOs lacking physical access to spaces where there is a need, according to one NGO respondent, "is a myth."[92] Where security might be an issue, "foreign agencies and aid workers would be respected and protected by communities."[93] One NGO staffer, discussing their work in Afghanistan since 1999, recalled an encounter in the early 2000s:

> I had to come in through Tajikistan, and upon crossing through I ran into a US military guy. "What the hell are you doing here?" he asked me. I said, "what the hell are *you* doing here?" The US military guys are just standing there, as an old Afghan man invites me into his home and offers to bake me chicken.[94]

Therefore, NGOs might lack access because they may be restrained by budget and resources, not because they are denied by the local community.

There are several other dynamics at play in fragile spaces. First, as discussed earlier, private money is a large part of what constitutes development programming, but when it comes to fragile states, there is evidence that political instability reduces private aid.[95] The opposite is true for public donor funding. Also, as fragile states are ripe with corruption and weak governance, donors' commissioning of NGOs to perform work on their behalf often bypasses the local government and goes straight to the people, as a way to improve effectiveness.[96] In 2016, the Organization for Economic Cooperation and Development criticized U.S. assistance for dealing mostly with non-state actors, instead of with governments in fragile settings.[97] Donors also leverage their ability to influence economic legislation, which is often at the root cause of weak governance in recipient countries.[98] In sum, when it comes to fragile spaces, there is little difference between publicly funded NGOs through UNDP, DFID, GIZ, or USAID, in fragile settings, and the publicly funded military in these same fragile settings. As donors try to pull all the levers in fighting corruption, strengthening governance, or financing basic services—directly or indirectly—they are essentially seeking to reduce fragility and prevent insecurity. This is not unsimilar to the military whose missions in training a country's security forces and building its defense capability aims to do the same. Both of these entities are attracted by tackling sources of insecurity in the gray space, causing them to converge once again.

Second, unlike the military, which tackles security and sources of insecurity by deploying a specific branch—SOF—not its conventional military, there is no tidy separation for *which* among publicly funded NGOs deploy in fragile settings. The blurring of conflict and non-conflict also leads to a blurring between the temporary and the permanent. When it comes to NGOs' work as humanitarian or long-term development actors, there are clear distinctions in mandates between meeting immediate community needs and programming for long-term development objectives. For NGOs, humanitarianism "is often thought of as response to natural and manmade disasters such as hurricanes, earthquakes and typhoons [and] it was once almost exclusively related to military conflict."[99] In the last seventy years, development NGOs have been implementing long-term social and economic programs, where organizations such as Oxfam and World Vision have sought to improve food security, improve healthcare, or lift people out of poverty.[100] The differences between these two organizations are predominantly reflected in how flexible these entities' funding structures are, their short or long-term programming, or whether a rapid response is deployed. But this tidy separation is only in theory. Some have argued that "the distinction between 'sudden', 'creeping' and 'chronic' disasters is one filled with ambiguity and broad areas of grey-ness."[101] Donini suggests that when it comes to whether they call themselves humanitarian or development, "NGOs tend to opportunistically choose a label of convenience depending on where they work."[102] This is also clearly demonstrated by how their programming is occurring. For instance, in doc-trine, the Stabilization Assistance Review, notes that stabilization activities "are intended to be short-term in nature (typically between one and five years)."[103] Yet, today, 70 percent of all aid is spent on programs that have been running for more than five years and 40 percent on programs that have been running for more than eight years.[104]

The spillover between short-term humanitarian assistance and long-term development aid programming has diversified the typical NGO project port-folio. There are instances where the continuum between short-term and long-term is bridged by public and private money becoming extensions of each other, with one tacking on to a project where the other left off. This is logical, as following official aid money, "major humanitarian crises in the past decade have prompted unprecedented amounts of private donations."[105]

Working increasingly in fragile settings, NGOs are also providing long-term services, not just the traditional immediate needs of health and educa-tion, taking the place of governments. This allows NGOs to go beyond just assisting suffering populations with "humanitarian work, security efforts, development programming, and rule of law promotion, working not just with, but alongside the UN, governments, other NGOs, civil society, in a shared space."[106] Ultimately, NGOs have been pulled into performing multiple func-tions in both peaceful and conflict-ridden settings.[107] How has this impacted the civil-military relationship?

The Hybridization of NGOs and the Changing Civil-Military Relationship

With the variety and scale of organizations under the development sector and the NGO umbrella, there are so many complex relationships and varying magnitudes in size, funding, and diversity that "the scope and breadth of this sector's typological landscape is lost."[108] On the side of the military, chapter 1 shed light on security scholars who argued that the functions of the warrior diplomat would span beyond the traditional role and into ungoverned spaces for the military, leaving the military with an equally expanded scope and breadth of where it operates and what it does. These low-intensity conflict, fragile and ungoverned spaces are the canvas of the civil-military relationship. The question is: If the space in which civil and military organizations operate has changed, how have NGOs themselves adapted?

From Short to Long; from Urgent to Important

NGOs are adapting themselves in several different ways. They are adapting skills and knowledge from one context to another, and from one type of specialty into another. On one hand, NGOs deploy development programs to prevent fragility. Or in fragile and insecure contexts, they deploy humanitarian relief to meet immediate needs, which if left unmet can lead to insecurity. On the other hand, they are also constantly navigating long-term development and short-term humanitarian assistance. This hybridity is causing NGOs to wear many hats in terms of short- and longer-term assistance provision. This comes with its own challenges. Take for instance NGOs' responses to natural disasters and conflict. NGOs that work as emergency responders in conflicts and disasters, may not necessarily "distinguish between the two in terms of relief."[109]

King and Mutter argue:

> NGOs will apply the same modus operandi, the same tool kits, and come with the same solutions. A water problem is a water problem within a conflict or natural catastrophe. It's the same with malnutrition. They will address the consequence, and they don't care what causes the problem.[110]

While true for short-term humanitarian relief transitioning into long-term development, this is more challenging in the other direction, as "development interventions rarely scale well from one context to another."[111] But considering the earlier mentioned blurring of short- and long-term assistance, the blurring and duplication of development and humanitarian frameworks is only a natural occurrence in fragile spaces. On their side, military respondents made no qualms about sharing how contexts transfer, and that the conflict they tackled in Mali was treated just as the conflict in Afghanistan. What becomes clear is that the gray space is an opportunity for *all* of these actors to tailor their traditional approaches to the spaces where they work and to their craft. This is because the boundaries between long-term and short-term engagement, the urgent need and the important military, development, and humanitarian programming and assistance have become increasingly porous.

Because SOF seek out sources of insecurity, some SOF projects *are* preventive in nature, even if their primary purpose is for access and placement. As a result, NGOs' work with the military is not necessarily only driven by emergencies, and their collaborative relationship can be multilayered and well-developed. Such can be the case with some local NGOs whose small footprint allows for more independence, making them much more entrepreneurial and less hesitant about engaging with the military. If not beholden to donors, these smaller, locally funded NGOs do not necessarily need to abide by the restrictions of international conventions or donors' preferences. In one instance in Guatemala, a local NGO had approached the military to take over a water purification project, as they were no longer able to absorb the cost of maintenance. This is not unusual, as staff who have spent a long time working on initiatives that are no longer to be funded seek ways to transfer the investment of time and knowledge over to another group that can ensure their continuity. Some NGOs are much more comfortable working alongside militaries, for instance in providing medical training programs, skills, and courses developed by Department of Defense (DOD) and taught to the HN military, medical being a necessary capability for both security and non-security actors.[112]

Agents of Convergence

One group is particularly integral to the civil-military space—retired military veterans, or those who served in the military, who join the staff of NGOs upon retiring or exiting military service, or found their own NGOs that focus on humanitarian and development efforts. Their leadership and technical skills are often attractive qualities for NGOs and are sought after when an NGO needs staff who know the arena in which they operate. These veterans are savvy ground operators and are hired either as direct implementers or headquarters office staff. The experience they bring to the table as they cross over from a career in the military to one with an NGO makes them convergence agents of the gray space.

NGOs that operate in fragile settings create a natural gravity for employing people who have already worked in these spaces, especially among younger officers or Non-Commissioned Officers, who seek to embark on a new career after active service. Team Rubicon, an international NGO specializing in disaster response, "unites the skills and experiences of military veterans with first responders to rapidly deploy emergency response teams."[113] Spirit of America (SoA) seeks to hire staff "with US government and/or military leadership experience."[114] Organizations such as these which provide smaller-scale relief response or contribute with goods to the community, overtly advertise that they are "staffed by veterans who have served in the toughest conflict zones in the world," as they seek skills "to operate in challenging, kinetic conditions in developing countries."[115] Just a few weeks into the Russian invasion of Ukraine in February of 2022, Global Surgical and Medical Support Group (GSMSG) remained to be the only U.S. surgical team on the ground in Ukraine, where GSMSG teams of retired SOF medics and medical/surgical professionals provided the spectrum of training on combat casualty care to the local population.[116]

It is not only on the ground level where organizations seek to place former soldiers who have the skills for conflict environments. As of the autumn of 2021, of the fifty advisory board members of SoA, more than half were retired, high-ranking military officers.[117] Retired high-ranking military generals are part of helping these organizations shape their vision and strategy, but also provide visibility to the work. These well-known public figures are to the security and development nexus, what Hollywood actress Audrey Hepburn—the long-established face of UNICEF—was to philanthropy—bringing attention and visible currency to the work of the organizations. James Stavridis and Evelyn Farkas already note that organizations, such as SoA, among several others, have "less compunction about teaming with militaries."[118] The Director of the Impl.Project, an NGO with a reputable track record of work globally focused on recognizing sources of insecurity, is a former U.S. Deputy Assistant Secretary of Defense.[119] Entities such as these are not typical NGOs or development partners of USAID, but they are widely known in the SOF community. They are also agile and highly skilled actors, even if on a smaller scale.

Of the almost thirty NGO staff interviewed for this study, nearly one-third were retired active duty or former reservist military. Almost all interviewed spoke of the advantages of working with people they knew previously, who helped them navigate the hierarchies and bureaucratic constraints to which both of these entities belong. It may be argued that this creates an immediate bias for these actors' relationship, but in fact, it reduces misunderstandings and strengthens the civil-military relationship by converging these organizations. As one military respondent noted, when it comes to exchanging information between NGOs and the military, "I would prefer to reach out to my buddy who retired two years ago and is now working for the NGO."[120]

In addition to the external relationships that these retired veterans form with their former colleagues, there is an unexplored intra-organizational aspect of how retired veterans impact the organizations which recruit them. As one retired military veteran, now NGO staff, stated, "I want my team to look like an Operational Detachment Alpha (ODA)[121] and be able to navigate these spaces," drawing a very clear link between how their experience and institutional knowledge apply to the model of their humanitarian work, and how they are going about staffing the organization and forming teams.[122] As such, it could be argued that NGOs are engaging in mimetic isomorphism, whereby structural and behavioral attributes in one organization mimic those of another, as they face similar conditions in the environment in which they operate.[123]

I have already established that when it comes to the gray space, there is no robust or commonly accepted mechanism for an effective civil-military relationship. But organically, there appears to be a tight-knit network that serves exactly this purpose. Namely, retired military veterans who are recruited by NGOs are more likely to experience a strong relationship with their military counterparts, and vice versa. Furthermore, as SOF go about their planning mission, they have the opportunity to meet with various organizations before deploying. But when asked about which specific NGOs they met with prior to leaving for their mission, many of the respondents only recalled the organizations which have hired or are led by former veterans, namely former colleagues from within the military community. What became clear is that there are natural "go to" NGOs for coordination, even if they are on a smaller scale. Coordination is primarily based on pre-existing relationships between the staff and less on specialization and craft.

The process of familiarizing oneself while serving in the military with the work of ground operators mostly occurs through USAID, once the teams arrive in country. Once on the ground, the military seems to engage with the usual easy-button organizations, such as SoA, due to pre-established and strong relationships. SoA has established strong ties with the U.S. military. In 2018, SoA signed a Memorandum of Understanding with DOD, allowing it to transport private donations and privately funded relief supplies through DOD transport capabilities, and at the discretion of Commanders.[124] In 2019 alone, SoA completed 238 projects around the world,[125] supporting U.S. diplomats and the military. High-ranking practitioners write about how once a comfortable relationship is established, the military often seeks to work "with the same companies or organizations."[126] This pre-established between-organizations' modus operandi is not just within the one country to which a team is deployed, it also carries across continents, following relationships and people's experiences across the various phases of conflict—from Afghanistan to Colombia, to Lebanon, to Kenya.

I do not argue that the sole purpose of NGOs recruiting ex-military is to strengthen their relationship with the military. Neither is my purpose to examine *why* veterans seek to return to conflict settings. Veterans' skill set to operate in conflict-affected communities allows NGOs to recruit better-suited partners, presenting an image of reassurance to locals, donors, or governments. In taking this approach, NGOs' staff have a unique ability and maturity to operate in complex spaces, while not posing a risk or liability to the organization, or the population. This is the opposite of what is faced by international NGOs, who until recently were based in Western capitals, and whose staff hold a completely different profile to seasoned veterans.[127] International NGOs' recruits of young volunteers, college graduates, and early career staff with almost no experience in how to navigate the gray space could not compete with seasoned military professionals.[128] Ultimately, a cozy subculture between NGOs and retired military veterans, now turned humanitarian and development actors, may not bode well with donors. But behind the scenes, all these parties—donors, NGOs, and private money entities, recognize the importance of security in these settings and the complex skill set necessary to navigate them.

Donors may vet the NGOs with which they choose to partner based on their staffing practices, but NGOs have their own rules about whom they can hire. Organizations, such as International Committee of the Red Cross, which work with armed groups, or the United Nations Office for the Coordination of Humanitarian Affairs, which coordinates natural disasters and complex emergencies, naturally need a skill set that only someone with established experience in conflict settings can provide. These organizations' need for a military skill set should not be confused with NGOs' or development actors' reluctance to be seen as associated with the military. As NGOs continue to operate in more complex and riskier spaces, veterans become naturally attractive candidates. Thus, the competition among NGOs in the gray space becomes less about funding and more about having an edge in employees' skill sets. Recruiting those who can navigate environments under high threat makes drawing from a pool of experienced military more attractive and unique, justifying a good business decision. It also further breaks down these organizations' differences, blurs the space, and converges them.

The Use of Private Military and Security Companies by NGOs

If now hybridized and staffed with military veterans, can NGOs compare to the military in how they carry out their work?

There is a series of structural constraints explored in this analysis that drives much of the interaction between NGOs and SOF CA. But a multitude of other factors also drives these entities' own decisions and approaches to how they navigate the gray space. As they continue to operate in a variety of spaces, running NGOs has become "more costly (and in insecure areas the additional costs of security have escalated out of proportion)."[129] But this is for a reason. Almost two decades ago, Peter Singer warned that militaries from the West would have to learn how to deal with "privatized military firms"[130] in war zones, in much the same way that they had to learn how to deal with NGOs during humanitarian operations. Private Military Security Companies (PMSCs) have been around for hundreds of years. In the 1990s in the Balkans, PMSCs, in addition to their logistics services provision, "constructed and operated the refugee camps outside Kosovo's borders."[131] It is still the case that PMSCs are no strangers to the civil-military space, but their role has evolved. Several of the NGO respondents in this study argued that NGOs' inability to operate in insecure areas is a myth, as their low footprint inherently gives a competitive advantage and makes most spaces permissive. But NGOs *are* vulnerable to threats, especially in more violent settings. It is because of these security concerns that NGOs employ PMSCs for protection, giving them the ability to maneuver conflict-ridden places.[132] UN Peacekeeping operations are increasingly using PMSCs for security purposes. There is evidence to show that this is because of need, but also due to "financial flexibility and opaqueness in procurement procedures for peacekeeping operations."[133] In 2008, 41 percent of "major humanitarian organizations," such as Oxfam, Save the Children, CARE, and the ICRC had employed private security contractors.[134] Speaking about the use of PMSCs in Sri Lanka, Oxfam staff have expressed it as "a step toward a pragmatic rapprochement."[135] The $288 million which the UN spent on security in 2016 has increased almost fivefold from 2014. From that amount, "PMSC activity, totaled $166 million from 2012 to 2017."[136]

Earlier analysis discussed the diverging factors which the military and NGOs experience, especially when it comes to the collection and utilization of information. The military focuses on intelligence, and NGOs use information to gain an edge over competing for money. One military respondent described the stark difference: "Civil affairs gets trained on mapping networks. But there is no mapping of anything on the NGO side."[137] This may be so, but in fact, these entities are more convergent, once again mimicking one another. The loose rules around procurement for hiring PMSCs for security apply to more than just physical protection. These firms offer "risk management consultants and safety personnel that will enable governmental and humanitarian organizations to be well protected."[138] But they also offer the full range of other services—including intelligence gathering, strategic analysis, and planning.[139] Just like with retired veterans, former military personnel, now turned PMSC, have all the skills and training of the military.

PMSCs have a more strategic and permanent role, too. They fill a void. Because the gray space is neither peace nor war, militaries may not want to step up because the threat is not sufficient for the effort. On their end, NGOs may want to step back from a situation because stability is not sufficient, or because they may not have the resources or capabilities. This non-commitment leaves a void, which PMSCs would fill. This is also an opportunity, as when PMSCs encroach upon the humanitarian space, it is a way for them to fix their image as "dogs of war," seeking to align themselves with humanitarian actors more closely, as a way to "establish authority and legitimacy as humanitarians" among populations.[140] Conversely, PMSCs are used to soften the perception of aid, which would have otherwise been provided by militaries in uniform. But some have argued that the notion of PMSCs, versus the military, makes little difference in the eyes of local populations. This is particularly the case in high-conflict settings such as Iraq, which did not "allow the reconstruction and aid to be sufficiently differentiated in the eyes of the Iraqi population."[141]

There is a bigger point to this. PMSCs provide the hard-power capability to NGOs, in the way that CA provides the soft-power touch of the military, giving NGOs some of the hard-power tools of soldiers. This has increasingly allowed NGOs to operate in areas which before might have been more restrictive for them, giving them equal capabilities to those of the military, when it comes to fragile settings. Using PMSCs in spaces that are constantly shifting between conflict and stability creates another challenge. According to one respondent, in areas where the security situation is not severe, NGOs "bring in private security companies, which now create a security pressure."[142] PMSCs can also affect the intensity and duration of a conflict.[143] Professionals in the field have expressed concern over the lack of clarity when it comes to PMSCs engaging with NGOs, as PMSCs are "half military and half not."[144] Others have argued that "the lack of a sound regulatory framework within which these private security companies operate can indirectly exacerbate the aggression that those working in aid and reconstruction activities face, because of the questionable tactics used by private security personnel."[145] Or, as one respondent puts it, "these are guys with PTSD who got kicked out of the military."[146]

This mix of dynamics is muddy territory for any entity to operate in. U.S. presence under FID or any other security cooperation program is under strict legal agreements. NGOs who are implementing partners of official donors may be more constrained in how they engage with the military, or even PMSCs. But there is no guarantee of a requirement for such legal arrangements. As one respondent said, "anybody can be an NGO."[147] Similarly, there are no strict requirements on who can be a PMSC as "some are large corporations, while others consist of little more than an office, a fax machine and a few employees."[148] And as already established earlier, PMSCs also enjoy vague liability and legal status which allows them extensive degrees of operational freedom compared with regular forces, such as in war-torn Iraq and Afghanistan.[149] Indeed, PMSCs have long been bound by international convention constraints on their engagement with state actors,[150] but these rules do not apply to non-state actors, such as NGOs, and "PMSCs are poorly regulated by both individual states and the international community."[151] As mentioned previously, in addition to not always following stringent processes on whom they hire for their staff, not all NGOs have a stringent contracting agreement for PMSCs, either. Furthermore, the ambiguity and chaos of the environments in which PMSCs operate leave little room for accountability for PMSCs' behaviors and approaches in the gray space.[152] Others have altogether questioned the transparency and accountability practices of the NGO sector in that "humanitarian agencies are deeply unprofessional in the way they hire PMSCs."[153]

In PMSCs enabling NGOs to navigate these spaces, it appears that indeed NGOs and the military are on equal footing to some extent, strongly converging into the gray. But this is at first glance, and this analysis argues that the scale tilts in favor of NGOs. On the part of SOF, strict rules, under the arrangements of Security Cooperation and Bilateral Security agreements, drive their presence, movement, and interaction, at least in theory. Equipped with physical security, intelligence, and planning capabilities, NGOs have at their fingertips many of the tools that the military does. But they have another advantage. Their historically altruistic and impartial image, even if sometimes only in theory, conceals their newly gained hard power. In the eyes of the locals, one respondent described, "all of us foreigners look the same."[154] Local communities cannot easily differentiate between military and non-military who stand in security roles. John Mackinlay notes that when it comes to NGOs, many "do not require to be mandated by an authorising body in the way the military force does, to participate in the conflict zone."[155] As a result, it is easier for NGOs to downplay their hard power than it is for uniformed military actors to up play their soft power.

CONCLUSION

Having established that SOF cannot be humanitarian because they are self-serving, are NGOs altruistic or also self-serving in working in local communities?

As they have ballooned in scale and scope, and prolonged their engagement from short to long-term, NGOs have also diversified in how they fund their work through both public and private money. As a result, they are accountable to the people who fund them in different ways, causing a divergence within the development sector. Private funding and official donor funding uphold NGOs to different accountability mechanisms, where privately funded organizations have much more room to maneuver and fewer constraints than publicly funded ones. But publicly funded ones are more prevalent in fragile spaces, giving them more currency with military actors. This analysis finds that as they monitor and evaluate their work,

NGOs prioritize differently. They do not ignore the needs of the populations they serve, but often they are forced to prioritize staying in business, which frequently puts their recipients' needs as secondary to securing funding from donors. A series of local and international dynamics also disrupts what is desired by outside countries, and what is feasible or necessary for local communities.

Furthermore, the NGOs are constantly having to navigate a series of political, structural, and financial modalities and constraints. As mentioned earlier, SOF are the hard-powered instrument of foreign policy, despite their soft skills. NGOs, as implementing partners of donors, are simply the soft power of the same foreign policy. So, by definition, much of the development programming is political, as foreign policy always takes a side. NGOs that choose to operate in fragile spaces are diverging away from a purist development approach to working in communities and converging closer to the security space. To continue to operate, NGOs need to stay competitive by diversifying their funders, but also their skills. To navigate the gray space, they seek to staff themselves with those who are seasoned in operating in insecure environments, by hiring personnel with strong military experience, and through the utilization of PMSCs. While there are no official organizationally established or accepted mechanisms for a robust relationship between NGOs with the military in the gray space, there seems to be an organically formed and tight-knit network of "military gone NGO" professionals who serve exactly this purpose.

But this puts NGOs in insecure settings in yet another unique position, compared to their military counterparts. By hardening up, they can *downplay* their hard power much more easily than SOF CA can *up play* their soft power. Contrarily, this convergence is only evidence of what is naturally occurring in the gray spaces, and in line with what Collier argued—that external military presence may have a role to play in fragile states. Further on the development side, the convergence is also an organic by-product of a space that is constantly shifting between degrees of insecurity, as described by Duffield. On the military side, NGOs navigating this terrain highlights the necessary diversity of skills that those engaging in low-intensity conflict, namely the military, must have, just as the military progressives Scales and Sarkesian argued. For NGOs, this new hybridization gives them the freedom to program and engage as they choose, not as their funders choose. With the ability to hire staff that best operate in the places where they work, namely former military; with their funding coming through different channels, often with little accountability to those who fund them, namely private donors; and the lack of stringent requirements to contract private security companies, when it comes to the gray space, NGOs can often get a carte blanche.

NOTES

1. R 51—NGO Respondent, April 8, 2021.
2. McGann and Johnstone, "The Power Shift," 65.
3. Hanhauser IV, "Comprehensive Civil Information," 1.
4. Smillie, *The Alms Bazaar.*
5. Stephenson, "Nongovernmental Organizations."
    World Association of Non-Governmental Organizations (WANGO), "Worldwide NGO Directory."
6. Brass et al., "NGOs and International Development," 136.
7. UNSW Canberra, "Operating."
8. Church of Jesus Christ of Latter-day Saint, "2020 Annual Report," 6.
9. Personal research/diary discussion with a member of the Mormon Church. October, 2021.
10. Lawry, "Guide," 31.
11. Donini, "Local Perceptions," 172.
12. Büthe, Major, and de Mello e Souza, "The Politics of Private Foreign Aid," 571–607.
13. Abiew and Keating, "NGOs and UN Peacekeeping Operations," 89–111; Sphere, "Antonio Donini."
14. UNSW Canberra, "Operating."
    Doctors Without Borders, "Ways to Give."
15. Aall and Helsing, "Non Governmental Organizations," 60.
16. UNSW Canberra, "Operating."
17. Trent, *The Need.*
18. UNSW Canberra, "Operating."
19. *Ibid.*
20. Desai and Kharas, "What motivates."
21. Fehrenbach and Rodogno, "A Horrific Photo of a Drowned Syrian Child," 1121–55.
22. Aall and Helsing, "Non Governmental Organizations," 59.
23. UNSW Canberra, "Operating."
24. Lomoriello and Scott, "Chapter 4: What official development assistance went to fragile contexts?"
25. *Ibid.*
26. R 51.
27. Brass et al., "NGOs and International Development," 138.
28. Fox, Witter, Wylde, Mafuta, and Lievens, "Paying Health Workers for Performance," 96–105.
29. Brass et al., "NGOs and International Development," 138.
30. Roads for Life, Lebanon.
31. Franke, "The Peacebuilding Dilemma," 9.
32. Aall and Helsing, "Non Governmental Organizations," 59.
33. Brass et al., "NGOs and International Development," 138.
34. Aall and Helsing, "Non Governmental Organizations," 59.
35. Anderson et al., *Time to Listen*, 91.
36. Smillie, *The Alms Bazaar*, 172.
37. R 51.
38. *Ibid.*
39. Brass et al., "NGOs and International Development," 138.
40. Smillie, *The Alms Bazaar*, 184.
41. Donini, "Local Perceptions," 160.
42. Smillie, *The Alms Bazaar*, 147.
43. *Ibid.*, 162.
44. *Ibid.*, 186.

45. Brass et al., "NGOs and International Development," 137.
46. Donini, "Local Perceptions," 159.
47. Bell, Murdie, Blocksome, and Brown, "Force Multipliers," 401.
48. Anheier, *Nonprofit Organizations*, 226 and 115.
49. Donini, "Local Perceptions," 159.
50. Anderson et al., *Time to Listen*, 40.
51. *Ibid.*, 45.
52. *Ibid.*, 35.
53. Anderson et al., *Time to Listen*, 30.
54. Smillie, *The Alms Bazaar*, 158.
55. *Ibid.*, 159.
56. Marshall and Suárez, "The Flow of Management Practices," 1036.
57. Donini, "Local Perceptions."
58. R 67—NGO Respondent, April 26, 2021.
59. R 62—NGO Respondent, April 19, 2021.
60. Smillie, *The Alms Bazaar*, 159.
61. Gowrinathan and Cronin-Furman, *The Forever Victims?*; White Paper, *Colin Powell School for Civic and Global Leadership, as referenced in Autesserre*, "International Peacebuilding," 120.
62. *Ibid.*
63. World Bank, "World Development Report 2011," 9.
64. Autesserre, "International Peacebuilding," 120.
65. R 51.
66. *Ibid.*
67. *Ibid.*
68. R 62.
69. Platteau, "Monitoring Elite Capture," 223.
70. *Ibid.*
71. Anderson et al., *Time to Listen*, 39.
72. Lawry, "Guide."
73. Ebrahim, "Accountability in Practice," 813.
74. Donini, "Local Perceptions," 159.
75. R 65—NGO Respondent, April 21, 2021.
76. Anderson et al., *Time to Listen*, 40.
77. Smillie, *The Alms Bazaar*, 161.
78. R 18.
79. *Ibid.*
80. R 59—Development/Donor Agency Respondent, April 19, 2021.
81. Donini, "Local Perceptions," 161.
82. Médecins Sans Frontières, "How We Work - Médecins Sans Frontières," https://www.msf.org.uk/how-we-work. (last accessed October 5, 2021).
83. Egnell, "Civil–Military Coordination," 248.
84. Jeong, *Peacebuilding in Postconflict Societies*, 217.
85. International Federation of Red Cross and Red Crescent, "Code of Conduct."
86. Fawaz, "Hezbollah as Urban Planner?," 323–34.
87. Østensen, "In the Business of Peace," 33.
88. Seybolt, "The Myth," 522.
89. *Ibid.*
90. Guttieri, "Humanitarian Space."
91. Duffield, *Global Governance*; Petrik, "Chapter 8: Provincial Reconstruction."
92. R 40.
93. Donini, "Local Perceptions," 162.
94. R 40.

95. Büthe et al., "The Politics of Private Foreign Aid."

96. Baldursdóttir, Gunnlaugsson, and Einarsdóttir, "Donor Dilemmas in a Fragile State," S27–S39.

97. Organization for Economic Co-operation and Development, "OECD Development Co-operation Peer Reviews."

98. Desai and Kharas, "What Motivates," 507.

99. Rysaback-Smith, "History and Principles," 5–6.

100. Fowler, "Chapter 6: Development NGOs."

101. Smillie, *The Alms Bazaar*, 101.

102. Donini, "Local Perceptions," 170.

103. United States Department of State, *Stabilization Assistance Review*, 4.

104. Peter Walker, "Conclusion: the Shape of Things to Come – an Essay on Humanitarian Challenges," in Dilemmas, Challenges, and Ethics of Humanitarian Action: Reflections on Médecins Sans Frontières' Perception Project. Ed Caroline Abu-Sada, McGill-Queen's University Press, 2012, 119.

105. Desai and Kharas, "What Motivates," 507–508.

106. Aall and Helsing, "Non Governmental Organizations," 54.

107. King and Mutter, "Violent Conflicts and Natural Disasters," 1239–55.

108. McGann and Johnstone, "The Power Shift," 161.

109. King and Mutter, "Violent Conflicts," 1240.

110. *Ibid.*, 1243.

111. Brass et al., "NGOs and International Development," 147.

112. Roads for Life, "Tactical Casualty Combat Care," provides training to the LAF in Lebanon.

113. Team Rubicon Global, "Team Rubicon Global Gives Military Veterans."

114. Spirit of America Jobs, "Spirit of America Is Hiring."

115. Samaritan's Purse International Relief, "Careers for U.S. Military Veterans."

116. Epstein, "American Veterans, Medical Professionals Train Ukrainians."

117. Spirit of America, "Board and Advisors."

118. Stavridis and Farkas, "The 21st Century Force Multiplier," 10.

119. Impl.Project, "Our Team."

120. R 49—NGO Respondent, April 6, 2021.

121. An ODA (Operational Detachment Alpha) consists of a twelve person special operations forces team, which includes operations, intelligence, weapons, communication, medical, and engineering.

122. R 36—NGO Respondent, March 11, 2021.

123. Mizruchi and Fein, "The Social Construction of Organizational Knowledge," 653–83.

124. Civil Affairs Association, "2021 Civil Affairs Symposium Report," December 30, 2021. The MoU allows for special donations which have been financed by private money and are in support of US missions, to be transported by DOD, under DOD Section 1092 "Department of Defense Engagement with Certain Nonprofit entities in support of missions of deployed United States Personnel around the world." See OHDACA Section in chapter 4. Also, see National Defense Authorization Act for Fiscal Year 2019, H. R. 5515 "Department of Defense Section 1092. "Department of Defense engagement with certain nonprofit entities in support of missions of deployed United States personnel around the world."

125. Spirit of America, "2019 Annual Report."

126. Stavridis and Farkas, "The 21st Century Force Multiplier," 8.

127. NGOs are seeking to increasingly move to places such as Tokyo, Dubai, Abu Dhabi, Doha, and Delhi.

128. This is not to dismiss the security and pre-deployment training that NGOs provide their staff before sending them to insecure areas. This statement seeks to make the point that no amount of experience of a young civilian can replace what a highly trained military professional can bring to the field.

129. Donini, "Local Perceptions," 159.

130. Singer, "Corporate Warriors," 186.
131. *Ibid.*, 188.
132. *Ibid.*, 219.
133. Tkach and Phillips, "UN Organizational and Financial Incentives," 103.
134. Singer, "Strange Brew," 76.
135. Hellinger, "Humanitarian Action," 212.
136. Tkach and Phillips, "UN Organizational," 103.
137. R 30.
138. Bjork and Jones, "Overcoming Dilemmas," 782.
139. Singer, "Corporate Warriors," 186.
140. Joachim and Schneiker, "New Humanitarians?," 386.
141. Bjork and Jones, "Overcoming," 792.
142. R 51.
143. Tkach, "Private Military and Security Companies," 291–311.
144. UNSW Canberra, "Operating."
145. Bjork and Jones, "Overcoming," 792.
146. R 51.
147. *Ibid.*
148. Joachim and Schneiker, "New Humanitarians?," 369.
149. Mathieu and Dearden, "Corporate Mercenaries," 744–55.
    Cheadle, "Private Military Contractor Liability," 690.
150. United Nations, "United Nations Resolution 44/34—International Convention against the Recruitment, Use, Financing and Training of Mercenaries."
151. Malcy, "Publicly Available Information," 14.
152. Tkach, "Private Military."
153. Mears, "Private Military and Security Companies," 3.
154. R 1—NGO Respondent, December 29, 2021.
155. Mackinlay, "Co-operating," 29.

Chapter 4

Brothers from Another Mother

ARE SOF AND NGOS ORGANIZATIONALLY COMPATIBLE BUT INSTITUTIONALLY RESTRAINED?

Militaries are understood to be culturally authoritarian and part of well-defined hierarchies, and NGOs are known to be decentralized and autonomous. They converge in large-scale disaster response and complex emergencies, forming the crux of the civil-military relationship. It is also generally accepted that these entities differ in their objectives, principles, decision-making procedures, budget size, operational rules, and organizational strategies. Ironically, when examining the gray space where Special Operations Forces Civil Affairs (SOF CA) units and NGOs carry out many of their engagements, we see these entities demonstrate traits that contradict many preconceived differences. In examining SOF CA separate from the larger Department of Defense (DOD) organization to which they organizationally belong, and NGOs separate from their relationship with and accountability to donors, these actors possess a series of similar attributes, namely the ways in which they manage money, implement projects, and select personnel. Contrary to the accepted belief that DOD is larger in budget than development actors, at the project level, DOD expenditures for these small-scale efforts are comparable to those of their NGO counterparts, and often DOD is outspent. Both organizations' activities may overlap in conflict zones, but their approaches to the full cycle of consultation, implementation, and follow-up differ. Their presence in the communities where they operate is also more complex than what meets the eye, and both actors, to a different extent, suffer from a lack of permanence in the areas where they operate.

In examining how militaries and NGOs go from large-scale coordinated interactions, to small-level and ad-hoc engagements, the gray space once again converges, rather than diverges these entities. The lack of traditional sequencing has changed the traditional roles of these organizations, causing them to adapt to the order in which they understand and respond to pre-conflict or post-conflict efforts. Just like with short- and long-term assistance, these boundaries, too, have become obsolete. In examining these organizations for their diversity, autonomy, generalist versus specialist expertise, transparency, organizational independence, and scale, these entities appear to be organizationally compatible, but institutionally restrained.

FROM WHOLESALE TO RETAIL

When looking at NGOs and the military, "the two principal circumstances that draw these institutions together are peacekeeping operations and responses to humanitarian emergencies."[1] Unlike large-scale, sudden disasters or complex emergencies, the gray space is smaller and subject to scarcity of resources which leads to insecurity. In such instances, there are few crises in number, but they are chronic, long-term, and affecting people more.

So, compared to large-scale crises, how does coordination occur differently in the gray space, if at all? To understand, let us contrast them.

In the traditional context, military and civilian actors have the oversight of coordination agencies, such as United Nations Office for the Coordination of Humanitarian Affairs or pre-established guidelines by other organizations (see table 4.1). The military is involved in handling "disaster relief, nation assistance, and drug interdiction to peacekeeping, noncombatant evacuation, and peace enforcement."[2] In natural disasters, such as typhoons or earthquakes, the military's role is to restore a void of services for the population. As mentioned in chapter 2, it does so by performing a sophisticated and robust mission tasking matrix (MiTaM) to quickly mobilize a response to emergencies, people displacement, hunger, and so on, when national emergency capacity is at a limit. In these large-scale interactions, civil-military cooperation (CIMIC) guides how to engage with civic actors, local populations, NGOs, and INGOs, in order to meet the needs of the population, not the objectives of the military.[3] In the early days of the war in Afghanistan, CIMIC was the coordinating structure between the Afghan ministries and the coalition.[4] CIMIC is in addition to a variety of other formal coordination mechanisms, such as "humanitarian operations centers (HOCs), civilian military operations centers (CMOCs), on-site operations coordination centers (OSOCCs), and humanitarian affairs centers (HACs)."[5] These have been used in many contexts, including in Haiti, Somalia, Rwanda, Albania, Kosovo, and Afghanistan.

Since the early 1990s, many efforts have been made for the best way to get the military and NGOs to coordinate in humanitarian crises (see table 4.1). Many of

Table 4.1   Main Frameworks, Guidelines, and Initiatives for Civil-Military Interactions

1993 Military Support to Civil Authorities (MSCA)

1994 Guidelines on the Use of Military and Civil Defense Assets in Disaster Relief "Oslo Guidelines"

1997 The Sphere Project: Humanitarian Charter and Minimum Standards in Humanitarian Response

2001 The ICRC Guidelines for Civil-Military Relations (CMR)

2001 US Army Civil-Military Operations Joint Publication 3–57

2001 Discussion Paper and Non-Binding Guidelines on the Use of Military or Armed Escorts for Humanitarian Convoys

2003 Guidelines on the Use of Military and Civil Defense Assets to Support United Nations Humanitarian Activities in Complex Emergencies "MCDA Guidelines"

2003 Good Humanitarian Donorship (GHD principles 2003)

2004 UN Humanitarian Civil Military Coordination (UN CMCoord)

2004 IASC Non-Binding Guidelines on the Use of Armed Escorts for Humanitarian Convoys

2004 Civil-Military Relationship in Complex Emergencies—An IASC Reference Paper

2004 Multinational Force Standard Operating Procedures (MNF SOP)

2005 Guidelines for Relations Between U.S. Armed Forces and Non-Governmental Humanitarian Organizations in Hostile or Potentially Hostile Environments, United States Institute of Peace (USIP)

2005 Asia-Pacific Regional Guidelines for the Use of Foreign Military Assets in Natural Disaster Response Operations 2007 Civil-Military Coordination Officer Field Handbook

2007 United States Institute of Peace, Guidelines for Relations Between U.S. Armed Forces and Non-Governmental Organizations in Hostile or Potentially Hostile Environments

2008 Civilian Military Cooperation Policy (USAID)

2008 United Nations Office for the Coordination of Humanitarian Affairs, Civil-Military Guidelines Reference for Complex Emergencies. Inter-Agency Standing Committee, New York

2009 US Army Foreign Humanitarian Assistance Joint Publication 3–29

2009 VOICE Working Group on EU Civil-Military Relations

2010 Civil-Military Coordination in UN Integrated Peacekeeping Missions (UN-CIMIC)

2010 Allied Command Operations Comprehensive Operations Planning Directive (COPD)

2010 Pakistan Civil-Military Guidelines

2013 NATO's Allied Joint Publication on Civil-Military Cooperation (AJP-3.4.9)

2014 Humanitarian Civil-Military Coordination—A Guide for the Military

2015 Policy on Cooperation with the Department of Defense (USAID)

2015 US Agency for International Development, Joint Humanitarian Operations Course (JHOC), Civil-Military Roles in International Disaster Response

2016 Interorganizational Cooperation (Joint Publication 3–08)

2018 US Department of Defense Joint Chiefs of Staff, Peace Operations. Joint Publication 3–07.3, Washington DC: Joint Chiefs of Staff

Source: Author, adapted from Jaff, Margolis, and Reeder, "Civil–military interactions during non-conflict humanitarian crises," 6.

these have been unsuccessful, either due to their failure to engage the host nation (HN) government, or abide by the principles of neutrality and impartiality when it comes to a HN military being involved in internal conflict.[6]

To be clear, these guidelines are not specific to large-scale coordination. There is nothing to prevent their use in the small-scale civil-military engagements which are not subject to many actors and resources. However, there are two complications: first, SOF's use of development and humanitarian projects is to meet their own security objectives; second, SOF's initiatives are the product of U.S. interagency coordination, if such coordination occurs at all.

In the gray space, the military continues to conduct disaster prevention or development efforts, such as building cyclone shelters, vaccinating cattle, or conducting preventative health checks of communities, to mention a few. These can happen in any operating environment, and are useful specifically in rural areas, which tend to be vulnerable to extremism, as they are often neglected by governments. There, CA, as a way to support the HN partner, can focus "on military needs and provides suggestions for how to gain the support of civilians for the military mission."[7] Placed under the auspices of stability operations whose purpose *is* to ensure an environment is seen as legitimate, acceptable, and predictable, Civil-Military Support Elements (CMSE) perform tasks across the gamut—from supporting programming designed to prevent youth to join extremist groups, to medical services, to assessing the readiness of armed forces in peacekeeping operations, such as in Kosovo.[8] A CMSE in a counterterrorism operation in Lebanon, or a training mission in Colombia, where Acción Integral is the CMSE for the Colombian military, all have different mandates, but at the same time they all involve similar actors.

So, what is different in the gray space?

Coordination in the gray space does not occur to the extent that it does with large-scale humanitarian responses, if it occurs at all.[9] While large-scale response operations have someone who serves as the translator between the NGOs and the military, the small-scale missions may not have an established role for this purpose.

First, when examined separately, and the extent to which CA and NGOs follow pre-established guidelines, each of these entities has its *own* idea of how and to what extent it should coordinate with the other. Some of the most common terms used by respondents—from both the military and NGOs, were *coordination, consultation, cooperation,* and *collaboration.* Most of the military interviewees spoke of doctrine informing how the military *should* be working with NGOs, but also that much of how such doctrine is implemented is ad hoc, and dependent on the individual. This is despite the doctrine for rules of engagement, where the stringent and structurally oiled machine that is the military brings together personnel, intelligence, operations, logistics, planning, and communications. On their end, NGOs may not necessarily have a central doctrine to dictate their rules of engagement with security actors,[10] but they have a lot of agency in *where* and *how* they choose to coordinate, and "may decide to participate in systematic information-sharing with military actors to avoid potential hazards, such as providing the coordinates of hospitals to avoid inadvertent targeting of these facilities by the military."[11] Such deconfliction mechanisms can also transfer over in the gray space, but they are most likely to be driven by the ad-hoc relationships formed by operators' personalities, not structures.[12]

Second, because the gray space is mostly steady—lacking the danger and volatility of high-intensity conflict, both of these entities—NGOs and SOF CA, can choose where to engage. For SOF, as they try to meet their objective first, the gray space may not always have the necessary strategic currency to justify investing in resources and personnel. In Nepal, for example, remote villages in need were neglected by development actors because they are hard to reach. This is in line with what previous studies have also shown that "populous locations have many NGOs."[13] But rural communities lack everything all around. Although the military *has* the capability to reach these areas, it likely will not put the resources to doing so if the area is not strategically important, and does not seem vulnerable to threats.

Clearly, between the lack of large-scale presence and resources in the gray space, and the possibility of low-intensity conflict fragile spaces lacking strategic importance, the gray space can be subject to neglect. But this offers another possibility. It leaves room for coordination and improvisation at the individual level. As a result, both military and NGO individual operators have a great deal of agency and autonomy, allowing them to converge, and making them the masters of this space in equal measure.

SEQUENCING

Chapter 3 referred to the constantly shifting short- and long-term programming of NGOs. When it comes to CAs' role, traditionally their work has been mostly associated with "what happened after the shooting stopped."[14] This all follows a linear approach to how conflict begins, occurs, and ends, and which actors get involved with which activities.[15] But the reality of such a linear approach, in any context where security and civilian actors are involved, is much more complex, rarely following a tidy separation of activities.

Let us take, for example, disaster response, where there are no political complexities to navigate. There, the neatly sequenced phases of *who* gets involved and *when*, should be much more straightforward. But this is not always the case. There is already a tendency for boundaries of natural disasters to bleed into situations of conflict, or counterinsurgencies, to turn into complex emergencies.[16] Most of the activities for restoration, rebuilding, and reconstructing are not "discrete events that run sequentially, or activities that necessarily run in parallel."[17] In long-term relief, resettlement, and development programs, too, stages may be predefined as "too rigid."[18] Christopher Holshek confirms this to also be true about peace operations:

> If conflict prevention failed then one moved on to various means of peacemaking; once there was an agreement to pursue a peaceful solution then traditional methods of peacekeeping could be applied; and finally, once peace had taken hold, peace-building could begin. . . . The reality of today's operations, however, is that there is essentially no such tidy sequence. Conflict prevention, diplomatic peacemaking, peace enforcement actions, classic peacekeeping, peace-building and nation-building (development) are often all taking place simultaneously.[19]

Antonio Donini describes a similarly chaotic and ambiguous definition of these phases in more conflict-ridden Afghanistan, which today we interpret as high-intensity conflict. But in fact, sub-regions of the Afghanistan conflict fit into different definitions of the phases of conflict:

> The situation in Afghanistan in early 2006 presented an astonishing blend of conflict, post-conflict, humanitarian and development characteristics. In Kabul and in the North, where security is not a serious issue and the legitimacy of the government is broadly accepted, agencies are in post-conflict, even development mode.[20]

This is further complicated as Donini also claims that such separation undercuts the complexity of how conflict and instability can occur. In his writing about Afghanistan, he notes that:

> One of the problems confronting aid agencies working in Afghanistan, and researchers trying to make sense of what is going on, relates to the ambiguities with which the overall situation is defined (or not). Is it a humanitarian crisis or a post-conflict, peacebuilding and/or development situation? This is not just an issue of semantics. The way in which the situation is defined impacts directly on the posture that agencies assume vis-à-vis the government and the other forces at play.[21]

In Afghanistan, the military was in charge of what development actors would have normally done, from "trash removal to restoring basic sanitation, distributing rations, and repairing and rebuilding schools and hospitals."[22] But many have been the critics of the conventional military doing the job of development actors, classifying it as unfit. So, are SOF a better fit for performing this work?

Chapter 2 argued that they are not. This is not because they are not equipped, but because their own need to meet their mission trumps the needs of populations, and the need of having a healthy and sustainable relationship with civic entities, which are not their main interlocutors. When it comes to the gray space, one military respondent expressed the challenges of constantly having to thread the intricacies of places that are neither full-on war nor full-on peace—"where we the military are in charge, it's so much more straight-forward."[23] The logistical work of rebuilding and reconstruction, which can seem much more complex than the combat and security work, ordinarily occurs only once fighting has ceased, and the environment is permissive for development actors to step in. But, in demonstrating the start and end of conflict, and everything in between, the "notional operational plan phases cannot address the layers and levels of complexity in any environment."[24] The blend of actors, phases, needs, and touchpoints between these entities is equally complicated.

From an intra-organizational standpoint, earlier I discussed the dynamic nature of SOF units trading places. Specifically that for SOF the civil-military relationship can occur between any member of the SOF team, and a civic actor—from the softest power component, namely CA, to the most lethal, namely SF. The sequencing and touchpoints of *who* gets involved and *when*, can change quickly, as it is driven by the threat of the dynamic nature of the three-block war. As one military respondent mentioned:

> SF might be the first to access an area because of its kinetic risk, and the first ones to speak to the population and NGOs. SF are in areas where CA are not. The same is true vice-versa. Once one of these more dangerous areas is assessed by SF, civil affairs would engage in this same area by talking to elders, elites, and trying to understand the locals' needs.[25]

But this carries its own risks and optically "a lot of people see SF as a threat."[26] Thus, once again, depending on the context, whose volatility can shift from one day to the next, the phases, activities, and perceptions within the civil-military relationship are difficult to predict or control. Because of this, once again, the factors which cause these entities to converge closer together, or diverge away from each other, are fluid and constantly shifting.

To most staff on the ground, and academics who have studied the civil-military relationship at length, this disconnect between the military and civic actors is not at all surprising. But if SOF are different than conventional forces, as established in chapter 2, and if NGOs are increasingly navigating spaces which SOF are as well, as established in chapter 3, are these entities in fact as different as we have been traditionally led to believe?

STRANGE BEDFELLOWS OR FAMILIAR STRANGERS?

Donna Winslow argues that militaries are culturally authoritarian, centralized, large, robust, and part of a well-defined hierarchy. On the other hand, NGOs are "flat, consensus-based with highly decentralized field offices."[27] Most militaries are strict and linear in objective setting and execution. In contrast, civilian organizations are concerned with a "process of fulfilling changeable political or social interest."[28] Their metrics for success are not the same. The military's definition of success may be measured by the number of terrorists killed or captured. For NGOs, success may be the number of lives saved or improved. For civil society and advocacy, an NGO's success is measured by social change in the communities where it operates.

Donna Winslow suggests that there are five main areas in which the differences between NGOs and the military are the starkest: "(1) organizational structure and culture; (2) tasks and ways of accomplishing them; (3) definitions of success and time frames; (4) abilities to exert influence and control information; and (5) control of resources."[29] This list is similar to the typology of civil and military actors described in appendix 2 (table A.2), which contrasts the attributes of small SOF teams and NGOs. This analysis challenges Winslow in that these entities are opposite. When examined closely, we will see these actors are quite similar. Undeniably, SOF's lethal power, as described in chapter 2, is one of its core competencies. NGOs' focus on humanitarian and development needs, despite the findings in chapter 3 of their hard power, also cannot be denied. But how these organizations function, adapt, budget, and operate is quite similar. It is this occurrence that causes them to converge.

First, unlike large-scale bulky conventional forces, SOF's agility, and ability to navigate spaces without a heavy footprint give them an advantage in the inconspicuous gray space, where visible or high conflict is less likely. CA teams, as part of SOF, are four to five members each. Much like NGOs, CA, too, can have a focus on health, education, or basic infrastructure, particularly among CA reservist units. At the time of the Persian Gulf War in 1991, and during Operation Provide Comfort, the military ran OBGYN clinics.[30] At the time of the Afghan Evacuation in 2021, during Operation Allies Welcome, U.S. Marines were responsible for distributing baby formula and diapers to mothers with infants.[31] These are instances where the military provided a service, similar to what an NGO would provide. Furthermore, SOF's training of other militaries is also about building capacity, equipping, and strengthening the resilience of a country's security sector. For NGOs, too, their focus is on supporting services in health, education, and governance, to name a few—all designed to build resilience in those sectors.

Second, contrary to Winslow's argument about a difference in hierarchy and bureaucracy between NGOs and the conventional military, the picture of NGOs and SOF is quite different. As one respondent noted about their small NGO, "we have bylaws, but we go mostly by our gut reaction. There is no formal bureaucracy yet."[32] On their end, SOF are "much flatter than what is found in much larger conventional forces."[33] They have "direct lines of communication to decision-makers and are organizationally small."[34] Winslow argues that the military "do not believe in their role as 'global street workers.'"[35] Yet, Shamir and Ben-Ari, refer to SOF as "street-level integrators,"[36] capable of connecting not just with other militaries but "with non-military and non-governmental organizations, or other civilian arms of government."[37] In other words, SOF have the ability to work well with others.

Third, contrary to Winslow's argument of how the military are not diverse, SOF are quite heterogeneous. CA's cross-cutting nature, as part of SOF, is comparatively diverse. The officers and non-commissioned officers (NCOs) can be both highly educated and highly trained, and indeed, have some specialization comparable to that of NGOs, especially when it comes to the field of medicine. SOF CA are organized across functional areas, and across geographic commands, they are expeditionary and multifaceted, making them well-qualified generalists. Contrarily, when it comes to how their personnel compares, for internationals, "an NGO operative is typically a well-educated person with a BA [bachelor of arts] or above and has usually been selected to work with his/her group while in college."[38] The military's recruitment is strong from within rural communities in the United States,[39] whereas voluntary and philanthropic organizations, such as the Peace Corps, receive many of their recruits from within urban areas.[40] Headquarters' staff for INGOs in Geneva or New York also seek highly qualified personnel who hold a master's degree and years of experience in a region. Local NGOs on the ground, especially those receiving funding from donors, also tend to draw on elites from within communities, where the more educated can be more highly sought after.

Furthermore, SOF are considered "specialized generalists" who can perform a large array of tasks. As non-experts, they are taught to learn an abundance of things and "become very good at something specific, very quickly."[41] This quality is further reinforced by the autonomy they are given and their ability to go outside the boundaries of their craft by leveraging civic actors. Similarly, a small health NGO, vetted by a donor, serving in a specific country or region would specialize just in that. Between their mandates, principles, codes of conduct, standards, coordination, and accountability, NGOs are very diverse, and some have argued difficult to work with because of this diversity.[42]

What is interesting is that while NGOs are perceived as specialists, in fact they can also be generalists. In one study of twenty-eight international development NGO managers, across eleven NGOs in fields such as finance, health, and nutrition, respondents were asked what factors drive the success or failure of international development projects undertaken by NGOs. The most important factor that came up was adaptability, followed by the ability to carry out multiple tasks.[43] In the same study, one of the key findings was a large response in favor of the ability to perform a range of tasks. "As an expert, you end up being involved in everything when you're abroad . . . You need to know how to write, you need to know about computers . . . I even took a street work course."[44] The ability to perform various tasks was one of the defining traits of SOF operators, as described earlier. Despite the different specialties which SOF and NGOs provide—SOF as generalists, and NGOs as specialists—as operators they both recognize the importance of a generalist skill set. There, these actors *are* heterogenous, vis-à-vis one another, but also within their respective organizations. SOF and NGOs are not so distinct. It is rather their institutional objectives that causes them to diverge, not the attributes, or the backgrounds of the skill set of the personnel who serve within them.

Fourth, despite being flat, both these entities are held accountable to larger organizations, and they both can be very top-heavy. For SOF, it is the multiple layers consisting of the Embassy, the Taskforce Special Operations Command (TSOC), the Geographic Combatant Command (GCC), and the larger DOD. For NGOs, the country team, the regional office, and higher headquarters, all add layers of bureaucracy. Yet, both SOF and NGOs hold a great deal of autonomy as ground operators, and away from their larger hierarchies, a topic which is further discussed in chapter 5. As such, they *are* and *have to be* extremely adaptable. Respondents in a study argued that:

> NGOs tend to, especially the more humanitarian ones at the field level, [they] make it up as they go along. Now they'll have plans, programs, those kinds of things that come from the top, but the implementation, is not nearly as disciplined as it is in the military.[45]

Another one noted that NGOs are:

> [M]uch more able to problem solve and to make decisions in the field because they have very in depth knowledge of what's going on in that particular community or a particular region, particular culture. Whereas once again, the military tends to have to ask people, NGO workers are given much more latitude and much more autonomy and responsibility.[46]

Chapter 3 provided an analysis of how NGOs are highly adaptable to fiscal uncertainty. Later I will discuss similar fiscal constraints for small SOF teams. But overall, this need to adapt is not unsimilar to much of what SOF respondents described as SOF's adaptability and known problem-solving skills at the team level. SOF possess a great deal of autonomy in the function of their flat and field-focused structure. They have the "abilities for action in a variety of fields straddling high- and low-intensity engagements, nation-building and humanitarian missions, and training indigenous forces and liaising with other national forces."[47] It is because of these skills that some argue SOF should be able to have an effective role to play under UN mandates as part of peacekeeping operations.[48]

Fifth, when it comes to one element of diversity, Winslow and others argue that the military is a male-dominant culture. It is extremely difficult to disprove or prove comparisons of these complicated sectors, but some evidence is available to challenge them. In peace operations, while the military are predominantly male, NGO relief workers tend to be female in their late twenties to early forties.[49] In many countries, more than 75 percent of health workers are women.[50] Women are more drawn to social work than men.[51] As discussed in chapter 2, SOF are known to be older, more mature, and indeed, male dominated. The gender imbalance among NGOs is sometimes within the community where they operate, not necessarily within the organizations themselves. As one NGO respondent in a study noted:

> It seems to me that the problem with gender issues with NGOs, is actually in the countries and in the fields where one is working. So it's not actually in the NGOs themselves, it's in their beneficiary populations, host countries, etcetera, and national contexts.[52]

A study in Nigeria of rural development NGOs confirmed that two-thirds of respondent personnel in a local NGO were male and between the age of thirty and fifty.[53] This all exposes the notion that drawing conclusions on gender balance of any actor—NGO or military, local or foreign, is difficult. And such dichotomy goes against some of Winslow's conclusions.

Sixth, when it comes to transparency, again these entities share more commonalities than differences, but for different reasons. Both private and publicly funded NGOs, if based in the United States, must abide by a set of rules to maintain their tax-free status. NGOs' fiscal transparency in how they spend their money is largely absent from privately funded NGOs, but we see more transparency from the publicly funded ones. Their main requirement, as imposed by sanction rules by the U.S. Treasury is to "refrain from working with governments or individuals under U.S. Sanctions, as well as with groups designated as foreign terrorist organizations, but otherwise, they are free to collaborate with foreign NGOs or foreign governments to achieve their purposes."[54] Chapter 6 gives further insight on the rules around the military working with vetted NGOs. At the same time, NGOs "need not provide notification to any government agency about its membership, activities, or outreach."[55] Contrarily, oversight by Congress for the military includes both budgetary and performance policy. Programs funded under Title 10, which covers many of SOF's activities discussed in this analysis, "contains more than 300 reporting requirements to be made to Congress, ranging from spending breakdowns to readiness assessments and strategy reports."[56]

Seventh, independence is most associated with NGOs, many of which seek to be independent of political parties or agendas in how they operate. While independence is usually considered in the context of political affiliation, there is another independence, which is organizational. How are SOF *independent* from DOD, and NGOs *independent* from donors? In the context of organizational independence, NGOs are much more constrained than the military, contrary to Winslow's argument. In certain instances, contracting and implementing the projects of donors is less straightforward. For instance, once contracted to perform projects, NGOs can further subcontract their work, taking their cut in the process. This makes them less organizationally independent, as they must be accountable to the donor, while also dependent on the quality of the subcontractor's work. Conversely, SOF's maneuvering of the physical terrain, and the ad hoc nature of how they select their projects make them much more independent in their work, even if this freedom is highly criticized by development actors. SOF's constraints are due to coordination with the Embassy, which varies depending on the strength of the interagency, and the leverage of DOD in the specific mission. When SOF uses other organizations to support its mission, in the way that United States Agency for International Development (USAID) uses NGOs to implement development projects, the closest to this comparison is SOF's work with the HN partner. This is the case with Acción Integral in Colombia, or with the Lebanese Armed Forces in Lebanon. In these cases, DOD provides the funding to the CA branch of the HN military, who carry out the actual implementation of projects. In short, when it comes to independence, both of these actors can be constrained in their day-to-day business operations.

But in both instances, there is a common denominator—accountability to populations. Taking into account chapter 3 on how donors often bypass consulting with the HN government in fragile states, to whom then are these actors accountable? If SOF builds a well in a community, and it dries up, has it met its security objective? What does now become of the decrepit structure, and who do the populations living inside of the communities where it was built hold accountable? If a bridge built by an NGO but funded by a donor, collapses, which of these two entities is held accountable and by whom? If the World Bank funds the building of an electric grid, which causes recipients' electric bills to increase, is this reducing poverty? If the Gates Foundation in Malawi only decides to vaccinate a specific demographic of the youth, who, among these players is to stop it from doing so, and on what legal grounds? The concept of "do no harm" is discussed in later chapters, but much of the debate around the *appropriateness* of projects has been pinned on the military, especially with the large Commander's Emergency Response Program (CERP) efforts in Iraq and Afghanistan where schools were built without teachers, and clinics were equipped without doctors. As one military respondent noted, "Commanding officers are not experts at most things. So, the question becomes how do the people in charge give guidance on something they are not experts at?"[57] Another military respondent referred to their time in Afghanistan, "I was given half a million dollars in CERP money to spend. I was 25 years old. I didn't know what I was doing."[58] These are *all* issues of accountability, but also of the ability to cause harm. What becomes clear is that both of these actors are equally prone *not* to thinking through the consequences of their programming. By default, this makes them accountable to their objectives, first, not to the population. When the recipients' perceptions are examined in chapter 6, this will be discussed at length.

Eighth, when it comes to scale, there is a similarity in the footprint of the projects which NGOs and SOF conduct. More precisely, the size and impact of a project are relative to the scale of the community where it is carried out. Small projects of just several thousand dollars may be a drop in the DOD bucket, but at the micro level they can make or break the relationship in a small village of several hundred. "The term 'small-scale construction' in a recently issued guidance for authority 333, means 'at a cost not to exceed $1,500,000 for any project.'"[59] Such an amount may be a maximum ceiling for a well-funded DOD, but exceeds NGOs' and grassroots initiatives' financial capabilities multifold. As one respondent said, within the scale of DOD, "10,000 dollars may translate into a meaningful project in Burkina Faso or be a money pit in Afghanistan's Helmand Province, where billions have poured in over the last 20 years."[60] This is the fundamental difference between large-scale nation-building efforts conducted through CERP, and the gray space, where projects can be much smaller scale.

Lastly, perhaps one of the most recognizable but practically frustrating contrast between militaries and NGOs is their use of language. The word "targeting," one of the most frequently used by military respondents to describe populations in interviews for this study, refers to "an entity or object that performs a function for the threat considered for possible engagement or other action."[61] This term, according to NGO respondents, could only be interpreted as elimination or killing. By definition, military collateral damage "is an effect that causes unintentional or incidental injury or damage to persons or objects that would not be lawful military targets."[62] However, it is often used to mean unintended consequences of armed conflict.

NGOs have their own terms and language, where certain types of assistance have evolved from "charity" to "capacity building," from serving "victims" to supporting "survivors," from "war relief" to "conflict transformation," from "asylum" to "protection," from decrying ineffective governments to the promotion of "good governance."[63] For the military conflict is "hot" or "red."

For NGOs, states which are affected by conflict are considered "fragile" and "unstable," a turn from the 1980s when they were simply "weak." For the military, those living outside of their home of origin due to displacement from conflict were once described as "dislocated civilians,"[64] but for NGOs, they are Internally Displaced Persons (IDPs), or if they have crossed an international border, they are refugees. During a panel focused on the coordination between the military and NGOs, NGOs expressed their hesitation when at first they were open to sharing assessments of local conditions with USAID, "until and unless they hear military colleagues use terms like 'intel' and 'exploitation of the local population' associated with their data."[65] It is in these instances, that SOF, and specifically SOF CA demonstrated their lack of understanding of how the language they use impacts their relationship with civic partners.

OVERSEAS HUMANITARIAN, DISASTER, AND CIVIC AID

It has already been established that NGOs have the advantage of receiving different streams of private and public money, contrary to the military which is publicly funded. Yet, one of the key differences between these entities is scale. DOD has a large amount of funding, while NGOs have small amounts. As one journalist argues, "We send soldiers where we need civilians because the soldiers get the resources."[66] But examined more closely, how big is the military budget for development and humanitarian activities, *really*?

The military's involvement in humanitarian work is authorized but not limited to one main budget authority—the Overseas Humanitarian, Disaster, and Civic Aid Programs (OHDACA). OHDACA is the go-to budgetary tool to address post-reconstruction, humanitarian disasters, and instability prevention, to mention a few. It is designed for "training military personnel, serving the political interests of the host nation and United States, and providing humanitarian relief to foreign civilians."[67] Congress passed OHDACA in 1992 as a sub-program of DOD, making its primary purpose to enable "PN provision of essential human services to their indigenous populations."[68] Covering the full gamut, OHDACA includes a series of health, education, humanitarian demining, and infrastructure projects for the Partner Nation (PN).[69]

Between training, equipment, operations, maintenance, and personnel, DOD's spending spans anywhere between $700 to $800 billion each year. GCCs, which "evolved into the modern-day equivalent of the Roman Empire's proconsuls,"[70] have their own budget systems. From the $719 billion spent by DOD for 2019,[71] $4.5 billion was allotted to and controlled by the five GCCs. OHDACA's actual spending for the same year was just under $118 million, of which roughly $86 million were committed to foreign disaster assistance, and $15 million were committed to humanitarian assistance and humanitarian mine action, respectively.[72] To compare, the president's 2019 proposed budget for USAID and DOS, combined was $39.3 billion.[73] The 600 NGOs which USAID partnered with in 2016 received just under $27 billion in support from USAID and private donations.[74] The 2022 proposed budget for the Office of Transition Initiatives (OTI) is $92 million,[75] nearly 80 percent of what DOD spent on OHDACA in 2019. None of these figures are comparable to the large amounts spent on CERP in Afghanistan or Iraq.[76] What is of note is that U.S. government development assistance in fragile states for programs with a development or humanitarian objective versus military assistance—for programs for armed forces, is 78 percent to 22 percent, respectively.[77] This design is contrary to what is often viewed as the military outspending, outdoing, and outmaneuvering its civic interlocutors.

Furthermore, in addition to the accountability measures mentioned earlier in this chapter, OHDACA is more prescriptive and restrained in *how* the military can spend its funding. OHDACA spreads across seven funding authorities—401, 402, 404, 407, 2557, 2561, and 2649, each carrying different purposes on *who* can approve money and *how* money can be used. These authorities support anything from large-scale humanitarian projects with pure logistics, such as the Japan earthquake in 2011 or Haiti in 2010 to hundreds of small-scale projects around the world (as listed in table 2.1) and the transportation of civilian supplies.[78] OHDACA allows some flexibility in regard to humanitarian activities around the world,[79] but such spending is allowed only as long as it does not replicate other U.S. government agencies.[80] Furthermore, these budget authorities are restricted to ensure that donations are not "being used to gain access or preferential treatment or, put in the most extreme terms, as a bribe or inducement to spur official action,"[81] by DOD in its role as a transporter of humanitarian supplies, or donations. These rules are further enforced for Section 401 of Title 10 funding,[82] the one most concerned in this analysis. It requires Department of State (DOS) approval, leading to close interagency coordination between what DOS as the lead sees as a priority first. Some among the above-mentioned authorities are overseen by the Defense Security Cooperation Agency, while others are overseen by Office of the Secretary of Defense or Joint Staff.

Both the restrictions and flexibility of OHDACA demonstrate its utility as an agile instrument across the interagency. The challenge is that the programming cycle which dictates *how* money can be spent, does not match with the needs cycle of the area of operation. Simply put, according to one respondent "what recipients/communities may identify as a need may not be what spending authorities or authorizers would allow, or when they would allow us to do it."[83] Or, as another respondent shared, referring to their work in West Africa, "We had money for masks, so this is what we gave. Now there is a vaccine for COVID 19, but we can't use it for the vaccine because our funding restrictions won't let us."[84] Restricting money by earmarking what it can be used for also applies to NGOs, as discussed earlier in chapter 3.

Contrary to DOD's stringent spending rules on *what* can be done and *how* it can be done in the gray space, the picture for NGOs is quite different. What NGOs might lack in funding, they possess in flexibility. As one NGO participant in a symposium noted, "there is no faster money than private money,"[85] and "while DOD is prohibited from soliciting assistance even in humanitarian emergencies, USAID and State can solicit donations of goods, services, and even money."[86] For the OTI—the expeditionary arm of USAID, more likely to deploy in conflict settings, it takes two months to stand up a program in a fragile state, versus USAID, which can take up to twelve months. This flexibility is by design, as the OTI provides "fast and flexible short-term assistance," and it allows it to engage "quickly and robustly, often where additional contingency funds are less readily available."[87] As such, OTI can cut a grant in six hours,[88] a flexible trait which helps it mitigate fragile contexts swiftly. While SOF have at their disposal more flexible tools than the conventional military to carry out their humanitarian support projects, they need approval through their Overseas Humanitarian Assistance and Shared Information System (OHASIS)—discussed later.

Chapter 2 provided evidence of how the military launches OHDACA projects, with little consultation with beneficiaries. NGO projects, according to chapter 3, provide little visibility on how they are funded or whether they meet desired effects. But *are* these projects serving their intended benefit? Who is accountable to whom in the deployment of OHDACA, and how?

OHDACA is not a black box, and it contains its own and *internal* accountability measures related to assessment, monitoring and evaluation (ME), which are closely followed in OHASIS.[89] This is only in theory, however. OHASIS is the knowledge repository for thousands of projects, and it is used by the interagency community of more than 6,000 users for the full project cycle—development, coordination, approval, and evaluation.[90] In 2018, nearly twenty years into its launching, from the 16,000 active projects in OHASIS, 7,000 were completed and were valued at over 2.3 billion.[91]

To exist in the system OHDACA projects are assigned a series of fields— "name, number, year, funding program, approval status, combatant command, country, cost, person of contact, key words, and a free-form project description."[92] There is a discrepancy in this system, however, as the needs assessment, ME guidance included in OHDACA does not always translate into the required fields of the OHASIS system,[93] and "there are no congressional or internal DOD reporting requirements in terms of outcomes or impacts of projects."[94] DOD's framework is to assess "security cooperation through humanitarian assistance."[95] The military seeks to "track, understand, and improve returns on DOD security cooperation investments."[96] Moreover, a Government Accountability Office report found that "DOD does not have complete information on the status or actual costs" of its OHDACA activities. And between 2005 and 2009, "DOD had not completed 90 percent of the required 1-year post-project evaluations for its OHDACA projects, and about half of the required 30-day evaluations for those projects, and thus lacks information to determine projects' effects."[97] So it should be of no surprise that respondents described "when we got in country, there were 30 proposed projects in the system [OHASIS], and none of them were approved—partly due to the cumbersome and long approval process."[98]

It is evident that once again, these projects are designed with DOD objectives in mind, not with development and humanitarian goals for the civic environment. So, if OHDACA projects are done with reconnaissance in mind, and they are not for the benefit of populations, then how *are* OHDACA projects sufficient in informing the military's mission? The opinion is mixed.

Some respondents spoke about how OHDACA projects *do* provide SOF with the access and placement needed for the military to carry out its missions. But others have argued that the information produced is *only* information, *not* knowledge. Some have already argued that "there is no definitive doctrine that explains how to collect, analyze or warehouse Civil Information,"[99] be it for intelligence purposes or simply to meet local needs. Respondents overwhelmingly agreed that OHASIS provides data and information, but *not* knowledge. There is no robust interface between information captured in OHASIS and the other information repository—Palantir—the human network and intelligence system.[100] One military respondent emphasized that, "As good as any of these systems are . . . they don't talk to each other. Why even bother putting in information if they don't use it. We are running everything on a printed out excel spreadsheet."[101] Military respondents also reflected on the weakness of how the "current stovepipe systems and data sharing systems of the U.S. government cannot meet the need for persistent knowledge and awareness."[102] As one respondent described it:

> What do I need to gather on the outside in terms of information, to help me feed the system inside. Not what is in the system inside that can help me recognize unique aspects of the context in which I am operating.[103]

In short, much of the effort is spent on finding ways to fit the context to the tools which are at hand, not utilizing such tools to understand the setting. As such, operators are often unable to draw a holistic picture, and the gathering of information process overrides the desired product that is the context.[104]

It is clear that the system and process used by DOD is not fit for purpose. So, do development actors have a more efficient mechanism to create and utilize knowledge for their programming?

I must mention that it is a stretch to make an apples-to-apples comparison between DOD's OHASIS and USAID's ME mechanisms, or individual NGOs' ME instruments, which were discussed earlier. USAID's systems are for the effectiveness of its programming, whereas DOD's are for managing the knowledge about the operating environment. But OHASIS *is* the program tracking system that comes the closest to USAID's project oversight databases. USAID's matrices are inclusive of performance indicators, targets, and baselines, which are carefully thought-out throughout the lifecycle of a development project[105] and against which implementing partners report. But this lacks on the DOD side. When it comes to NGOs' own central exchange, knowledge, and monitoring of development projects, there is no one centralized hub for data that creates knowledge about the effectiveness of programs, rather there are individualized reports which are submitted to the funding donor. This is logical as these are disparate entities, unlike the DOD which, despite its size, is still a single organization. On the humanitarian side, there is one common data exchange platform that allows NGO access to humanitarian data.[106] The closest to a centralized hub for this information is the UN, which helps to identify and publicly share sources of insecurity and instability. No centralized system on the impact of NGOs' programming on communities exists. This is also the case with DOD's OHASIS system, or the individual tools—Political, Military, Economic, Social, Information, and Infrastructure (PMESII) and Areas, Structures, Capabilities, Organization, People, Events (ASCOPE)—which was discussed in chapter 2.

What becomes evident is that, as with the military in carrying out its PMESII and ASCOPE assessments, there is little evidence of a centralized knowledge creation mechanism for NGOs to share assessments of the social and economic consequences of their activities.[107] It is further evident that NGOs are often left to achieve a hard balance between staying accountable to the donors who fund them, and the population they serve. On the military side accountability is toward the U.S. taxpayer and upward hierarchical structures, not populations. Consequently, both of these occurrences cause SOF CA and NGOs to converge.

There has been some question around—"What does 'locally accountable' mean in fragile states or places where the government and/or local actors participates in exclusion/conflict?"[108] As mentioned in earlier parts of this chapter, no structure exists to hold either the military or NGOs accountable for the results of their work by local communities. With that, it must be emphasized that accountability should not be confused with transparency, which is argued to be one of NGOs' weak points,[109] and which is off-limits for DOD, as OHASIS is a government-only system to access. As discussed previously, NGOs are accountable to donors, but much of their private funding allows them lesser levels of transparency. For DOD, transparency is also a challenge, due to the classified nature of their work. Together, all these enti-ties—the military, NGOs, and their funding donors, are to various degrees, self-serving.

QUICK IMPACT

One last comparison of SOF and NGOs as development actors is in order. This is the utilization of Quick Impact Projects (QIP). As their namesake implies, the idea of QIP projects is for populations to see quick and tangible improvements within their communities. QIP are used across the gamut in peacekeeping operations to keep the peace[110] and in counterinsurgency opera-tions to gain access,[111] by both HN and foreign militaries and development actors. For SOF, QIP are the projects under OHDACA, and are carried out around the world as a way to engage and win over populations and build trust.[112] Another organizations that uses QIP is the United Nations. The UN uses QIP as a way to achieve a quick and long-lasting effect meeting priority needs of the population and building confidence.[113] But QIP are approached differently by the military and development actors, and there is a question about their quickness *and* about their impact.

Chapter 3 discussed the fluidity between NGOs' short- and long-term projects for humanitarian or development purposes. The military, too, experi-ences a similar spillover between short-term and long-term implementation. Here is how: once OHDACA is obligated, it becomes available funding for projects to be implemented within five years. A five-year obligation is the length of a development program, not a short-term QIP program. These proj-ects also become subject to a lack of continuity, due to the erratic deployment cycles of the military. A five-year period adds up to several teams' rotations of six to nine months each. Added to this is the sporadic change of vision brought on by "commanders swapping out every 2 years or less, when they may completely pull the plug on these projects."[114]

For NGOs, QIP has a longer attention span. NGOs and development actors' concern is about the local community's ability to sustain the goods or services provided in the long term. This is particularly the case with the gray space, within which absorption capacity can be limited.[115] In a series of UN QIP projects executed in the early and mid-1990s—in Mozambique, twelve health posts and fifteen primary schools were still functioning fifteen years later.[116] But for the military, one noted, "nobody knows what really happened to a school we built in Somalia 15 years ago," one respondent said.[117] In one instance, one former military respondent shared that a school that the U.S. military had built in South America had been repainted, and a giant poster of Fidel Castro had been displayed for the locals to see. In Afghanistan, QIP projects under CERP "were a way for the Taliban to stop shooting at us,"[118] according to a senior officer.

Following up on projects by the military is sporadic, and lacks systematization,[119] much like the initiation of projects. When it comes to measuring impact, several military respondents noted, and one put it succinctly, "There is none. We used money as a weapons system."[120] This could sometimes also have the opposite impact, where the most violent areas benefited from investments, and the ones making the most progress were neglected. This is the example from Afghanistan, where the areas which were the most violent were ones where the most money was invested in the hope to improve security. The opposite happened. One lively NGO official described her view of these investments in Afghanistan, "today, I will slap you in the face, you will give me 10 dollars. Tomorrow, I will kick you in the ass, you will give me 100 dollars. Why should I stop kicking you in the ass?"[121]

THE UNBALANCED CIVIL-MILITARY BUDGET

Examining how even small-scale DOD projects compare in terms of spending and budgeting against NGOs would be a difficult task. Taking into account local NGOs, who "tend to have few staff and are most likely to hire local people for administrative requirements,"[122] and the small footprint of a CA team, how do these entities compare when it comes to the cost of personnel?

When it comes to how rich in resources each of these entities perceives the other to be, there is another misperception. From the point of view of NGOs and civilian agencies:

> [T]he military seems quite resource-rich, with its helicopters, large numbers of vehicles, transport aircraft, robust communications and computing equipment. From the military perspective, civilian agencies seem resource-rich because they have aid money to disperse—and, after all, dispensing money is the role of many civilian organizations.[123]

DOD's large and sophisticated machine separates funding allotments between projects and personnel, but an exact amount of how individual DOD projects and individual NGO projects compare in terms of cost would be difficult. This is in particular because of what was discussed earlier on NGOs' lack of disclosure on their spending. However, the military's costs for activities under OHDACA are appropriated for projects, and to some extent for the travel of personnel and transport. Where salaries are paid, they are primarily according to rank. A soldier digging a well, repainting a school, or performing a medical exam will be paid according to their rank, not their specialty, and be paid anywhere from one-third to two-thirds less of what their civilian counterpart is compensated.[124] Where the military carries out these projects directly and not through contractors, OHDACA funds are strictly allocated for the goods or services attached to a project. They do not include the cost of the salary, accommodation, transportation, or travel expenses of a soldier.

Just like the military, NGOs have their own funding authorities for deliverables and operations. Hiring experts, consultants, or even permanent staff requires careful budgeting and planning for years out. As DOD draws from specialist units, NGOs may draw from a pool of rosters with specialists ready to deploy. Because military ground operators are expeditionary by nature, they are trained to perform a variety of tasks. An E5 logistician and E5 medic make essentially comparable salaries. But an MSF nurse and a driver do not. It is a long stretch to make a dollar-to-dollar comparison between an NGO and a CA unit. But as one NGO respondent puts it, "for each 100 dollars of what an NGO spends, 80 of that will go to keep the lights on or fuel up the vehicles to get staff to where they need to be."[125]

As mentioned, to compare civilian and DOD spending at the project level is difficult. In his 2002 article about the Stabilization Force in Bosnia and Herzegovina (SFOR), Adam Siegel compares the cost of one member of the UN International Police Task Force (IPTF) versus one soldier. He argues that members of the IPTF are often the envy of soldiers, as they earn tax-free salaries, allowances, and long vacations. But when compared, IPTF staff cost the same to their organizations, as a soldier with a minimal tooth-to-tail ratio costs to theirs,[126] where one member of personnel needs several others to support them in carrying out the mission. Tooth-to-nail ratio typically applies to combat, but not always. Considering the cost that the military invests in training, recruitment, and administration, to prepare a soldier to deploy, it *does* outspend NGOs multifold in the range of $240,00 to $720,000—see table 4.2. This figure does not take into consideration a

Table 4.2   Describing Yearly Deployment Cost of IPTF Personnel versus Military

	IPTF	*Military NCO 3:1 ratio*	*Military NCO 11:1 ratio*
Base salary	$80,000	$30,000	$30,000
Per diem	$40,000		
Training + miscellaneous	$30,000		
Support (recruitment, travel, supplies, admin) required	$100,000	$180,000	$660,000
Benefits		$30,000	$30,000
Total	**$250,000**	**$240,000**	**$720,000**

Source: Author, data from Siegel, Adam B. "Civil-Military Marriage Counseling: Can this Union Be Saved?." Special Warfare. 15, no. 4 (2002): 28–34.

soldier's dependents' allowances, health insurance, basic housing allowance, and other costs borne by the organization when a soldier is on deployment.

As discussed earlier, it is difficult to make a one-to-one comparison, as such analysis are mostly done at the agency level, not at the project or program level. What becomes clear is that the riches of the military are not because of its funding pool for humanitarian and development projects. Quite on the contrary, DOD's colossal investment is in the military's conventional capability, and personnel, not in funding allocations for building schools, digging wells, or taking out the trash. The discrepancy is more evident *within* the NGO sector, especially with the public-to-private money relationship discussed in chapter 3. With this sort of flexibility, one NGO may spend the majority of its money on staff while another may mostly carry out tangible projects.[127] Various factors, such as the length of deployment and benefits to the individual also must be taken into account. Other factors such as the number of civilian contractors, civilians in international organizations, military and Private Military Security Companies, as well as short- or long-term employment, temporary international staff of national secondments, will also drive many of these figures.[128]

The Non-monetary Civil-Military Budget

Thus far this analysis has mostly focused on the financial differences between SOF and NGOs' programming in local communities. But there is another currency that differentiates these actors—the human one, which, as much as the financial one, can drive these organizations' success. Let me explain.

Unlike NGOs, who must raise or compete for money, GCCs receive consistent streams of public funding which get disbursed to SOF missions, even if such amounts fluctuate from year to year. As one respondent noted:

> Each year commanders ask for more money for stability ops. Some of the things we are giving are commodities that these communities can get from elsewhere—the Taliban brings people stuff, Al Shabab brings people stuff. We as the US military shouldn't be in the commodity business. Besides, because this stuff is not sexy, we are not very good at it, as it's not in our DNA to do hearts and minds. This is in addition to stability operations not being the appetite of commanders.[129]

This is consistent with a study in the 1990s, which assessed that among U.S. military leadership the majority felt comfortable with the military's role to be *only* about fighting and winning wars.[130] All of this is to say that while money may not be an issue, unlike for NGOs, the military is emotionally detached from its role as a development actor. Those with expertise to understand and implement civic projects, namely CA units, one military respondent noted, "have been kicked to the curb with the draw down on the big wars,"[131] and there is little appetite for finding a solution to how to organize, train, deploy, and overall utilize them.[132] There is no CA champion in the U.S. Army. It is not a command, and much has been moved to the reserve component. As one military respondent noted, "In my entire year during my last deployment, the SF Colonels were like a bull in a China shop, with CA colonels basically being told to only speak when spoken to."[133]

On the NGO side, there is little lack of appetite to carry out their core activities. NGOs have at their disposal individuals willing to volunteer their time, making this one of NGOs' most precious commodities.[134] A woman from a local NGO in the Gambia expressed:

> It's difficult to get support from donors. And this is why we can't have many staff. There are no funds to pay salaries, good salaries. It is difficult. But we are managing. I have managed to work as a volunteer, and I go to here to work as a volunteer. I put up a small bakery, and that's how I manage. Some relatives here and there assist me. (Director, local NGO)[135]

Contrary to NGOs that greatly benefit from volunteers,[136] the military get assigned to carry out their missions, and whether those include stability operations or not, they have little choice except for circumstances in health and family situations. There is more leeway with private contractors, and civilians in their assignments overseas. During my own time in Afghanistan, my military colleagues, who were sent there by their Ministries of Defense, were often surprised to know that I had competed for my job as an international civilian, which was compensated, but mostly that I had expressed the desire to deploy to a warzone.

Scholars and practitioners *do* question the military's purpose in performing stability operations, but not for the various reasons mentioned above. Mac Ginty argues that stability operations are a concept designed for control by outside interveners who sought to achieve immersion of locals into Western values,[137] not as a mechanism to find and help local solutions. This is fair. Most of the discussion is about development actors' emphasis on the importance of using local capacity to carry out community projects,[138] something which the military is often accused of not understanding. But some in the military *do* understand the importance of using local capacity.[139] DOD may be a direct participant or direct funder of projects through Operational Contract Support, acquired through support from the HN, directly by the United States or a third country, or through a private security company or a business enterprise.[140] This is partly because the military recognizes that they must include other actors in carrying out activities they are simply not equipped to do.[141] In Guatemala, building and reconstruction are frequently handled by engineers, due to the lack of security concerns. Thus, in a lot of these cases, the military is not looking to gain access and placement in threat areas—the primary objective behind engaging with populations is to be in areas where "the local population already views the US military favorably."[142]

Alternatively, while military commanders may dismiss stability operations as something outside of their repertoire, there can still be a non-security or non-military objective behind them getting involved in the construction business. Employing locals to carry out construction projects can have intentions that are not overtly or directly related to security. During my deployment to Afghanistan, I experienced first-hand the constant renovation and reconstruction in front of the Yellow Building—the home of International Security Assistance Force High Command. I could not understand the efficiency of constantly rebuilding, repainting, and reconstructing the little courtyard in front of my office. When I approached the Major in charge, she said, "it is a jobs program we are running, it's not about efficiency. We are all trying to help these people."[143]

Finally, as the military seeks to gain intelligence and understanding of the spaces where it operates, clear evidence shows that their approach to measuring success is self-serving as chapter 2 discussed at length. OHDACA projects' effectiveness is measured against the extent to which air space, sharing of assets, or intelligence occurs between the U.S. military and the HN. There is no measuring, however, of the extent to which a long-term relationship has been achieved, either with NGOs or the population.[144] Neither is there such a measurement by NGOs for their relationship with populations or the military. In short, both actors are self-serving in their accountability to the larger hierarchies to which they each belong. When it comes to impact, the picture is similar. These organizations' imbalance is in the non-monetary relationship which NGOs have with volunteers, giving them an edge in the civil-military relationship by having at their disposal the human will to do good.

Placement Without Permanence

One of the requirements for effective interaction between NGOs and the military, and for effectiveness of the projects they deliver is the longevity of their presence on the ground. The lack of structural enmeshing between the NGOs and the military's decision-making authorities is further exacerbated by the timelines and longevity of these actors' programming. Soldiers only rarely get deployed to the same place, leaving little room for continuity in building institutional knowledge. For interviewees on both sides, almost everyone unanimously agreed that this is one of the biggest mistakes that the military makes. To form meaningful long-term relationships there must be a degree of permanence. This is a challenge for this type of military actor, who is there on short-term assignments. Officers who return to the same place are sufficiently higher up through the ranks. But they are no longer navigating relationships with populations or NGOs in villages. Instead, they are posted at the operational or strategic levels and they are likely to engage with their counterpart elites from the HN—other high-ranking officers or heads of organizations. As such, it is the young, less experienced ground operators who roam the gray space. "Imagine a 30-year-old meeting with a 60-year-old elder in the community!" one military respondent quipped.[145] While many expressed their wish for longer deployment cycles, as a precondition to be most effective, others did not agree with this suggestion, "We are not humanitarian or development actors, we are soldiers. It should be an in and out job."[146]

Short-term deployment cycles can also have an impact on the ability to develop expertise. Earlier, this chapter discussed the balance between specialist NGOs and generalist SOF. But under normal circumstances, those posted in-country longer are bound to have the institutional knowledge, which a short-timer might struggle to achieve. Almost every respondent in both the NGO and military groups confirmed that the military's short-term deployment cycles are one of the most significant obstacles to effectively engaging in humanitarian and development work. Rotations can last from three months to nine months at the most. The challenge of short-term deployments are also recognized by NGO staff and development workers, some of whom brief the military during the training and preparation for their missions. One such trainer noted, "My conversation with the military, and everything I've briefed them on in 2007 is no different than everything I brief them on today in 2020—it's the same thing over and over again."[147] For those NGO respondents who recognized the importance of sharing and working with the military, the challenge according to them is that, "When I train the people who are deploying, I end up talking to the people who go to the field. Not enough is done at the Colonel and General officer levels. It's really a bottom-up approach, not top down."[148] With this, clearly transfer of knowledge is personality dependent, as every strategic decision-maker was once an operator.

This revolving door is a detriment not only to developing the institutional knowledge necessary to do the job but also to the confidence of civic actors toward the military—be it NGOs or populations. This lack of continuity is also about "temporal" reconnaissance.[149] Sensitivity and understanding of the sociocultural landscape they work in are vital to a successful outcome of a project. Whether it be Ramadan or other culturally or religiously significant events, the timing of engagement and project implementation matter. As one respondent notes, "a third of my deployment was during the month of Ramadan. It was impossible to get anything done."[150] Disruption can also be due to other priorities, where during one individual's few months of deployment, they were pulled to complete training which took several weeks. Continuity is also about the consecutiveness of personnel's deployments and avoidance of disrupting the mission.

For NGOs, continuity is less of an issue, as civilians "typically sign up for a longer duration. Civilian employees, with the exception of emergency teams, typically consider a year to be the minimum commitment."[151] But as discussed earlier, even in emergencies, the longevity of civic actors' involvement may vary, as emergency response and long-term programming often cross over into one another. Longevity appears to be the least of an issue for local NGOs, who are also part of the community. Donors are increasingly looking to partner with local organizations as implementers of their programming. But when it comes to staffing, NGOs can be equally short-timed, particularly when they work in emergency response. In tackling emergencies, NGOs have at their disposal "databases of CVs, which are kept on file for a certain period"[152] as a resource for when they need to hire experts. This is common practice, as "NGO contractors will often bounce between different NGOs in different emergencies around the world, holding 3-, 6- or 12-month contracts before moving on to their next assignment."[153] Some have already found that "INGOs often operate in an environment of short-term contracts, dampening organizational accountability and any oversight that could limit rent-seeking practices."[154] So just like the military, NGOs can be short-timers. In addition to staffing, NGOs' mandates are equally disruptive, as "many aid agencies (especially those engaged in humanitarian assistance) equate efficiency with 'timeliness,' and timeliness is regularly interpreted to mean speed. In development, peace-building, or human rights activities, programs are usually funded in one-, two-, or three-year cycles," as there is pressure to deliver in short periods of time.[155] And because of the donor model which NGOs follow and the need for speed to deliver and get on with the next planning cycle, this makes some NGOs' attention span equally short, and comparable to that of the military.

CONCLUSION

Considering their similar attributes in the operating space, are SOF and NGOs organizationally compatible or institutionally restrained?

In examining how these entities go from large-scale coordinated interaction, to small-level ad hoc engagement, the gray space, once again converges, rather than diverges these entities. The lack of traditional sequencing has changed their traditional roles, causing them to adapt to a new and chaotic sequence of development, diplomacy, and security happening simultaneously, replacing an obsolete order of pre-conflict, conflict, and post-conflict events. In examining these organizations for their diversity, autonomy, generalist versus specialist expertise, transparency, organizational independence, and scale, these entities appear to be organizationally compatible at the ground level, but institutionally restrained by the larger bureaucracies to which they belong. Contrary to popular belief, in the gray space, DOD *can* be underfunded compared to NGOs that have ample resources. Both of these entities thread the boundary between short- and long-term engagements, less by the function of their presence, but more by the flexible budget authorities available to them.

Both development and military actors are savvy in trying to develop quick and impactful projects for quick wins, but by their inherent nature, such approaches give little credence to accountability. On their end, the military lacks the necessary permanence needed to see these efforts through, even if its budget authority can have a longer life. With lack of permanence also comes lack of knowledge about the places where the military is operating. On the NGO front, too, deployment of staff can vacillate between quick touch-and-go projects, emergency response, and long-term commitments. Local NGOs do not face such a challenge, as they are nested into the communities where they operate. Yet, international staff who are in and out of the country are equally prone to failing to understand the contexts of the places where they work.

Finally, these actors are not deliberately designing themselves to adapt to each other. Their organizational compatibility is organic, while their institutional restraints and their contrasting objectives are by design. In examining these entities, Winslow has given plausible reasons as to why these organizations' values, languages, and cultures clash. But in the last twenty years, these organizations are inadvertently mirroring one another to adapt to the needs of Duffield's described space of permanent instability. This is the unavoidable reality in fragile states where, as argued by Collier, security actors have a role to play as a way to break up the vicious cycle of fragility and insecurity. But this blend of civil and military efforts, and as a result civil-military interaction, is at odds with traditionalist thinkers on both sides—Sachs for development and Huntington for security. In their own way, both of these scholars believe that these entities have no business doing each other's jobs. Yet, unsurprisingly, the organizational similarity and compatibility of these actors share much of the same DNA. And it ultimately confirms what Brooks has argued all along—that the boundary between those who carry guns and those who carry stethoscopes is fading.

NOTES

1. Aall and Snodderly, "Introduction," 13.
2. Kober, "Low-Intensity Conflicts," 17.
3. Franke, "The Peacebuilding Dilemma," 8.
4. Flavin, "Civil Military Operations," xi.
5. Lawry, "Guide," 198.
6. Madiwale and Virk, "Civil–Military Relations in Natural Disasters," 1085–105.
7. Franke, "The Peacebuilding Dilemma", 8.
8. R 38—Civil Affairs Officer, March 16, 2021.
9. This implies coordination at the field level, beyond the walls of the Embassy, not the coordination which occurs through the U.S. interagency which was discussed earlier.
10. Such doctrine may occur through some of the guidelines mentioned before, or through coordination structures such as OCHA, but such requirements may not be necessarily enforced.
11. Schopp, "Guidelines for NGO Coordination."
12. This speaks to small US SOF CA teams, not the large coordination efforts that exist under the UN structures, such as UNOCHA, which coordinates international humanitarian response through the cluster system.
13. Brass et al., "NGOs and International Development," 137.
14. Brewer, "U.S. Army Civil Affairs," 5.
15. Department of Defense, *Joint Operations*, V-7.
16. The tidy sequence may exist in contexts which have strong capacity and structures for response. For instance, there is no evidence that the 2011 Japan Tsunami resulted in conflict. This is contrary to violence and criminality being on the rise following the 2010 earthquake in Haiti. Bremer and Cawthorne, "Haiti"; Vergano, "Mudslide Buries;" King and Mutter, "Violent Conflicts."
17. Pettit and Beresford, "Emergency," 317.
18. *Ibid.*, 316.
19. Christopher Holshek, "Humanitarian Civil-Military Coordination," 274.
20. Donini, "Local Perceptions," 161.
21. *Ibid.*, 160.
22. Stewart and Brown, "The Pentagon and Global Development," 5.
23. R 15.
24. Otto, "The End of Operational Phases at Last," 78.
25. R 17.
26. *Ibid.*
27. Winslow, "Strange Bedfellows," 41.
28. Holshek, "Humanitarian Civil-Military Coordination," 276.
29. Winslow, "Strange Bedfellows," 38.
30. Armed Forces Staff College, "Anthony Zinni."
31. Author's deployment to USMC Quantico during Operations Allies Welcome October, 2021.
32. Fyvie and Ager, "NGOs and Innovation," 1396.
33. Breede, "Special (Peace)," 229.
34. *Ibid.*
35. Winslow, "Strange Bedfellows," 40.
36. Shamir and Ben-Ari, "The Rise of Special Operations Forces," 355.
37. Breede, "Special (Peace)," 229.
38. Scheidt, "NGOs," 5.
39. Philipps and Arango, "Who Signs Up to Fight?"; Savell and McMahon, "Numbers and Per Capita Distribution of Troops."
40. PeaceCorps, "Peace Corps Announces Top States," December 7, 2009.
41. Breede, "Special (Peace)," 229.
42. UNSW Canberra, "Operating".

43. Brière, Proulx, Flores, and Laporte, "Competencies of Project Managers," 120.

44. *Ibid*; Brière et al., "Competencies," 120.

45. Holton, Febbraro, Filardo, Barnes, Fraser, and Spiece, "The Relationship," 19.

46. *Ibid.*

47. Shamir and Ben-Ari, "The Rise," 336.

48. Burduja, "Use of Special Operations Forces."

49. Miller, "From Adversaries to Allies," 181–97.

50. World Health Organization, "Gender and Health Workforce Statistics."

51. Fischl, "Almost 82 Percent of Social Workers Are Female."

52. Holton et al., "The Relationship," 17.

53. Angba, et al., "Performance," 35–46.

54. US Department of State, "Non-Governmental Organizations (NGOs) in the United States," Fact Sheet, Bureau of Democracy, Human Rights and Labor, January 20, 2021; "Deputy Secretary of the Treasury Wally Adeyemo's Roundtable Discussion with Human Rights and Anti-Corruption NGOs." US Department of the Treasury. April 29, 2021.

55. *Ibid.*

56. Hathaway, Kuehne, Michel, and Ng, "Congressional Oversight of Modern Warfare," 155.

57. R 53.

58. R 54.

59. *Ibid.*

60. Cornell Law School, "10 U.S. Code § 333 - Foreign Security Forces."

61. Department of Defense Joint Chiefs of Staff, *Department of Defense Dictionary*, 235.

62. *Ibid.*, 35.

63. Anderson et al., *Time to Listen*, 34.

64. US Department of the Army, *Civil.*

65. Civil Affairs Association, "2020 Civil Affairs Symposium Report."

66. Suri, "History Is Clear."

67. Drifmeyer and Llewellyn, "Overview of Overseas Humanitarian," 275.

68. Defense Security Cooperation Agency, "Chapter 12."

69. Defense Security Cooperation Agency, *Strategic Plan 2025;* Defense Security Cooperation Agency, *Evaluation.*

70. Eaglen, "Putting Combatant Commanders."

71. Statista, "U.S. Military Spending from 2000 to 2020," November 10, 2021.

72. Defense Security Cooperation Agency, *Overseas Humanitarian, Disaster, and Civic Aid.* Fiscal Year (FY) 2021 Budget Estimates. OHDACA funds are partially reserved for disaster response (about 30 million) and for small OHDACA humanitarian projects which the military carries out.

73. US Agency for International Development, *Fiscal year (FY) 2019 Development and Humanitarian Assistance Budget.*

74. Aall and Helsing, "Non Governmental Organizations," 60.

75. US Department of State, *Department of State, Foreign Operations and Related Programs.*

76. Special Inspector General for Afghanistan Reconstruction https://www.sigar.mil/.

77. D'Alelio, "US Aid."

78. US Library of Congress, Congressional Research Service, *Japan 2011 Earthquake.*
Cecchine et al., "The U.S. Military Response"; Defense Security Cooperation Agency, *Evaluation*; Thaler, McNerney, Grill, Marquis, and Kadlec, *From Patchwork to Framework.*

79. Defense Security Cooperation Agency, "Chapter 12," Section 9561.

80. *Ibid.*, Section C12.3.1.

81. Stavridis and Farkas, "The 21st Century Force Multiplier," 15.

82. US Library of Congress, Congressional Research Service, *International Crises.*

83. R 61.

84. R 16.

85. Civil Affairs Association, "2021 Civil Affairs Symposium Report," Discussant.

86.   Stavridis and Farkas, "The 21st Century Force Multiplier," 15.

87.   US Department of State, *Department of State, Foreign Operations and Related Programs,* 85.

88.   These are exceptional circumstances. For example, if an attack occurs, conflict heightens between two adversarial tribes, OTI would cut a grant to mobilize money to rapidly address the situation through a radio address or other public outreach means. This specific example is similar to how the military would deploy MISO and PSY-OPS.

89.   Defense Security Cooperation Agency "Chapter 12," Sections C12.2.4.3, C12.2.4.4 and C12.2.4.5.

90.   Defense Security Cooperation Agency, *President's Budget 2019 Defense Security Cooperation Agency.* Exhibit R-2.

91.   *Ibid.*

92.   Bourdeaux, Lawry, Bonventre, and Burkle, "Involvement of the US Department of Defense in Civilian Assistance," 68.

93.   Koffi, "Effects of DOD Engagements."

94.   Bourdeaux et al., "Involvement," 67.

95.   US Department of Defense, *Assessment, Monitoring, and Evaluation Policy for the Security Cooperation Enterprise,* 3.

96.   *Ibid.*

97.   US Government Accountability Office, *Humanitarian and Development Assistance,* Highlights.

98.   R 18.

99.   Burke, "Civil," 1.

100.   "Palantir empowers intelligence agencies to securely derive actionable insights from sensitive data and achieve their most challenging operational objectives." https://palantir.com/offerings/intelligence (accessed on February 25, 2024).

101.   R 30.

102.   Hanhauser IV, "Comprehensive Civil Information," 22.

103.   R 18.

104.   Hanhauser IV, "Comprehensive Civil Information," 17.

105.   US Agency for International Development, "Project Monitor and Evaluation Plan."

106.   Human Data Exchange, "All Organisations."

107.   Such assessment is not to be confused with the monitoring and evaluation and donor reporting requirements discussed in chapter 3.

108.   Seferis and Harvey, "Accountability in Crises," 23.

109.   Keating and Thrandardottir, "NGOs, Trust, and the Accountability Agenda," 134–51.

110.   Kassem, "22: Peacekeeping, Development, and Counterinsurgency."

111.   Baker, "Quick Impact Projects," 1–21.

112.   *Ibid.*

113.   Kassem, "22: Peacekeeping," 467; Baker, "Quick Impact Projects."

114.   R 53.

115.   Newbrander et al., "Rebuilding," 639–60.

116.   Oda, "Speed and Sustainability," 6–7.

117.   R 32 Senior Officer (Retired), March 9, 2021.

118.   Professional Communication/Interaction with a US Marine Corps Officer USMC Officer—July 2021.

119.   Shilling, "Development Activities Locator and Assessment Method."

120.   R 39, R 61, R 30.

121.   Author's own experiences on military deployment in Afghanistan June 2012 to June 2014.

122.   Scheidt, "NGOs," 7.

123.   Siegel, "Civil-Military Marriage Counseling," 32.

124. Stortz, Foglia, Thagard, Staat, and Lutgendorf, "Comparing Compensation of US Military Physicians."

125. R 67.

126. Siegel, "Civil-Military Marriage."

127. Smillie, *The Alms Bazaar.*

128. Author's own deployment to Afghanistan, ISAF 2012–2014. It related to comparing the employment and compensation of NATO international staff versus seconded diplomats from NATO countries for the position of NATO Political Advisor. In some instances, the pay and leave for temporary staff who were part of the NATO international staff was higher than the pay and leave for staff who were under national arrangements, but had job security beyond their mission deployment to Afghanistan.

129. R 53.

130. Holsti, "Chapter 1: Of Chasms and Convergences," 47.

131. R 30.

132. Jacobs, "The Army's Civil Affairs Problems."

133. R 75.

134. Brown and Korten, "Understanding Voluntary Organizations."

135. Fyvie and Ager, "NGOs and Innovation," 1389.

136. Farmer and Fedor, "Volunteer Participation and Withdrawal," 349–68.

137. Mac Ginty, "Against Stabilization," 23.

138. Pinnington, "Local First in Practice."

139. Gregg, "Employment."

140. Trevino, Greathouse, Siefkes, Ting, "Leveraging Our War-Fighting Capabilities," 4–14; US Department of Defense Joint Chiefs of Staff, *Operational Contract Support.*

141. Glenn, "Band of Brothers," iii.

142. Bourdeaux et al., "Involvement," 71.

143. Author's deployment at ISAF High Command in Afghanistan 2012–2014.

144. This strictly refers to measuring the success of the relationship between NGOs and the military as a contributor to positive development and humanitarian outcomes. Further chapters discuss at length NGOs' approach to measuring impact on recipients.

145. R 16.

146. R 39.

147. R 52—Development/NGO Respondent, April 9, 2021.

148. R 40.

149. This refers to the breaking down of time segments or timing of occurrences, specifically there is a temporal aspect to when conflict may be on the rise, or when it may decrease. For example, the rise of attacks during Ramadan in Afghanistan and Iraq. Ramadan is also a time of fasting, when "minimal physical action is taken." See Burke, "Civil," 64 and 77.

150. R 56—Civil Affairs Officer, April 15, 2021.

151. Siegel, "Civil-Military Marriage," 31.

152. Lawry, "Guide," 58.

153. *Ibid.*

154. Bell et al., "Force Multipliers," 401.

155. Anderson et al., *Time to Listen,* 40.

Chapter 5

Ground Operators

Between a Rock and a Soft Place

WHAT DRIVES THE SUCCESS OF THE CIVIL-MILITARY RELATIONSHIP IN THE GRAY SPACE?

Given that both Special Operations Forces (SOF) and Non-Governmental Organizations (NGOs) need to reach desired beneficiaries, chapter 4 explored how in the gray space, SOF and NGOs converge due to their function, but then diverge because of the significant differences between the larger institutional objectives which they serve. But despite their structural differences or similarities, both of these entities' missions are carried out by individuals—the ground operators—whose unique skills and abilities drive the civil-military relationship, and who cultivate their own culture, far away from the strategic and operational headquarters where mandates are formulated. In examining the conditions under which these entities coordinate at the individual level, personnel can demonstrate cultural awareness, openness in communication, and understanding of one's interlocutor. Although they undergo rigorous cultural and language training, SOF are often perceived as lacking the necessary skills to engage beyond the lethal components of their mission. This is both because of the types of alpha personalities who serve the mission, and because of less emphasis being given to the cultural and emotional over the physical requirements for the job. On the other side, NGOs which do not undergo anything close to the vigorous training of soldiers, often come to the mission with a preferred set of professional and personal qualifications best suited to implement effective humanitarian and development project work.

Taking into account that mission success may be determined by the individual conduct and character of both civil and security actors, rather than by prescriptive mandates and structures, this chapter examines a series of individual attributes between the military and NGOs. Civil-military interaction is shaped by organizational cultural-pattern orientations of employees depending on their loyalty to, and connection with, the dominant paradigms of the entity to which they belong. At one end are those who, in some sense, embody the ethic and *espirit de corps* of their organization, a group termed as the *loyalists*. At the other end are those whom the loyalists would consider deserters: those who have absorbed the mores and values of the other organization, a group termed the *converted*. In the center of this spectrum are those who are cognizant of the rules and norms of the other group, and who seek out programmatic intersection by which coordination, communication, or consultation, in various phases of their missions, may allow for accommodation and compromise. This is the group of the *bridgebuilders*.

Contrary to high-intensity conflict, which traditionally draws clear lines between the military and NGOs, in the gray space, these actors are more equipped to improvise and engage with one another in less threatening environments. Yet, because security is a lesser issue or concern in the gray space—areas that are neither at peace nor at a point of full-on war—these actors are more able to navigate it. Ultimately, the very existence of gray spaces causes these entities to gravitate to and converge there, but this is mostly driven by the personalities of the individuals whom these organizations deploy in this space. Contrarily, where divergence occurs, it is not only due to the lack of amiable personalities, but also due to core differences in these organizations' missions and the fact that in the gray space, NGOs do not need the military to provide their security.

THE GROUND RELATIONSHIP

Chapter 4 discussed how the relationship between civilian and military entities materializes differently in the gray space. Before delving into the interaction between SOF and civic organizations on the ground, it must be mentioned that U.S. military personnel abroad either fall under Chief of Mission authority, where they are part of the Embassy and answer to the Ambassador, or under the Geographic Combatant Commander (e.g., EUCOM, CENTCOM). Except in war zones where the Department of State (DOS), and by extension the Ambassador, may play more a supporting role, the Combatant Commander will normally not authorize operations in country without the concurrence of the Ambassador, even where SOF Civil Affairs (CA) are not under Chief of Mission authority, but where SOF CA *are* present.

In the gray space, SOF hold strong autonomy. So, then how *do* SOF and civic entities happen to interact? And what is it about the gray space that changes the civil-military relationship?

Once again, these entities organically tie into one another through a series of specific tasks, daily interactions, and pre-agreed engagements at the ground level. It may at times occur when these entities deliberately consult with one another or seek each other's assistance. These touchpoints occur on two fronts—at the operational and strategic levels of the Embassy, *when* and *if*[1] CA teams are in country, and at the ground level, hundreds of miles away from headquarters and Embassies, where soldiers are deployed.

The primary purpose of coordinating with NGOs and donors, is "alignment, coordination, and deconfliction," as one military respondent noted.[2] Quite often, there is no robust coordination in the gray space,[3] and according to a military respondent, SOF CA are simply "maintaining movement of maneuver, which is a catch-all phrase to say that there is nothing to do."[4] Yet much of the coordination with NGOs depends on the mission, even in the gray space. In certain parts of Africa and the Middle East, SOF are carrying out development and humanitarian projects, but their engagement with NGOs is driven mostly by the level of security. Even if NGOs were able to access the space as much as SOF are, they are wary of appearing to be too close to the military, as they would not wish to put themselves or locals at risk, especially in more violent extremism contexts.[5]

Where coordination does exist with NGOs, it often starts with the Embassy, where the United States Agency for International Development (USAID) maintains a list of cleared and acceptable NGOs with whom the military can work. But SOF teams do not clear every activity through the Embassy, and operators often find themselves engaging with NGOs in their generalist role. During a 2020 Civil Affairs Symposium, a view was shared that CA teams:

> [C]an sometimes provide access and security for civilian colleagues to unstable regions (e.g., in the coastal regions of Kenya). They can check in on projects and populations of interest to civilian agencies on their behalf, when conditions are unsafe for civilians (e.g., Northeastern Syria). CA teams can even benefit from indirect access, through their civilian contacts, to enhance civil reconnaissance in areas that military personnel may not be authorized to visit (e.g., parts of the Sahel following the Tongo-Tongo ambush).[6]

When it comes to consultation with NGOs, or development actors, where SOF do play a critical and welcomed role is in security assessments of the ground for USAID's activities. SOF serve to advise on the security situation in non-permissive areas of the ground operating space, where USAID and DOS are not present. This is the only role that USAID would prefer SOF to have, according to respondents. While SOF are not in the lead, by a sheer function of their access to actors and events on the ground, they can become the connective tissue between all ground operators, and all other entities—Embassies or International Organizations. As one military interviewee posited, "We went out to do the security assessment, and USAID would have stood up an office if the security situation allowed it. They would have coordinated with us about the setup, but they would have still maintained a separate space."[7] Since CA can serve as the eyes and ears for the Embassy, they assess through a security lens. Ultimately, most of the time, and depending on the context, and the U.S. Embassy country team, SOF would not deploy a project without having cleared it through the DOS. By coordinating with other agencies which are contributing parts to the functions of an Embassy—USAID, DOS, or even the Environmental Protection Agency and the U.S. Department of the Treasury—SOF CA become part of a Cross Functional Team (CFT). CFTs have their own tools to assess the operating space through the Interagency Conflict Assessment Framework (ICAF). The ICAF is used "to support steady-state engagement or conflict prevention planning," and it is based on this assessment that SOF decide where to deploy projects.[8]

Away from the strategic headquarters of the Embassy, in speaking about the dynamics of the on-the-ground relationship, one respondent said, "DOD does not leverage NGOs well, and neither do NGOs leverage the military well."[9] Another military interviewee shared:

> If the security situation is poor, most NGOs have security restrictions and are not able to make the assessment of needs. NGOs cannot access an area and mostly stay limited to their office and do not have the full picture of what is going on. As a result, they are unable to spend their resources. It's a vicious cycle.[10]

Conversely, there are instances where CA and USAID (as the donor who contracts NGOs) have a strong relationship. In one instance in Jordan:

> Based on the extensive research and analysis conducted by USAID's D-RASATI education program, the CA team helped identify schools that needed assistance, but were out of USAID's immediate reach. While the CA team's [Liaison Special Operations Forces] LSOF partners provided extra security in higher-risk areas, it was able to lay the groundwork for future assistance programs that reach the common goals of the U.S. Central Command, USAID, LAF, and the Ministry of Education.[11]

In another instance, CA were working with an NGO in a higher-intensity conflict setting, but where the security risk was much like the gray space:

> [W]e gave them access and placement. They were quasi working in the red zone, and the NGO loved the information sharing. They gave us access to information that we didn't have. It was very much just information sharing.[12]

It is evident that there is a touchpoint between the NGOs and the military when it comes to security, information sharing, coordination, and logistics. This connection "can form a strong and potentially lasting bond"[13] between the two groups. But the interdependency between military and NGOs looks and lasts differently in the gray space. The military do not necessarily rely on NGOs to get the information they need. As softened hard-power actors, CA are able to get information directly. As one military respondent noted:

> The military does not need the NGOs in the permissive environment, but you would be stupid to not talk to them. We want to make sure we are not doing any repetitive work that the NGOs are doing. NGOs are a great repository for information. But in a sovereign permissive environment, the NGOs don't need us.[14]

What is key to remember, however, is what was mentioned in chapters 2 and 3. The military personnel's idea of working with NGOs, and generally operating in the civic environment, is largely driven by soldiers' previous individual experience, not necessarily by the technical requirements of missions. As one military respondent noted, "It's operational art,"[15] and soldiers are often left to their own devices to figure out what to do, how and whom to do it with, when operating in these environments. This is on top of insufficient understanding of the civic environment.

On their part, NGOs have more room for maneuvering in the gray space than in a high-intensity conflict space, as mentioned in chapter 3. As a result, the gray space converges and allows both actors to operate, without the obligation to a pre-existing relationship, or pre-established structure. Where there is a pre-existing relationship, it is where SOF has a strong tie with the donor agency, namely USAID, but potentially others. The strength of this relationship is also driven by how secure or insecure the environment is. As a result, SOF and NGOs are subjected to push factors, where both can access what is needed on their own, and pull factors, where they can share information and support each other when it suits them. As discussed in chapter 3, the relationship with NGOs *can* be driven by pre-established relationships with retired military joining NGOs or individuals who were pursuing non-military careers before joining the military. However, as discussed later in this chapter, the amicability of the civil-military relationship transfers less between contexts and more between people, as argued by Mackinlay.

Table 5.1 demonstrates the types and frequency of communication which respondents described as helping them interact with one another. This begs the question: What does the *informal* process of consultation look like?

Table 5.1　Types and Frequency of Communication between NGOs and the Military

Types of Communication	Frequency of Communication	Reasons for Success/Failure
• Meet at office • Meet at a coffee shop • Encounter in a social setting • By text • By phone • By email	• Ad hoc • Regular • No coordination	• Previous relationship • Established system/process • Once worked in the same organization • Successor provided a good introduction • Personality based

Source: Author, based on interviews.

Civ-mil over Coffee?

It is argued that in addition to the already mentioned interagency coordination, operators have their own culture, which is removed from the Embassy and strategic headquarters. Respondents, certainly on the military side, overwhelmingly shared the reality that the further away from the headquarters they are, the easier keeping each other informed becomes, even in the absence of official mechanisms. As one military respondent said about NGOs and development actors, "We would bump into them on the street, or out in the town, if we are out."[16] Also, as one NGO respondent said, as they talked about the interaction between the military and NGOs working in the same country, "some of them [the military] live in the same hotels, or have guest houses in the same neighborhood. The military hang out at the pool of the hotel, having drinks with the NGOs."[17]

Even when it comes to NGO-to-NGO collaboration, there is a certain trust that can only be established in a casual environment. "You must not only be an administrator. There is the relational aspect . . . there are things that you will understand only when going out for a beer of singing some karaoke."[18] These unofficial restaurants, cafes, and social settings are the "archipelago of expatriate social life,"[19] and are valuable opportunities to meet, exchange, and network. According to respondents, these unofficial situations are equally productive ways to engage and work alongside NGOs, as during official business hours. Informal relationships or priorly established relationships in informal settings and circumstances, or relationships formed around a common interest—in this case, expatriate life—provide for valuable circumstances for engagement. They are also the unofficial, but often reliable and converging ways for business to occur between these entities.

Ultimately, it must be noted that contact does not necessarily translate into efficient, continuous, or permanent coordination. Specifically, these casual interactions do not replace the coordination mechanisms mentioned in table

4.1. However, a convergence of such coordination occurs on two fronts. As discussed in chapter 4, these guidelines are often criticized as being unable to follow pre-agreed principles. But it may be that these individual interactions and personalities fill the void where structures and guidelines fall short. Conversely, casual relationships are just that—casual, but not institutionalized mechanisms, and where they may fall short, official guidelines step up. What ultimately becomes clear is that *both* of the official and unofficial have an essential role to play.

INTERACTIONS AMONG GROUND OPERATORS

Chapter 4 gave insight into the organizational attributes of SOF and NGOs and how as separate entities from the larger organizations to which they belong, these two are more similar than different. In table A.2, these differences are also examined at length. Chapter 4 also established that in contrast to large-scale disaster response and complex emergencies, SOF and NGOs are often left to their own devices on how to coordinate, leading these entities to converge in their interactions, taking them beyond the enforced constraints or allowed liberties by higher headquarters, such as the Embassy or the Geographic Combatant Command.[20] These tactical interactions lead to the cultivation of a culture among those *doing* the work. In these instances, a lower rank member of the military may have the freedom to lend aid to ensure the health of local livestock, for example, no differently than an NGO field operator may have the autonomy to provide service to a clinic. As a result, there is an opportunity for these individuals to look beyond the differing ideologies of their organizations.

In conducting the interactions described in table 5.1, SOF and NGOs form a series of individual relationships, which involve verbal and non-verbal communications, and which become effective drivers of their engagement. This is driven "largely by personalities involved in the field."[21] Mackinlay, too, is of the view that the military and NGOs working well together is difficult to establish at higher organizational levels, but is possible at the working level. As discussed in chapter 4, the success of coordination structures or guidelines established to help these entities coordinate, has been mixed. Mackinlay posits:

> Despite the same actors participating in each emergency, the co-operative linkages between them relied on the personalities at the interfaces between them rather than the institutionalization of their relationships. The structures they created were ephemeral and had to be recreated for each new contingency.[22]

Chiara Ruffa takes this stance further and argues that doctrine comes second to soldiers' own behaviors and personalities, which change depending on the context in which they are operating.[23] And, considering that Robert Egnell argues that doctrine often dictates to soldiers *what* to do, but not *how* to do it, this analysis argues that the artistry of the civil-military interaction in the gray space, which is fluid, is often improvised, and left entirely up to operators. Thus, if mandates or official structures are not reliable predictors of the civil-military interaction, which human skills are best fitted for the job? There is some knowledge concerning the interpersonal qualities which are needed to meet the objectives of these organizations. Those mostly have to do with how these entities are to interact with local populations, especially on the military side. What is still unknown are the precise skills needed for these entities to interact with one another. Before demonstrating how the types of behaviors, perceptions, and approaches of SOF and NGO impact their relationship, let us examine what we currently know.

Special Operations Forces

When we turn our focus on what it takes to make a successful tactician, it is important to examine both innate traits and formal training and education. Some argue, that "not all soldiers possess the natural ability to effectively interact with civilians."[24] But as discussed in chapters 1 and 2, SOF members are generally characterized by their training and ability to navigate multicultural settings. Examination of military operations other than war (MOOTW), the term used as a precursor to stability operations in the 1990s, suggests that soldiers should understand the political consequences of their actions.[25] There is also a need for soldiers' ability to perform "effectively in different cultures, learning new languages, values, traditions, and politics."[26] Such a debate became recently most prominent with the wars in Iraq and Afghanistan, and with the recognition that soldiers and specifically leadership needed cultural awareness and social intelligence, as these wars required "non-dominatory, respectful culture, structures and processes."[27] War, in general, some have argued, calls for "awareness and management of affect—fear, rage, anger, hatred, grief, joy, and love."[28] War also requires the soldier to exhibit a high level of emotional intelligence; the ability to "adjust interpersonal style to achieve goals when working with new teams, coworkers, or customers."[29] Almost all of the SOF respondents spoke to the need of demonstrating empathy with local populations. This is supported by evidence where "cross-cultural success requires such traits and skills as empathy, respect, interest in other people, behavioral flexibility, tolerance for ambiguity, initiative, open-mindedness, and sociability."[30] According to General Scales, Iraq and Afghanistan were human failures, not technological ones. As one respondent

Table 5.2 Traits of Civil Affairs Personnel

- Trustworthiness—21%
- Creativity—41%
- Honesty—9%
- Flexibility—40%
- Independence—26%
- Interpersonal skills—70%
- Leadership—24%
- Maturity—52%
- Patriotism—4%
- Physical fitness—14%
- Organizational skills—13%
- Persuasiveness—22%

Source: Author, adapted from selected information from Garric M. Banfield and Jonathan G. Bleakley. "The role of civil affairs in unconventional warfare." Master's Thesis., Naval Postgraduate School Monterey, CA Defense Analysis Dept, 2012.

noted, "many of the SOF do not speak the language. They have anything technology wise. But human intelligence is something different."[31]

This dilemma has been tackled by military practitioners in their own studies of how to better acquire such skills, or what skills practitioners see as most valuable. In a study of over one hundred CA soldiers, respondents were asked to select the three most important character traits CA personnel should possess as candidates in operational roles (see table 5.2) They identified them as follows: interpersonal skills, 70 percent; maturity, 52 percent; and flexibility, 40 percent. Yet only 9 percent and 21 percent, respectively, believed that honesty and trustworthiness were key.[32] This is a concern among NGOs, who take issue with the military withholding information, even when it is not of classified nature, simply because a military operator touched it.

In their study, Garric Banfield and Jonathan Bleakley also suggest that within SOF CA's five core tasks—population and resource control, foreign humanitarian assistance, civil information management, nation assistance, and support to civil administration—none of them reflect how "to identify, develop and motivate the people who can best do that from within the target environment."[33] In other words, there is no institutionalized practice for SOF CA to best leverage and develop a positive relationship with actors outside of the military, who are most able to carry out development and humanitarian work.

Similarly, twenty operators, from across one hundred engagements in counter narcotics, foreign internal defense, and counterterrorism in twenty-three countries, revealed similar themes regarding developing these skills.[34] Respondents reported failure in almost one-third of the nearly one hundred civic engagements, mostly due to the ground operators lacking cross-cultural and interpersonal skills. The extent to which the lack of humility, respect, and compassion leads to failure should not be underestimated. Likewise, helping others, having the capacity to listen, keep an open mind, ask questions, and put oneself in another's shoes, cannot be easily measured, yet the value of these traits on the ground is enormous. Another study reconfirmed that "there is no magic way to change the interpersonally challenged individual on a team from a 'bull' to a 'canary' in the China shop."[35] But this should not be a surprise. U.S. troops are not always trained to effectively manage the degree of complexity they face in the gray space. This is further exacerbated by the fact that commanders do not see stability operations as their main job. Instead, soldiers must rely on their instinct, as they are "forced to improvise, show flexibility, and quickly adapt to changing environments and threats. For this, American troops are not prepared."[36]

As rigorous as the selection of SOF recruits is for physical abilities, it is nearly non-existent for interpersonal skills. "Interpersonal skills won't fail you, the physical stuff will fail you," one military respondent noted.[37] The Special Forces Assessment and Selection (SFAS) course that SOF undergo is a way to measure the physical and psychological resilience needed to be admitted into SOF. There is even evidence of science being able to predict one's level of physical ability based on cortisol, sex hormone-binding globulin, and C-reactive proteins.[38] It is a way for future soldiers to be evaluated on "behavioral and physiological predictors of success in a multi-stressor environment with real-world occupational consequences," measuring physical performance and grit—as non-cognitive traits to predict intelligence, aptitude, and resilience.[39] They do not measure, test, or select based on the ability to express empathy, and understanding toward populations, NGOs or culture. While, as part of the plot during training exercises, soldiers had to interact with civilians in the Middle East, military personnel in charge of coaching trainees and reinforcing the scenario "often dismissed the role-players' actual, lived experiences—the substance of their worlds—as irrelevant."[40] This further supports findings that these tests assess how personality impacts motivation, performance, or persistence. As one military respondent noted:

> We do not get measured on empathy. We are mostly assessed on how we would handle a situation, if we see a civilian in distress, like a mother whose child is sick, or injured, for instance, not how empathetic or understanding we would be towards them.[41]

Non-Governmental Organizations

When it comes to the interpersonal skill sets of NGO staff, there is a general assumption that civilians would automatically know how to behave with other civilians. As far as the civil-military relationship is concerned, no thorough holistic analysis of NGO staff's ability to engage with military actors exists. The inquiries which have been done on this topic demonstrate more insight into the types of skills necessary to run programs, especially when it comes to developing and sustaining the capacity within countries so they can become less dependent on outside foreign assistance.[42] Furthermore, "because all NGOs are not able to invest in the training and development of their project-based staff due to resource constraints (USAID, 2014), ensuring personality–job fit in these organizations is of utmost significance."[43] As NGOs are often resource-constrained and small in footprint, they usually have to do more with less to manage their projects. This imparts a different dynamic to the type of skills necessary to run these organizations. In short: "The NGO's management style is specific, because of the lack of resources, the decentralized and participative management, a low level of formalization, few reporting levels and a network-style work pattern."[44]

In a study of international development managers across a dozen NGOs, a similar set of human skills and behavioral competencies are observed with NGOs as they are with the military: negotiation, leadership, motivation, creativity, and political awareness, to mention a few.[45] Just like in the military, interpersonal skills for NGO workers are needed to advance teamwork, the ability to negotiate, and establish trust.[46] Some studies have examined the leadership traits exhibited (e.g., assertiveness, open-mindedness) within an organization, and how NGO project success can be predicted based on them.[47] There is no data, however, that correlates positive leadership traits within NGOs with more productive and effective relationships with the military. Large donor organizations, or coordinating bodies, have as part of their organizational structures specialists whose job is to liaise and communicate with armed forces. Unlike the military which have, as part of their structure, units and entire brigades whose job is to specifically engage with civic actors, generally there is no such specialized unit for NGOs. The exception is NGOs which have it as their job to negotiate access and security guarantees with armed groups, such as the International Committee of the Red Cross, for example. Also, by and large, there is little in terms of what specific skill set NGOs as organizations must possess to navigate their relationships with security actors. In existence is a series of courses provided by the United Nations Office for the Coordination of Humanitarian Affairs, targeted field mid-level professionals.[48]

When it comes to the importance of interpersonal skills inside these organizations, both NGO and military respondents voiced the need for cultural awareness, and for working together in a team. These interpersonal skills must include cultural sensitivity and the ability to understand nuance, with which the gray space is saturated. One respondent in a study of international development NGOs, spoke about how they interacted with locals, "signing a contract does not mean the end of negotiations, but rather the beginning of negotiations."[49] What becomes clear is that interpersonal skills are valued by both these organizations, leading them once more to converge.

THE LOYALISTS, THE CONVERTED, AND THE BRIDGEBUILDERS

There are general operating rules for how to engage with NGOs and the population, but officially, there is no touchpoint doctrine on how to do this on the ground. It's operational art.[50]

Interdisciplinary thought on group identity suggests that broader social transformations play a major role in social and political development. For Ferdinand Tönnies, this change involves movement away from *gemeinschaft*, or the world of small-scale units (household, clan, village, etc.), to *gesellschaft*, whereby connection to smaller, primary units is replaced by abstract identities such as markets or "nation-states."[51] For Emile Durkheim, the comparable change was from "mechanical" to "organic" solidarity, the latter associated with an expansion in the number and variety of interactions in which people participate.[52] Eugene Kamenka's interpretation is that, despite factors which unite a community in *gemeinschaft*, there are always potential rifts within society over the degrees of attachment to the primary group boundaries. In *gesellschaft* there are no factors which "manifest the will and the spirit of the unity even if performed by the individual," and, "everybody is by himself and isolated, and there exists a condition of tension against all others."[53]

While these thinkers considered movements away from group identity to be a fundamental component of modernity, the basis for their thinking is that transformations are driven by individual behaviors influenced by micro-level rewards, sanctions, and capabilities. It is possible, therefore, that individuals move in the opposite direction—that is, they abandon abstract identities to seek out narrower attachments that fulfill a sense of community. Sebastian Junger, for example, has identified a loss of "belonging" as an explanation for the rise in psychological trauma among soldiers returning home.[54]

Taking into account responses from and interaction with over seventy interviewees from NGOs and SOF for this analysis, I categorize them across a similar spectrum regarding their own orientations toward their primary "in-group." At one end are the *loyalists*, or those individuals who are committed to the objective of their organization and are least likely to question the merit of the organization's approach, namely working with civic or military actors as is the inquiry of this study. At the other end are the *converted*, or those individuals who have either transitioned to work from either of these organizations into the other—the military or civilian, or those, who no longer subscribe to the values of their organization. In the center are the *bridgebuilders* who understand and often practice the uncomfortable reality of questioning the status quo, as they seek to not only meet the objective but also make every effort to maintain the relationship with civic or military actors. These three categories are underpinned by the gray space, which leads these individuals to either converge closer or diverge away from the preconceived notions they each have about the other.

The Loyalists

Donna Winslow discussed loyalty among soldiers as the strong bond between a social group that all share a common goal and a necessary ingredient for cohesion in combat. But she warns:

> Once overseas the group will be asked to participate in a number of operations which will bring it into contact with a wide variety of actors with different organizational cultures (other national military forces, UN representatives, NGOs, local representatives, etc.). If the smaller group cannot overcome its insularity, it becomes increasingly difficult to work in a collective security operation.[55]

It is commonly argued that there is an inherent loyalist culture in the U.S. military, which "demands subordination of the self to the group."[56] In engaging with interviewees, respondents from both the military and NGOs expressed unquestionable loyalty to the mission and their respective organizations; for the *loyalists*, this is a shared and admirable trait which influences how they each approach the task at hand. For the military, loyalists expressed the difficulty in engaging in spaces where the military is not in charge. On the NGO side, too, the loyalists do not make a secret of their disdain toward any military presence—something they believe impedes their work. On the military side, the loyalists are the ones who would predominantly focus on "getting the job done"[57] under any circumstance. Military loyalists are also the group, which most evidently recognized themselves as masters of the operating space, but demonstrated little analytical inquisitiveness, as to how their actions might negatively or unintentionally impact other actors.

This lack of inquisitiveness demonstrates a disregard for the work done by those in other organizations. For example, as a regular function of planning their missions, SOF receive briefings by the interagency and the NGOs. The SOF teams have "a unique opportunity to spend time in Washington, D.C.," and find synergies between their mandates and development and humanitarian programs.[58] But when asked to specify which NGO they met with, some of the military respondents could not recall an instance of any memorable engagement, except one NGO entity, which was established and run by former military veterans.

The loyalists are the least sensitive to questioning the idea that the military takes on development and humanitarian projects as a way to gain access and placement first, not as a way to improve the lives of populations or supplement the work of civic actors. They recognize the military's behavior to use *whatever* it has at its disposal to achieve the mission. As a result, in its attempt to meet its aim, the military neglects its relationship with NGOs, viewing interaction with them merely as a means to an end. One NGO respondent described their observation:

> With the military the individual attitude is that of what's in it for *me*, to help *me* achieve *my* mission. You almost can't blame them for being so self-centered, you have to be narcissistic to survive what Green Berets do. The problem is that this spills over into all of their activities.[59]

This is further supported by the overwhelming response from military respondents on how the projects they provide to the population are labeled as humanitarian, and expected to serve a humanitarian purpose, but only to the extent that they serve the military's mission first. Any other benefit is only secondary.

For the loyalists, a clear commitment to the objective of the mission was demonstrated. As discussed later, unlike the bridgebuilders, who question the status quo, or the converted who outright reject it, the loyalists demonstrate a strong conviction for the cause, with little question for its merits. On the military side, when speaking about engaging with NGOs, respondents did not refer to an outwardly negative or positive experience. On the NGO side, respondents felt freer to speak about their frustrations with the military in instances where they felt that during engagements the military was trying to collect information on them and offering little in return. Because of the strong focus to stick to their own kind, the loyalists tend to be insular, seeing little value in consulting with the other side.

It is not just their personalities that are self-serving, as the tools which SOF deploy are also in their interest. The deficiency of Areas, Structures, Capabilities, Organization, People, Events (ASCOPE) and PMESII-PT, which is explored in chapter 2, is in that these tools fail to understand "how social power flows in the operational environment, thus missing important sociocultural linkages among subsystems."[60] Andrew Bibb describes these tools as ends in themselves,[61] where thinking through the second-order effects, as long as the mission is achieved, is of less importance. On the military side, this group is about mission first. They believe that if the military achieves what it needs to, there is no need for long-term relationships with NGOs or any entity in these spaces. Even if there were such interest, the military's short-term deployment cycles would erode any hope for a long-lasting productive relationship. The loyalists also do little to demonstrate whether the second-order effects of their engagement with NGOs or the populace would have meaningful consequences down the road.

The loyalists' understanding and mobilization of the civil-military interaction are demonstrated through the level of commitment they have to the relationship. What the loyalists lack vis-à-vis one another is hustle.[62] To explain, when asked about the effectiveness of the initial point of contact and meeting with NGOs, some SOF CA interviewees spoke about achieving little success in establishing a continuing relationship. It was also evident that little to no effort was put into forming these new relationships with civic entities and destigmatizing the military's reputation with the NGO community. When they needed to, SOF CA most frequently called on those NGOs with which they already established relationships, not because of the quality of the relationship but likely because of the convenience. On the NGO side, there was almost no demonstration of proactivity by the loyalists to coordinate with the military.

Even if there are specific characteristics exhibited by these individuals to make them less loyalist-like, the culture of their respective mother organizations is inherently such that it fails to positively predispose them to each other. As discussed previously, SOF as a whole, have become more lethal, namely, special forces have become "harder." This has resulted in a deepening divide between them and SOF's soft arm, namely CA, causing CA to become ostracized in the process. As one military respondent described it:

> Yes, SOF is in a crisis, as they've gone so lethal, so CA are in a crisis, too, because we have to align ourselves close to the lethal. But our job is how to provide alternatives to lethality to meet the objective. So, a lot of these guys will sacrifice their relationship with civic actors in order to meet the security objective and get themselves promoted. So, the question is *not*: how do I help the NGOs? The question is: how do I tie my operation to lethality, so I can align closer to the boss?[63]

So, it is not a surprise that naturally the need to align with the organization under any circumstance, costs SOF the ability to have a productive relationship with NGOs. Consequently, the loyalists are not the ones making up the adaptable, converging cluster in the gray space. Rather, their individual approaches and behaviors uphold the values of serving their organization first, without much question of the impact of such objectives on others operating in a space of conflict. As a result, the loyalists cause a divergence in the gray space.

The Converted

The *converted*, as the term might imply, are not deserters of their organization. Instead, like the bridgebuilders, they are critical thinkers as it relates to questioning the merits of decisions within the organization to which they belong. As discussed in chapter 3, they could be individuals who have served in the military, and upon retiring, established themselves in the development and humanitarian professions by providing their skill set beyond the organization where they gained it. The converted military, now gone NGO, fully subscribe to the mission of their newly joined organization, whether it be religious, philanthropic or for-profit sectors.

The same occurs for NGOs, even if in a slightly different order. The converted are those with an earlier non-military career in organizations, such as the U.S. Peace Corps, for example, where language, cultural skills, regional familiarity, and already established relationships and networks in the places where they worked and volunteered are leveraged by the military.[64] The converted are not to be confused with going native, a phenomenon often associated with SF, or military advisors, who, after spending long periods in the field begin to perceive themselves as being on equal footing as their advisee, or the local population.[65] As intellectual mavericks, the converted have no qualms in criticizing the organization, as demonstrated by one military interviewee who openly expressed, "I've come to the conclusion that war is immoral."[66]

Chapters 2 and 3 established that the separation of military and development organizations based on their differing values of impartiality and neutrality is not so straightforward. Yet, there is a self-perception *within* these organizations about *who* and *what* they truly are. A military respondent reconfirmed that in fact, it is this fundamental difference between the military as killers and NGOs as altruists which drives a wedge between them:

There is absolutely a different calculus between NGOs and civil affairs. NGOs are genuinely there to help and improve people . . . even if it's politically driven. Civil Affairs is there to meet military objectives. Civil Affairs will naturally try to control. When objectives don't align between these entities, then there is friction.[67]

While the loyalists were agnostic when it came to their proposed projects benefiting their civic interlocutors or populations, the converted were just the opposite. Especially on the military side they view and exercise their position as one where they could help, regardless of whether their actions meet a security objective. One military respondent was very clear about the constraints of the bureaucracy, but also mentioned the room to exercise personal perseverance:

I would decide for myself, this is what I can affect. This village has an outbreak in malaria, they don't have the right medicine, and there is no healthcare. I would write an OHDACA project. If it doesn't move, I would get on a plane to Stuttgart and make it happen.[68]

While the loyalists, who demonstrate inclinations of *gemeinschaft*, namely, staying close to and within the community, as opposites, the allegiance of the converted is not lost to another organization. Instead, they demonstrate a much more holistic view, beyond the group, such as transferring skills, knowledge, perceptions, and valuable insight outside their own organizational objective. Their expanded perception of the relationship vis-à-vis one another does not translate into their lack of commitment to their organization. Instead, it puts them outside of their element, where they are recognizing and working toward a larger objective to benefit both sides through their knowledge of the system, influence on the environment, and recognition of priorities outside of their immediate mission.

The Bridgebuilders

On both the NGO and military sides, the individuals interviewed understood the myopic and self-serving approach that each of these entities can take when working with the other, and with the communities they serve. This group is the *bridgebuilders*. The individuals in this group are highly self-aware and recognize the pitfalls of self-interest. On the military side, respondents spoke of the ability to take on a collegial approach when working with their civic interlocutors, namely, to find ways how *they*—the military—can help NGOs, be it with information, security, or assets. They recognized the toxic self-serving approach of "what can you all [civic actors] do for *me* to help *me* meet *my* mission."[69] The bridgebuilders understand and truly live by the fact that "plans for military operations are based on an imperfect understanding and uncertainty of how the commander expects the military situation to evolve."[70] Specifically, they are comfortable with the notion that they do not have all the answers. On the military side, the bridgebuilders recognized how their behavior to get certainty and answers in the short-term can be perceived as aggressive and cost them the relationship in the long-term. What is more evident is that members of both the NGOs and the military in this group recognize that insularity can backfire, as it creates disconnection with other organizations.

On the NGO side, the bridgebuilders were self-effacing in describing the naive thinking of NGOs about the impartiality or neutrality of their mission, recognizing that these are often indefensible values, as everyone serves an interest. On the military side, too, there was wide recognition of how the military's hard-power mentality may blind its ability to understand the psychology of civilian organizations.

Military respondents did not deem interaction between NGOs as positive or negative, but simply as necessary. This necessity was in part for the military to complete its task, but was also an opportunity to provide their civic interlocutors with valuable insight into the space in which they are operating together. The military bridgebuilders knew that NGOs have a stronger understanding of the sociopolitical context. Likewise, NGOs knew that the military has valuable information beyond just security. In addition to the exhibited self-awareness of this group, the bridgebuilders appeared to be the most at ease with the ambiguity of the gray space. They recognized the need to remain open and transparent as a condition for a productive relationship, even if the mandate at hand may not necessitate or recognize it. The bridgebuilders understood that more interaction means a better understanding of the operating environment, but they also recognized that gaining information is not a one-way street. In several interviews, military respondents emphasized how important it was to share useful information with NGOs. One NGO respondent recognized the value their organization added to the relationship by saying, "the NGOs speak the local language, and the military relies on getting access to the populations through them."[71]

The bridgebuilder NGO interviewees did not view the military in purely negative terms. They recognized the military's paramount role as a security provider in high-intensity conflict areas. They also understood its unique role in filling a void in low-intensity conflict, and in spaces where development actors would not go. Some of the NGO bridgebuilders also expressed a much stronger preference for the military providing security instead of private security companies doing so, citing the issue of ambiguous rules and sometimes lack of professionalism by Private Military Security Companies, as discussed in chapter 3. The NGO bridgebuilders also recognized that in their need for a unique skill set to help them navigate insecure environments, such as skills in security, information gathering, or logistics—NGOs are similar to the military in terms of their structure and modus operandi on the ground.

On the military side, SOF recognized the misperception they may create with their approaches in seeking to influence the civic environment. For example, elements of SOF and specifically CA, are known for wearing civilian clothing in operations. This was particularly the context for SF through the Village Stability Operations program in Afghanistan, as it was a way to engage with locals.[72] NGOs have outwardly expressed concern, as one worker from Catholic Services did in saying that, "when soldiers go around wearing blue jeans, sandals, hidden weapons, long hair, it blurs the line—people don't know who they are."[73] CA teams' engagement may not always be for the purpose of civil reconnaissance used to capture terrorists, but having soldiers roam around in civilian clothing is unsettling for civilians.

This begs another question: how are military units that wear civilian clothing but are armed, different than civilian private security companies that also wear civilian clothing and are also armed? Chapter 3 discussed this at length, and there are still questions about whether in this scenario these soldiers would be protected under international law.[74] If one strips away the laws of war in the gray space, which is not considered an international armed conflict, what is left is a space for maneuver by these actors, and essentially, as one respondent described it, "the Wild West."[75] Ironically, it is the ambiguity of these rules which leads these actors to converge, even if only optically.

What is interesting about the bridgebuilders is that despite the sometimes categorical disapproval of how the military behaves, they did not see the civil-military engagement as a zero-sum game. The bridgebuilders on the military side recognize the value of both entities and believe that they *can* and *should* help each other. One respondent spoke frankly of the importance of maintaining the relationship with NGO interlocutors, regardless of the military mission's outcome. Specifically, that the relationship should be maintained, independent of whether the military is achieving tactical gains with its interaction with civilian organizations.[76] On their end, NGO bridgebuilders did not demonstrate the willingness to embrace the military as equal partners or suggest ways in which a more permanent or equal partnership could occur. Instead, they found themselves closer to the military by recognizing that both provide similar services. This was particularly when it comes to the military's competence in carrying out vital activities, such as in the field of medical services, which NGOs provide as well.

Another attribute of the bridgebuilders is their handling of information. The military are caught in a Catch-22 situation. While for J2 (Joint Staff Intelligence)[77] everything connects to vital intelligence information related to the security threat, CA recognize that not all information is for the purpose of performing lethal tasks. They also recognized the danger of treating everything as a target and the harm of overclassifying information—which once classified, can no longer be shared with the NGOs. One military respondent shared:

> Not everything on the ground is intelligence. Treating it as such is the pitfall of the simple bureaucracy. We classify something as secret only because an operator touched it. Is this really a productive way to be? Ultimately, it's up to the judgment call of the person collecting/analyzing the information on what should be done with it.[78]

Another military respondent shared how overclassifying information impedes the relationship, "A lot of times the NGOs and all of our relationships are on the red [high classified system]. There is no need for that."[79]

Another military respondent exclaimed how "there is no one overarching repository on how to handle information. We as Civil Affairs should have a Wikipedia-like living document that keeps a log that the NGOs can access. But if it's unclassified or open source, it loses its credibility."[80] There is little available information on how NGOs keep information close hold, or classify it for their own use. Chapter 3 discussed how in competing for money, some organizations treat information as proprietary, keeping it only to themselves.

Of all three groups, the bridgebuilders were most interested in solutions to help them improve their craft vis-à-vis one another. Many of them viewed their participation in this study as a way to help them understand how the civil-military relationship works. Unlike the loyalists who saw themselves as strictly going after the clear objectives of the mission, the military bridgebuilders openly shared frustrations on the army's inability to find a good utility for CA. They recognized the shortcoming of the utilization of tools, such as PMSEII and ASCOPE, which are not designed to take into account the military's impact neither on the population nor NGOs. Ultimately, the bridgebuilders came the closest to recognizing the human side of listening to the grievances of another, and that meeting their objective of engagement with the populace is an art, not a science. On the military side, the bridgebuilders recognized that not gaining immediate or useful information from the other side did not necessarily result in a bad or unproductive relationship in the long term. Rather, they believed that the act of continuing to engage with their civil interlocutors, no matter the outcome, was the definition of success.

The relationship between these entities is not always tumultuous, and they often converge in how they view one another. Some respondents noted the impressive speed with which the military supported them with logistics in the hottest places in Afghanistan.[81] This appreciation of the military's effectiveness is not unusual among NGO circles, and the respondents in this study positively commented on the professionalism of their military counterparts. Where a divergence does occur, is where we see a difference in operational tempo between NGOs and the military. In describing one account between a UN agency and a NATO Commanding General in Sarajevo in 1996, Siegel writes:

> The military view that civilians are lazy because they go out to dinner, go away for the weekend or take a vacation is one that emerges almost without exception in post-conflict operations. The perception is evidence of a failure to understand that military personnel deploy for a limited period as individuals, while civilians might remain in a post-conflict environment indefinitely—it becomes, in essence, their home.[82]

Perhaps the most dominant attribute of the bridgebuilders is the intellectual rigor through which they see the relationship. They recognized the status quo of the traditionally tumultuous civil-military relationship, and proactively sought to question it, or correct it. On the military side, the bridgebuilders believed that humanitarian and development activities do not have to be an access and placement function only. They recognized that the military's transactional focus may backfire, and one should always seek ways to establish a long-term relationship with their civic counterpart, despite constraints. They believed that the order of priority for meeting security objectives first, then humanitarian and development ones, did not diminish the military's success, or their fighting edge. Just the opposite was possible, as they believed the gray space provides ample opportunity for the military to provide development and humanitarian assistance first, which would establish a long-term relationship, organically providing for access and placement and meeting security objectives. And, that this can still occur without turning the military into a quasi-NGO, or by making development part of their core business.

Ultimately, the bridgebuilders recognized the deviating views between high command and the tactical level, and described instances when they sought to convince their chain of command of the value of the proposed activities on the ground. On the NGO side, there was recognition of the at-times contradictory view of what donors sought to implement, with the NGOs' understanding of the local reality being very different than what donors understood. For NGOs which do not work through donors, it was higher headquarters, be in Geneva, Paris, New York, or Nairobi, and the constant need to ensure that whatever decisions were being taken in the field would be accepted by headquarters. Additionally, the bridgebuilders hold the strings to convergence in the gray space, as they are most likely to seek out, and understand the value of the other side (table 5.3). But even in this open-mindedness about one another, they are not blinded to their differing objectives.

Table 5.3   Impressions of Interacting with Respondents

The Loyalists	The Bridgebuilders	The Converted
• Confident	• Confident	• Strongly convinced
• Has all the answers	• Asks more questions	• Openly critical
	• Humble	
	• Appears uncertain at times	

Source: Author.

Note: Attributes are described based on impressions during online and in-person verbal interaction with interviewees. These are based on the tone, interpersonal skills, natural curiosity expressed, and overall behavior of the respondents. These are not psychologically and scientifically assessed, but rather based on autoethnography, and the author's own experience of working in military and NGO cultures. Notably, attributes do not necessarily reflect behaviors. A humble, self-doubting individual may also be a shrewd operator and negotiator, as well as highly skilled at taking others' perspective into consideration.

ON TRUST

Earlier chapters compared how both the military and NGOs use information to their advantage. For the military, the objective is to plan and plot against potential threats, and improve the outcome of security objectives. For NGOs, it is to improve programming activities, and to strengthen their ability to compete for money and access target delivery. Because of the highly classified nature of the military planning process, this analysis is not privy to the extent to which information gained from the civilian space is predominantly used for the military's most lethal missions. It is also not clear whether this is information that could have been gained in other ways, without compromising the relationship with NGOs. In contrast, considering the lack of transparency in the NGOs' own processes, namely that they are not available as public information, it would be difficult to prove or disprove NGOs' utilization of information gained from the military. Yet, one thing stands clear—much of the interaction between these groups revolves around trust about information sharing.

As previously mentioned, the military's high turnover cycle does not allow for the opportunity to form long-term and long-standing relationships. So, what is left is what Egnell argues to be trust driven by people unfamiliar with one another:

> It represents reliance on weak ties and is based on the assumption that another person would reciprocate and comply with our expectations of his or her behavior, as well as with existing formal and ethical rules.[83]

As previously said, personalities, not contexts or organizations, are the backbone of the civil-military relationship. There is a consistency with this when it comes to trust in exchanging information, but there is also evidence, as Mackinlay described, that preconceived notions of previous relationships, from other contexts, between the military and NGOs, materialized. Respondents in a seminar discussing the relationship between civil and military entities collectively noted that:

> [T]rust is usually based on previous experience. Trust is the most important precondition for information exchange, which is usually based on non-negotiated agreements and occurs behind the scenes. Once information is shared, we lose control. Information sharing is further complicated by the fact that most guidelines which exist on it are unclear on what should be shared and how. Where it does exist, it is specific to an agency, and there is no one overall approach.[84]

Despite the porous nature of the structures and mandates of these entities, the need for information acquiring and information sharing revealed a series of vulnerabilities that these entities have toward one another across all mandates. As one NGO seminar participant noted, "There are common goals that we want to achieve. Access—we all need it to complete the work. Everyone needs to look at their mandate. Sharing of information can be done but it needs to be under trust."[85] Another seminar participant noted, "We need a good basic understanding of each other's roles and responsibilities. Whether it's from a humanitarian perspective, civil government or military—this helps us to understand what information can be shared."[86] Furthermore, both military and NGO interview respondents agreed that continuity and structure create trust—a challenging task, certainly for the military, whose short-term deployments prevent them from cultivating long-term relationship building with any other actor. Janice Laurence acknowledged this by saying, "Trust and relationship development are thwarted not only by lack of cultural exposure, experience, and discourse—cultural illiteracy—but by the rotation schedule of our Brigade Combat Teams (BCT)."[87]

The lack of permanence is not detrimental only to the ability of these actors to build trust. The short length of deployments also puts out of order what should be prioritized as urgent, over what is considered important. The military are inherently trained to be in a crisis mode, and as mentioned earlier, they seek to deliver swiftly within their deployment cycle. Following a meeting between the NATO Commanding General and the head of the UN in Sarajevo in 1996:

> The general had just arrived—anxious to achieve great things—for a six-month tour (during which he would be eligible for weeks of leave). The U.N. agency head had also recently arrived—not from a home base where he had a nice house in which his wife was waiting at the end of each day, but from another post-conflict environment. The military were ready to act immediately with the agreed way forward, while the UN staff were to enter into a holiday period, just before the New Year.[88]

Ultimately, it is these entities' perception of time and permanence, which also translates into perceptions of their commitment to the operation, which drives the trust in their relationship.

In a study of 11 respondents—5 from the military, 5 from NGOs, and 1 expert, the interaction of Canadian military forces and Canadian NGOs reconfirms much of the analysis here between U.S. SOF and civic actors. Specifically, the relationship is almost always driven by both formal structures and informal ones, which are largely driven by the personalities of its interlocutors.[89] It is these individual relationships, more than structures, contexts, cultures, and organizations, which bring these entities closer together in the gray space. In the same study, one NGO respondent noted that it was rather the longevity and frequency of interaction that drives trust between these entities:

> It's not something that's going to develop overnight and if you don't have a regular dialogue with people, you don't develop the trust. I mean, everybody appreciates that, so it becomes a question of making sure that you don't just see people once every 3 months and expect that something will come out of that, it won't.[90]

In the same study, respondents spoke of how trust is based on many of the same obstacles already discussed earlier. Respect for how the other group operates and exercises good judgment is one important factor in gaining trust. In speaking about the work of NGOs, one military respondent noted:

> When an NGO does what was from our perception a very uncoordinated and dumb thing, like bringing old people back to their houses, in an uncoordinated way with no provisions for security, you tend not to trust them.[91]

In Afghanistan, military personnel were continuously suspicious of NGOs potentially undermining their efforts "with whom are they really working? With the Taliban? We do not really know."[92] This lack of sharing of information led to mistrust, and the military categorically decided that separate and independent action was preferable to coordination with NGOs, and instead opted to help meet their own objectives, instead of helping the NGOs.[93] Therefore, the level of openness, as well as confidence in each other's judgment, actions, integrity, and commitment to deliver, is key to maintaining trust: "If you're making promises, or think you're making promises and don't live up to them it can be very damaging to what you're trying to do."[94]

As previously stated, SOF and NGOs engage differently in the gray space, than conventional military forces and NGOs. Many of the responses provided above concern conventional, or large-scale military engagement with NGOs in disaster response or complex emergencies through coordinating structures. But the mood around perceptions between these actors is only marginally different in the gray space. Development actors know the importance of security. Conversely, many SOF operators know the indispensable role which NGOs and civic actors at large play. It is when the military walk the fine line between being a helpful interlocutor to civic entities, and then treating them like intelligence assets, that is what breaks the trust,[95] a notion very clearly understood by both the bridgebuilders and the converted. As one NGO respondent puts it, even with a good working relationship, and the right personalities at the table, one thing is very clear—clarity on how information which is gained and is then used in this space directly influences trust:

At the end of the day, the NGO's information could be used to attack a village. On the other hand, some of this information is just open already. We just have to agree on a standard on how to share and interpret it. We need a really clear understanding of what is being done with this information. We just must remain within the boundaries of the different mandates. Also, military forces handing out goods and being a humanitarian actor never sits well with us [NGOs].[96]

As the military sees everything through the prism of security, one lively DOS respondent spoke about instructing their military team to prepare for a meeting with an NGO, "When you go in there, don't you dare just sit and take notes. You need to say something, or they (the NGOs) will think you are collecting on them. You need to make a contribution."[97] Another participant in a discussion noted that "it is difficult to encourage a mutual information sharing without making it seem like a tit for tat."[98] This often applies to complex emergencies, but these behaviors and practices transfer over to others. A participant in a NATO Civil-Military Cooperation forum noted, "Use common sense, be open and friendly, be social, and drink beer with your counterpart,"[99] further giving credence to the previous suggestion that causal relationship-building is a way to establish trust.

But trust can be much more complex than that, even in seasoned structures such as the UN, and especially at the multilateral level. A discussant shared:

In a normal humanitarian response situation, yes UNOCHA is great, but nothing can replace the bilateral meeting. As the team gets bigger, it is harder and harder to build trust, which requires one-on-one interaction. Then information sharing is done on the bilateral organization level. Organizing on a multilateral level is very hard. The Germans speak to Germans, the French to the French. The same is true with the NGOs.[100]

As discussed in chapter 4, the omnipresent CA missions that have been examined here are not usually coordinated within the UN structures, but within the interagency. Still, even on the small team tactical level, soldiers prefer to interact with those who understand their language and culture. This was the example noted in chapter 4, where SOF speak to NGO staff who are former SOF, much more easily than organizations whose staff are not former military, leading us to conclude that all these actors naturally seek to communicate with others like themselves.

When it comes to the gray space, some NGO observers at a forum saw little or no change in behavior between large-scale coordinated civil-military efforts and what was observed through interviews. In both of these contexts and actors, especially on the part of the military, they "show up to meetings just to take notes."[101] When asked about what would be the ultimate gesture for cooperation and consultation the military could make, one NGO member responded without hesitation, "When we get included in the planning process."[102] There has been a recognition for a more formal sharing of information, suggesting reforming intelligence sharing and the opening up of unclassified information "vertically, horizontally, and across domains" through the establishment of "Stability Operations Intelligence Centers (SOICs)," whose focus should be the sharing of information with NGOs.[103]

Ultimately, when it comes to trust, this pinnacle of human interaction is equally challenging to form across mandates. As much as the gray space provides more opportunities for forming trust between these entities because of the absence of high emotions, mostly associated with crisis settings and full on warfighting, trust building is an area which still remains difficult. What becomes evident is that once again it is the personalities that are at the table which drive the relationship, not the organizations. But by the steady-state of conditions that the gray space provides, where coordination is not urgent, these entities have the opportunity to form more systematic and productive interactions.

CONCLUSION

This chapter comes the closest to the anthropological angle of the culture of SOF CA and NGOs. It further posits that success of SOF and NGO interactions is the result of a series of personal qualities and attributes. These include a robust level of interpersonal skills, and intellectual rigor to question the status quo and preconceived notions from previous contexts—qualities associated with a group of interviewees in this study, coined the bridgebuilders. They demonstrate that the NGOs and the military can be helpful interlocutors. This is driven by their attitudes and recognition of the value that each brings to the relationship. It is less driven by the mandates of their organizations. This only reconfirms what Scales and Mackinlay have argued, that it is the personal, not the technical that forms this bond. The sensitivities around the relationship of the military with NGOs are not strikingly different than Montgomery McFate's analysis on the relationship of the military with populations, namely that it is the military's behavior which makes or breaks relationships. These findings also build on the knowledge which Ankersen provides on CIMIC in peacekeeping, where he suggests an exploration of civil-military interaction through the eyes of other actors, and other contexts. Namely, what this analysis finds, which confirms Ankersen's and Mackinlay's claims, is that the civil-military relationship is most powerful when people, rather than organizations, are conducive to its success.

NOTES

1. At the level of the Embassy, the touchpoint is with the interagency, where the Ambassador is in charge, and where USAID is the donor who engages with NGOs as implementing partners.
2. R 17.
3. As mentioned in previous chapters, coordination can occur through the structures of UNOCHA for large-scale coordinated efforts in complex emergencies or natural disasters.
4. R 38.
5. R 72—Donor Agency Respondent (Retired Military), April 29, 2021.
6. Civil Affairs Association, "2020 Civil Affairs Symposium Report," 12.
7. R 16.
8. US Department of the Army, "Civil Affairs Planning," 1–21.
9. R 15.
10. R 16.
11. Overstreet, "Building the Special Operations Force Enterprise."
12. R 57—Civil Affairs Officer, April 15, 2021.
13. Lawry, "Guide," 196.
14. R 15.
15. *Ibid.*
16. R 16.
17. R 67.
18. Brière et al., "Competencies," 122.
19. Aikins, "Last Tango in Kabul."
20. This can depend upon whether NGOs are implementing partners of USAID or not, but SOF will engage with both, depending on the context, SOF's presence or mission.
21. Abiew, "From Civil Strife to Civic Society," 18.
22. Mackinley, "Co-operating," 1.
23. Ruffa, "Military Cultures," 391–422.
24. Burke, "Civil," 5.
25. United States Department of Defense Joint Chiefs of Staff, Joint Doctrine for Military Operations Other Than War, III—02.; Egnell, "Explaining US and British Performance."
26. Laurence, "Military Leadership," 497.
27. Francis, "Culture, Power Asymmetries and Gender," 104.
28. Allen, "Leader Development in Dynamic and Hazardous Environments," 102.
29. Laurence, "Military Leadership," 497.
30. *Ibid.*, 492.
31. R 67.
32. Banfield and Bleakley, "The Role," 83.
33. *Ibid.*, 6.
34. Delcoure, "The Smooth Operator."
35. *Ibid.*, 65.
36. Egnell, "Explaining US and British Performance," 1060.
37. R 3.
38. Farina, Thompson, Knapik, Pasiakos, McClung, and Lieberman, "Physical Performance."
39. *Ibid.*, "Physical Performance," 2.
40. Nomi, "Imperial Mimesis," 539.
41. R 3.
42. Brinkerhoff, "Developing Capacity in Fragile States," 66–78.
43. Hassan et al., "The Impact," 75.
44. Brière et al., "Competencies," 117.
45. *Ibid.*
46. *Ibid.*

47. Hassan, Bashir, and Abbas, "The Impact of Project Managers' Personality," 74–87.

48. Humanitarian-Military Dialogue: civil-military coordination service, https;//www.unocha.org/civil-military-coordination.

49. Brière et al., "Competencies," 122.

50. R 15.

51. Tönnies, Community and Society.
    Kamenka, "Gemeinschaft and Gesellschaft," 4.

52. Thijssen, "From Mechanical to Organic Solidarity," 454–70.

53. Kamenka, "Gemeinschaft and Gesellschaft," 4.

54. Junger, "How PTSD Became a Problem."

55. Winslow, "Misplaced Loyalties," 346.

56. Greene, Buckman, Dandeker, and Greenberg, "The Impact of Culture," 958.

57. Losey, "After War Zone Scandals."

58. Overstreet, "Building."

59. R 40.

60. Whalley et al., Improving, 618.

61. Bibb, "Destruction."

62. This reference speaks to the passivity of the military, when it comes to engaging with civic actors. Specifically, examples of how operators did not take a strong proactive approach, going above and beyond, when it came to finding new civic actors with whom to engage. In some instances respondents described how they reached out to a specific NGO organization, but did not receive a response. They also did not conduct any follow-up. The assumption by the military is that the NGOs did not want to work with them, and investing in the relationship was not worth the effort.

63. R 3.

64. Civil Affairs Association, "Strange Bedfellows: CA and Returned Peace Corps Volunteers," Online Zoom Panel Discussion by Glenn Blumhorst, Dan Baker, and Michael Greer, February 22, 2021.
    McElligott, "Leveraging Returned Peace Corps Volunteers."

65. Simons, "Chapter 6: The Military Advisor as Warrior-King"; Newman, Army Special Forces: Elite Operations; Nomi, "Imperial Mimesis."

66. R 61.

67. R 30.

68. R 30.

69. R 20—Civil Affairs Officer, February 23, 2021.

70. US Department of the Army, "Civil Affairs Planning," 1.

71. R 67.

72. Farrell III, "No Shirt, No Shoes, No Status."

73. Brooke, "Vigilance and Memory."

74. Farrell III, "No Shirt." According to Ferrell III, the wearing of civilian clothing as a solider has legal implications. For a soldier, wearing civilian clothing leads him or her to fail to optically and outwardly demonstrate one as military, even if one does not do it with the intention to pretend to be a civilian. This leads soldiers to lose their ability to distinguish themselves from civilians, and causes loss of protection under Geneva Convention International Law and consequently be in violation of the law for LOW violation (perfidy) or the loss of POW status (spying). Farrell III's reference is to what is specifically in the Convention as it relates to combatants and civilians "having a legal distinctive sign recognizable at a distance." See International Committee of the Red Cross, Geneva Convention Relative to the Treatment of Prisoners of War. ICRC, Geneva, Aug. 12, 1949. (p. 41) Farell III's interpretation under Commentary article 4(A)(1), 6 U.S.T. 3316, 75 U.N.T.S. 135. https://ihl-databases.icrc.org/applic/ihl/ihl.nsf/INTRO/365?OpenDocument

75. R 44.

76. R 3.

77. Joint Chiefs of Staff, "J1—Personnel, J2—intelligence, J3—Operations, J4—Logistics, J5—Planning, J6—Communications."—https://www.jcs.mil/Doctrine/Joint-Doctine-Pubs/ (last accessed April 1, 2022).

78. R 18.

79. R 44.

80. R 30.

81. R 65.

82. Siegel, "Civil-Military Marriage," 31.

83. Khodyakov, "Trust as a Process," 115–132 as referenced in Egnell, Robert. "Civil-Military Aspects of Effectiveness in Peace Support Operations." Swedish Defense Research Agency, Defense Analysis: Stockholm, 2008.

84. NATO Civil-Military Cooperation Center of Excellence, "Engaging in Civil-Military Information Sharing Seminar," July 8, 2021. (Seminar)

85. *Ibid.*

86. *Ibid.*

87. Laurence, "Military Leadership," 495.

88. Siegel, "Civil-Military Marriage," 31.

89. Holton et al., "The Relationship."

90. *Ibid.*, 25.

91. *Ibid.*, 24.

92. Ruffa and Vennesson, "Fighting and Helping," 610.

93. *Ibid.*

94. Holton et al., "The Relationship," 25.

95. R 75.

96. R 29.

97. R 33—Department of State Respondent, March 10, 2021.

98. NATO Civil-Military Cooperation Center of Excellence, "Engaging."

99. *Ibid.*

100. *Ibid.*

101. *Ibid.*

102. R 43—NGO Respondent, March 27, 2021.

103. Hanhauser IV, "Comprehensive Civil Information," 1.

Chapter 6

The Center of Gravity

HOW ARE SOF AND NGOS PERCEIVED BY LOCAL POPULATIONS IN THE GRAY SPACE?

According to security scholars, the center of gravity is the most critical part of a military campaign, as it is the source of strength or balance in a mission.[1] But beyond strategy, capabilities and military might, one of those centers of gravity is the population, whose support to the military mission is paramount for success. For development actors in fragile states—beyond the recipient government, elites, and donor agencies—the center of gravity is the population, who are recipients of the goods and services NGOs provide. As they interact with populations, both NGOs and Special Operations Forces (SOF) are exposed to local communities who form perceptions of these actors' ability to understand the local context or listen to local needs. As a result, in interacting with populations, which the military is trying to influence with the use of humanitarian and development projects, and NGOs who serve in the place of local government, these entities experience a series of factors that lead them to converge or diverge in the fluid gray space.

This chapter explains how these entities converge in their attempt to understand the populations and their needs. Where they diverge, however, is in a systematic and robust method to assess outcomes and impact. On the one hand, NGOs deploy a series of institutionalized monitoring and evaluation mechanisms, which are lacking on the part of the military. Yet, when it comes to local populations as recipients, both of these actors are removed, to more or less of an extent, from the rank-and-file needs of the communities, and they both tend to help one group while disenfranchising another. At the same time, what takes precedence in forming the populations' perceptions is shaped by the practical implications of the projects in local communities, respect for the local context, and the inclusion of local citizens in the process. Perceptions can also be driven by the extent to which the military and NGOs are seen as working together, deconflicting and coordinating their efforts.

CONSULTING AND PRIORITIZING
POPULATIONS IN THE GRAY SPACE

In recent counterinsurgency operations in Iraq and Afghanistan, the U.S. military's deployment of development and humanitarian assistance projects was a way to compel the populace to reject the insurgency.[2] The same assistance was also mostly supply-driven as opposed to demand-driven, with little consultation done with locals. Chapters 2 and 3 have established that there is a difference as to why SOF and NGOs deploy humanitarian and development projects. For NGOs, development projects are their primary craft. These projects span cross-sectoral areas of health, education, and governance, to mention a few. For SOF, development projects provide a way to influence populations when deterring threats. SOF often refer to these projects as humanitarian and development, when in fact they are for fulfilling security objectives, not saving lives. On the side of the NGOs, where development and humanitarianism are often distinct, Donini argues that NGOs label themselves in whichever convenient way that suits the context, audience, or donors who hold the purse strings to NGO funding.[3]

Previous analysis of these entities also established that their actions are mostly accountable to the larger organizations to which they belong, and less to project beneficiaries. When it comes to field operations, as some have argued, "NGOs do not fit the mold of the grassroots, mass-participation vehicles idealized by many theorists."[4] But they are the "closest to engaging directly with those citizens most affected by but least heard in policy decision-making."[5] For the military, SOF is the entity that is in most direct contact with "local nationals, such as town and city dwellers, farmers and other rural dwellers, and nomads; local civil authorities, such as elected and traditional leaders at all levels of government."[6] As they engage with populations, NGOs and the military come in contact with locals who, as Dijkzeul and Wakenge note, are not just "passive recipients, rather, they mediate and act,"[7] upon the assistance provided to them. Louisa Seferis and Paul Harvey separate citizen groups into three broad categories of recipients—those who are passive, those who make decisions, and those who shape policy.[8]

Donini claims that many on the receiving end of assistance see outside efforts as bypassing them,[9] as aid mostly goes to those who make decisions and shape policy, not to beneficiaries or recipients. In Bosnia and

Herzegovina, citizens' negative perceptions of local government processes discouraged them from participation in making decisions about receiving aid to such an extent that only 20 percent expressed interest in participating in the local government process.[10] This is on top of most citizens believing that government decisions do not account for citizens' preferences or priorities. However, according to the earlier referenced study by Anderson, Brown, and Jean, local communities are vocal in their opinions, perceptions, and values about both NGOs' and the military's presence, behaviors, and priorities. It is this level of beneficiaries and recipients which this analysis examines here. The levels least examined as part of this analysis are the makers and shapers. This is based on the premise that in fragile settings, institutions are weak, and have weak social contracts with their citizens.

Populations

As described previously, the gray space does not suffer from a sudden loss of services or infrastructure caused by natural disasters or complex emergencies. Instead, it is subjected to state fragility and chronic sources of insecurity, which may be a consequence of larger problems. If not based on need, then how do SOF and NGOs prioritize populations?

In examining humanitarian response missions, Seybolt has already challenged how those receiving assistance are selected, whether or not the kind of humanitarian assistance that was provided was relevant and appropriate to the need, and whether the desired results of saving lives were achieved?[11] When it comes to prioritizing populations and which strata of society outsiders deal with, Hugo Slim argues that, "humanitarianism is always politicized somehow."[12] In Afghanistan in the mid-1990s, "NGO support for anti-government *Mujahuddin* refugees (and militants) far outweighed the NGO effort to relieve suffering within Afghanistan."[13] The military, for example, does not hesitate to discriminate between good and bad populations, when providing reconstruction and stabilization assistance,[14] which often leaves it open to criticism by non-security actors. NGOs are less likely to differentiate between good and bad populations, even in the absence of impartiality and neutrality of their agendas, but they are also not completely exonerated. Chapter 3 established that in the attempt to focus heavily on resolving one issue, NGOs will completely ignore another. Robert Hall argues that, for example, the interest of the international community to eradicate a type of disease may not align with *what* or *who* within a given country sees a given disease as a priority on the national health agenda.[15] NGOs are political influencers, often using the services they provide as leverage to affect internal to the host nation (HN) policy.[16]

Furthermore, even if such an alignment does exist between those providing the service and national policy priorities, sometimes NGOs myopically focus on one group of a community, while completely ignoring another. For example, one NGO respondent noted that in consulting with local communities about their health needs as part of starting up a health clinic, there was a disparity in the views between men and women in East South Sudan, as to what was most concerning to them:

> For women it was sexually transmitted diseases (STDs). Those were syphilis, as the women were in polygamist marriages, where the men would be away for long periods of time, often returning with new strains of STDs. As a result, syphilis would prevent these women and their husbands from having more children, compromising their standing in the community. Social standing in the community was based on how many sons you have.[17]

The same respondent continued to explain how when tasked with a survey to inquire about communities' security concerns, the responses between men and women were completely different:

> For the women, one of their main concerns was snakes on the road which they use to walk to fetch water every day. For men in that same community, the concern was mostly other men, who would steal their wives, as women are the economic engine of the household. So how do you build a program to address both of these problems?[18]

Addressing two very incongruous issues with one set of resources is near impossible, also for SOF. One SOF CA respondent was very direct in describing their work in Colombia:

> Even if we choose an area to influence because we want to counter a security threat, in Colombia, the question becomes—which population? The Catholics, the indigenous, the farmers? They all have different needs vis-à-vis the government and vis-à-vis each other. What about women? Depending on the community, they are almost never present at the decision-making table.[19]

Disenfranchisement of one group over another is not uncommon, and it clearly carries across contexts and actors—for both military and NGOs. Under conditions of horizontal inequality certain groups, because of their exclusion, may be overlooked in multi-ethnic or multi-religious societies.[20] Some have argued that, under these conditions, development assistance inevitably helps some groups while ignoring others, and raises the prospect of communal violence.[21] This was suggested by one military respondent who shared their experience in Colombia, "Sometimes a simple intervention of providing slippers for children can generate conflict. When you serve one group you automatically neglect another."[22] Similarly, another military respondent noted that, in Iraq, "if we did one thing for the Sunni area, we had to do the same for the Shia area, regardless if there was a need or not."[23] In speaking about Afghanistan, a military interviewee shared how aid was being distributed to cities and not rural areas, pushing people to migrate to urban areas as they also provided for better jobs, causing concern about having enough workers in farming communities.[24]

Local populations from Bosnia and Herzegovina noted how NGOs categorized and distributed aid based on ethnicity, which in turn created more tension between communities, specifically between refugees and those who did not flee the war.[25] A local man in Cambodia spoke about how the reinforcement of aid for the most vulnerable communities fueled the divisions between refugees and locals in the village, potentially even leading to envy among communities. He shared how "the refugee village has electricity; the road is better there, and here it is muddy. It makes me feel they are better than us."[26]

As mentioned throughout previous chapters, the military's approach to selecting populations is not based on need, but rather, on security objectives. Yet, as discussed earlier, even those are not completely without consultation with recipients, be it improvised by an individual operator, or institutionalized. Once populations have been prioritized, U.S. SOF, in coordination with the HN military, can execute effective, strong, and robust mechanisms to provide assistance in the gray space. One such example of this was demonstrated in a municipality in Mindanao—an island in the southern Philippines which is prone to natural disasters. Out of sixteen local community respondents interviewed for this study, eleven felt that the local public goods and services provided to their community—road construction, solar electrification, and solar-powered streetlights—were appropriate to the community. One respondent noted that the projects implemented by the local NGO, with the help of both the Philippine and U.S. militaries, increased social cohesion and trust in the community and were also an opportunity for local community members to come together. Almost all respondents thought the projects were appropriate to their community, and almost all alluded to participating in a public or private meeting where they were consulted about the planning or implementation of the local project. Those included local and regional government leaders or religious leaders. Almost all respondents reported using the projects provided to them and believed that they had increased trust in the community, and improved living conditions. Specifically, the roads provided better access, especially during the rainy season. One police officer noted, "The project serves as an essential conduit in promoting public safety thus enhances local police services expansion to their communities."[27]

But some of the impressions among local community members in Mindanao were not uniformly positive. This had less to do with the utility of the projects, and more with the fact that locals distrust their own government, without whom decisions cannot be taken. In sum, nothing can be done without having elites involved. In one instance, a local respondent spoke about the local development council meeting convened by the mayor, with the participation of the HN military and SOF CA:

> Sometimes these consultation meetings with the local community are facilitated by the local military for US civil affairs. This is important because sometimes civil-military programs are done for the sake of doing them, and these actors are not interested in helping the community. This is key because for example, there was a water project done by civil affairs. It was not successful, as they didn't really tap the underground waterways. After a few months, the water system dried up. They just wanted a photoshop opportunity. But did the people really benefit from the water system?[28]

Several outcomes are clear when it comes to providing community assistance, by both NGOs and SOF. With the simple act of implementing projects, whether their objective is security or development, each of these actors can be interpreted as being politically driven. For NGOs, as an extension of the donor's agenda, it is national policy and what the donors believe should be a priority. For the military, their influence is to ensure that both U.S. SOF and the HN partner are perceived positively by locals. But there is a huge gap between the locals' reality and the outsiders' understanding. As a result, these projects sometimes come down to window-dressing and lack substance. Also, when it comes to engaging with both decision-makers and beneficiaries, U.S. SOF and NGOs rely heavily on elites within communities.

Elites

Earlier chapters discussed the horizontal imbalance between groups—how by providing a service to one group, another is disenfranchised in the process. Yet, the gray space is subject to a vertical imbalance, where elites at the national level are the ones most likely to benefit from assistance, when in fact "locals often see the causes of conflicts and its solutions at the sub-national level,"[29] not at the national level. The vertical inequities within communities between elites and non-elites are referred to as "elite capture" as a form of corruption whereby public resources are biased for the benefit of a few individuals of superior social status.[30] Both military and NGOs recognize the problem of elite capture, mostly because elites are gatekeepers of the communities where the military and NGOs operate. On the NGO side, Donini suggests that, "Aid is going to the people who are 'connected', and to those who are rich and powerful and are able to occupy key links in the chain of intermediaries, not to the most needy."[31] In the 1990s, Somali humanitarian programming often interacted with powerful community members. Locally, "businessmen, political actors, senior members of the community, or clan or other powerful individuals—often decide who should receive aid or insist that recipients should hand over a portion of the relief they receive."[32] During the Pakistan floods of 2010, the assistance provided reached those who were generally better off, that is, with connections to the political elite and with salient political affiliations.[33] This coercion runs deep and often leads to threats and blackmail. Non-elites may not feel empowered to resist those in their own communities who disenfranchise them.[34] In speaking about conducting monitoring and evaluation work as part of one of their NGO projects, one NGO respondent shared about the complexities of who is identified as the most vulnerable: "It's whoever is the most disadvantaged, but all depends on the conflict. Most frequently the most susceptible to suffering are women and children."[35] In Somalia, humanitarian programming interacted with national and local politics and conflict, often benefiting more powerful community members. At the local level, gatekeepers known as black cats are defined as:

> [L]eaders who imposed themselves on vulnerable communities or minority groups and who control access, information and resources in those communities, but who are not of that group and who have their own agenda, which usually does not prioritize the welfare of the community.[36]

But the benefit is not a one-way street. For the military, most engagements and decisions are made in consultation with elites and elders. As one military respondent noted:

> The elites have a lot of good information. They are the first layer on the painting. Once we get their blessing, it's open and you can go anywhere. The mayor always needs to be involved. Just their presence alone is important.[37]

Respondents for this study confirmed they are not blind to the disconnect between those with power and influence, and those without, reconfirming that the social imbalance between elites and ordinary people, prevents everyday citizens "from speaking out the truth."[38] The way SOF respondents spoke about dealing with this disconnect is by describing how they [SOF] "validate the information with the peasants, shopkeepers, and everyday people. Communication is key, no matter what mission is being supported."[39]

Local populations are not blind to the vertical capture. One local community member and an NGO leader respondent spoke about the nutrition program they have been running for the local community, "Whatever program is implemented, it is to transform the lives of the elites, not the farmers. Where is the nutrition? It's only available for the Governor's children."[40] Working with elites is not isolated from the rest of the process. The same respondent noted that,

> Most of the NGO programs are already pre-identified, and already have their own bias. Whatever they do, they just present it to the chief mayor, and it just implements. This is important for them, as they need to give their funder a good report for them [the NGO] to continue to operate.[41]

LOCAL PERCEPTIONS—SOF AND LOCAL COMMUNITIES

These focused interviews confirm some previous evidence from community-based development studies, and suggest that inequitable outcomes from aid programming can be heightened in fragile states. Weaker state governance, naturally, creates room for opportunistic behavior by local elites despite the best intentions of aid providers. What is also revealing is that despite being focused on security objectives, SOF recognize that the assistance they provide, regardless of its primary objective being on security, is assistance, nonetheless. Despite their security-focused objectives, SOF make an effort to ensure that what is provided reaches those in need. Indirectly, even if not intended to be humanitarian or development in nature, the process through which SOF's assistance is distributed and NGOs' own practice of assessment and delivery, leads these organizations to converge.

Much of the perceived effectiveness of US military-deployed humanitarian and development assistance will depend upon public opinion within local communities as part of security objectives. To what extent are favorable perceptions possible?

Perceptions often serve as a catalyst for U.S. foreign policy and development actors to carry out their other objectives.[42] When it comes to the civil-military relationship, studies show that positive perceptions of the military and NGOs can be associated with more effective humanitarian disaster intervention.[43] But even when the engagement of the U.S. military, or any other agency, is not simply for logistical purposes, Guttierri argues, "the simple status of being an outsider generates a political signature."[44] The U.S. military's global collection of bases—old and new, has long been a cultivator of public opinion within the communities, where military personnel is deployed. Simple occurrences which are part of a soldier's deployment, such as visiting a village market, and speaking to a local shopkeeper, or generally interacting with locals, require interpersonal contact with the population, and can produce both positive and negative perceptions of U.S. military personnel.[45]

When it comes to the gray space, two areas are causing a potentially negative perception of SOF among local communities. First, the extent to which SOF understand the needs of local communities, or can go about addressing them, and second, how soldiers behave.

If the types of projects carried out by OHDACA are humanitarian, and SOF deploy them, then are SOF humanitarians? Chapter 2 already established that SOF are not humanitarians, at least not intentionally. The ability to carry out small-scale infrastructure projects, or provide goods and services, such as digging wells, and providing veterinary and medical services, puts them in a similar position to an NGO, even if SOF's objective is security. Yet, there is still a clash between the locals' view of outsiders' interventions, and outsiders' view of their role in the local community. In peacebuilding, it has been identified that there is a "major disconnect between how outsiders (aid agencies, peace support operations) and local communities understood the meanings of peace and security."[46] Similarly, one respondent noted:

> As outsiders, we may see that the greatest problem a village may face is a terrorist or criminal threat. To the host nation villagers, they may believe it is inadequate medical care or a drought that has been going on for years that prevents them from feeding themselves.[47]

In a 2016 presentation on the *Survey of the Afghan People*, panelists discussed how locals' first requirement for a school was a double-reinforced wall for the side of the building which faced the road. This was a priority even before quality teachers, or school supplies. The reason was to reinforce safety measures for students, in case a roadside bomb attack were to occur.[48]

Ultimately, it is evident that when it comes to understanding needs, soldiers' views of what is *broken* and *how* it should be fixed may be completely disparate and separate from those of populations. As earlier chapters mentioned, much of the understanding of these needs is systematized through efforts made by the individual, not the organization.

Then, if not suited for the commodity business, but claiming to be highly skilled warrior diplomats, does the behavior of SOF win them any favors with locals?

As argued previously, any moment a U.S. soldier steps foot on foreign land, he or she is bound to encounter civilians. As one HN military respondent from the Philippines noted, "Everyone that is not trained to kill is civil affairs."[49] Any interface between the U.S. military and locals creates a social touchpoint, where even the most benign gesture, such as "merely nodding at someone," generates a reaction.[50] But on the other hand, these interactions are not always positive. The initial negative impression that U.S. soldiers and their presence created among locals in East Africa, prompted the need for soldiers to make additional attempts to make a connection:

> When these soldiers were moving around with their vehicles, it happened one day that some boys stoned that vehicle. The children ran away. The soldiers stopped and went to some parents but we had no idea who did it. When the soldiers came to the school, I told them: "These children, they don't know you, your windows are tinted. . . . They need to know you, you are strangers."[51]

In Afghanistan, locals "complained about the presence of the military base, including the partying late at night."[52]

If it is not their behavior or dress code, it is the simple impression the military makes by default—the heaviness of their physical presence and sheer hard power which turns off local populations. As discussed in previous chapters, it is here where NGOs may have a comparative advantage. A local community respondent shared:

> Every time they [the US military] pass through the city, there are so many vehicles, and the local community is not happy about it. When they move around with all of their equipment, people are not so pleased. But if they go there with institutions like UNDP or USAID, the atmosphere is more welcoming.[53]

Interviewees for this study show that, SOF recognize that the optics of their hard power trumps any attempt of building an image of soft power actors. Several military respondents spoke about how they sought to mitigate this (see table 6.1). But there seems to be some evidence from population interviewees that when the military are seen to be working together, alongside, or in some sort of coordination with development actors, SOF's image softens, making them appear more accessible, approachable, and welcomed by the local community.

Table 6.1 Self-Described and Self-Employed Mechanisms for Engagement and Behaviors by the U.S. Military with Local Communities

Engagement by the Military with Populations
• Conversational
• Unscripted
• Ad hoc
• Consultative (seeking the other's opinion)
• Highly qualitative
• Highly personal—asking about personal life
• Offer bottle of water
• Downplay military association (use Department of State email if possible)

Source: Author, based on interviews.

But the individuals' approaches to engagement, as described in table 6.1, are not to be confused with the institutional decisions which impact populations' perceptions. Specifically, one member of a local community spoke of the lack of continuity and commitment of SOF where "most military commanders do interventions during their time. As soon as they are out, the next commander comes in and he sets his own agenda, and there is no continuity."[54] Another community respondent noted that "the locals should be in the process the whole time, but they are not. When the timeline of their tour in country is done, US civil affairs will get out, without telling the community."[55] The trust and confidence are broken. "Leaving without saying goodbye is just bad manners,"[56] as one local community respondent noted, and it is a poor reflection on the institution whose main objective is to initiate, form, and maintain relationships. So, both SOF and local communities recognized that the U.S. military's short-term presence is its Achilles heel. The military's short-term presence is in line with the concerns that NGOs had about the military, and which were described at length in chapter 5.

General McChrystal understood the importance of optics of the U.S. military in Iraq and Afghanistan, where he "refused to wear body armor, carry a weapon or wear sunglasses."[57] On her part, McFate's Human Terrain System work claimed that culture and social knowledge drove the success or failure of the United States' counterinsurgency efforts in those countries. Speaking with both local populations and military interviewees, it becomes clear that there is no secret ingredient that can sway populations in *our* favor. Everything the military does, and how it does it, all drives local communities' perceptions. As observed in the gray space through OHDACA, and in high-intensity contexts like Iraq and Afghanistan through Commander's Emergency Response Program (CERP), providing high-quality goods and services cannot make up for a lack of cultural understanding and skills. Later this analysis will explore the reverse—whether positive perceptions of soldiers can materialize, regardless of the utility of SOF's services in local communities.

LOCAL PERCEPTIONS—NGOS AND LOCAL COMMUNITIES

Chapter 3 explained the distinction between local and international NGOs, both of whom interact with communities. Chapter 3 also discussed how the NGO-population relationship can suffer from a lack of consultation on the needs of communities. Frequently, NGOs' program objectives are set up by what donors decide to be best for locals, not what recipients decide to be best for themselves. Chapter 4 discussed how the lines between long-term development and short-term immediate emergency aid can sometimes cross.

Scholars have argued that NGOs' approaches to engaging with local populations "mobilizes people, encourages increased information sharing, fosters alternative political ideas, and empowers the disadvantaged."[58] But this is often an ideal against which many NGOs cannot abide. How this occurs, what participation means, and what should be expected from such participation, is unclear.[59] Consultation with populations on the ground in conflict and fragile settings is even more difficult than in normal development contexts. This is because the quality of information can sometimes be poor, inconsistent, and unreliable, or there may simply be a lack of access to communities to have a fully representative sample. Also, the ability to maintain up-to-date information, which can quickly become outdated as populations may change public opinion, is strained.[60] Unlike the military, who are not limited to access, and whose consultation with communities is ad hoc and less scientific, for NGOs, consultations are not only a core part of their work, but also a costly endeavor. Smillie argues that how well NGOs monitor and evaluate the extent to which their programs are consulted with recipients is based on the NGOs' ability to deploy and fund sophisticated measuring mechanisms.[61] Alex de Waal claims that, during the 1984–1985 Darfur famine, millions died due to the inadequate humanitarian response to outbreaks of diseases—not starvation—as a consequence of misaligned priorities and expectations between the locals and humanitarians.[62] Similarly, during the 2004 Indian Ocean tsunami, "the main needs in Sri Lanka, India, Thailand, the Maldives, and Malaysia were for clean water, food and medical supplies. The initial surge of donations, however, was largely clothing."[63] A lack of understanding of how, and to whom, development assistance is distributed stalled efforts and caused a series of security consequences in the 1980s Somalian refugee camps.[64] The camps became fertile ground for the recruitment into the Barre regime's military, turning the camps into "de facto training camps."[65]

In a study of 6,000 respondents, very few of those who distributed assistance listened to the populations they sought to assist. Confidence in the missions on the part of local populations eroded:

> Villagers consistently expressed disappointment with outsiders for taking their time to ask questions and even make promises only to never return or provide the promised aid. This contributed to speculations that aid was somehow misused or redirected or that outsiders were not responsible and trustworthy.[66]

Where populations have been consulted, they may distrust the process, as their feedback is solicited but does not materialize in improvements for those concerned.[67] As mentioned earlier, in Bosnia and Herzegovina, this caused participants to decline to participate in the consultative process. They may also have feelings of being patronized by the aid agencies. Autesserre found that one Congolese businessman "thought foreign peacebuilders were talking down to local counterparts, and that they did not take the ideas of local people into account."[68] In instances where their voices *are* solicited, still, the objectives of the locals who are participating in the process, may not align with the intended objective of the NGO.[69] One seasoned NGO professional in this study confirmed what Anderson, Brown, and Jean had also reported in their study. They shared their experience working with a large international organization:

> The NGO assessment was on a community in East South Sudan. They needed a community health center. But the assessment came after the project. They had already put the people in place to do this community health center. So the cart came before the horse. I would go in and do a needs assessment. Whatever didn't fit into the project already, was discarded. The assumption is that they [the local community] are so much in need of everything, whatever you build or give them [they] are gonna use it anyway.[70]

This failure of fitting community requirements into programmatic ones is further exacerbated by how ineffectively these programs are implemented. One head of an international NGO at the former Thai-Burma border (currently Thai-Myanmar), described the relationship with donors, referring to how they "come with their new ideas, trends and we have to jump. . . . We end up with ridiculous time frames to do things. We cut out the process and spend the rest of the year doing damage control."[71] While the speed at which aid is provided differs between emergency intervention and longer-term development, the pace and consistency of distribution can be equally misaligned. The timing of assistance must be planned in such a way that the community can absorb it. This lack of strategic planning and mismatch between demand and supply is recognized by local populations. A local policeman in Thailand referred to it as "too much too fast,"[72] a phenomenon not specific only to development aid but security too, where "the amount of aid entering Afghanistan, and the ambitions for what it could achieve, clearly exceeded that country's capacity to use the aid for its intended purpose."[73] Because, as established in chapter 3, NGOs are often accountable to donors, not locals, NGOs try to turn over projects very quickly to prove performance to the donors. A villager in Myanmar shared that aid agencies "try to show how successful their aid delivery mission is"[74] to donors who fund them. As a result:

> Time pressures cause aid agencies to cut corners in terms of community consultations and to make assumptions about local circumstances. The pressure to deliver 'development,' 'human rights,' or 'peace' in short project bursts is again seen by those on the recipient side to be wasteful and unrealistic.[75]

This rush of NGOs to deliver projects in line with the timing of donor cycles is like the scenario described earlier, where the military acts quickly in carrying out a mission because its projects are tied to commanders' deployment cycles.

What becomes clear is that communities will automatically assess and evaluate any assistance they receive—be it "seeds, tools, boats, and even loans" and have an immediate understanding of *how*, and *if*, it will improve their economic situation.[76] In discussion with community members in Rwanda who received aid, one study found that refugees often spoke of humanitarian actors' lack of cultural understanding and inadequate responses to their needs. They note that:

> Yellow maize grain is bad for us, we prefer white maize as it can be pounded and given to vulnerable people. Yellow maize is no good for the poor and vulnerable, for only those with money can afford to have it ground.[77]

This is not unsimilar to what is discussed earlier as the military's lack of cultural understanding and local needs. Following the 1994 genocide in Rwanda, and upon their return from neighboring countries, Rwandan refugees were resettled in "marshy areas, on steep hillsides, and even in protected areas—unfortunately contributing to an ecological disaster."[78] In his account of the 1979 Cambodian famine, William Shawcross tells how despite agencies spending millions of dollars of aid, the needs of the populace were not related to development, but a political resolution as a way to end the decade-long civil war.[79] A survey of local Afghans concluded that what citizens expected was not what was delivered. What communities preferred were large ticket items, which were not possible for them to attain themselves, such as infrastructure, "not the small NGO rehabilitation projects that 'we can do ourselves.'"[80] And where infrastructure projects such as roads have been conducted by outsiders who lack understanding of the local environment context, the money is often wasted. In Afghanistan, a woman remarked on an infrastructure project, "Just look at the roads—they become like swimming pools in winter."[81]

Finally, from the view of aid recipients, it is often the case that NGOs lose their footing with the center of gravity. NGOs fail in the area of accountability for or follow-up on projects they start—just as the military does. According to one local account, "many NGOs 'just put up signs' but do not actually do anything substantive."[82] A local woman in Thailand shared, "There is only one time we saw staff of one of these international NGOs come and meet us—they came to unveil the sign about their funding here. We haven't seen anyone that belongs to that sign since then."[83]

As part of this analysis, the most dominant message coming from military and NGO interviewees about their experiences with development missions around the world was that no two places are the same, and that engagements all depend on the cultural context in which they are taking place. Yet, in interviewing nearly 6,000 respondents in more than twenty recipient countries, Anderson, Brown, and Jean found that when it comes to aid, "cumulatively, from all these conversations with all these people in all these places, remarkably consistent patterns and common judgments emerged."[84] This same message is clear from those interviewed as part of this analysis. As a result, like the military, NGOs, too, often lack the cultural know-how and context, leading to poorly designed programming. This misalignment causes these entities to converge through the shared challenges of their engagements.

ALL TOGETHER NOW

Success or failure of assistance in the human-centric gray space depends on the individuals more than the group. The challenges that military, development, and humanitarian actors experience, moreover, are across contexts—humanitarian assistance, disasters, food assistance, and infrastructure in high-intensity conflict. Chapter 5 discussed at length the struggles that SOF experience in exhibiting the appropriate cultural and social skills vis-à-vis civic actors, making it clear that the success of SOF's engagement is driven by individuals, and is not derived from their standard military training. On the NGO side, Donini notes that the personal behaviors of NGO aid workers, just like those of military personnel, can impact the relationships with the locals, where "even if the universalist values of the enterprise do not clash with local views of the world, the baggage, modus operandi, technique and personal behavior of aid workers often do."[85] A RAND study shows that "for Afghans who believe that NATO forces were not acting in Afghans' best interests, the main reasons cited were collateral damage and lack of respect for homes, leaders, and religion."[86] Ultimately, the grievances which populations expressed and which are common to both military and development actors are about outsiders' lack of cultural understanding, respect, and consultation when engaging in communities (see table 6.2).

Table 6.2   Attributes Identified as Most Valued by Locals When Engaging with the U.S. Military and NGOs

- Sincerity
- Respect for local culture
- Politeness
- Inclusion
- Consultation

Source: Author, based on interviews.

Generally, respondents attributed successful engagement with local populations to individuals' backgrounds and abilities to relate personally to the communities they are serving. For example, there is evidence for the military maintaining a strong recruitment pool from within rural communities in the United States.[87] Because of this, the military may be able to better assimilate with rural communities than some NGO workers from Western countries, who are often urbanites. One NGO respondent noted how:

> Herd culture is like cowboy culture. Those who live in cities could never understand the societies of the places where they are working and the local needs. For sure, they don't need tablets or kindles, they need safety for their livestock, which are treated as part of the family.[88]

This approach to providing "nice things"[89] for the population as a tactic to win them over has proven of little value. One SOF CA respondent confirmed this instance by expressing that during their time in Mauritania, the team provided the locals with electronics that were of no use to the local community.[90] This is in line with what previous chapters drew on how U.S. efforts to build schools without teachers and hospitals without doctors in Iraq and Afghanistan proved ineffective, leading to little use of the infrastructure.

An even more complex occurrence of assistance by outsiders is described by Sophia Sabrow, who argues that positive perceptions of an entity intervening do not necessarily translate into a positive perception about the assistance provided, and vice versa. In writing about peacekeeping operations in Mali, Sabrow notes that:

> The French intervention is highly appreciated for its achievements on the ground but discredited from an ideological point of view. ECOWAS' [Economic Community of West African States] perception is the reverse: regional troops are positively perceived on an ideological level but dismissed with regards to their practical outcomes.[91]

This sentiment is further confirmed in some of the positive responses by recipients in the Philippines about the benefits of projects implemented by the U.S. military. But that should not be confused with how locals perceive the U.S. military. As one member of the local community in the Philippines shared, "There is a difficult history. More than 1,000 civilians were slaughtered in Sulu by the US military, so that wound is still in the minds of the local population, regardless of what they are providing."[92] In short, these projects are not automatic mechanisms for swaying the population to support the U.S. efforts. Contrarily, not providing them does not automatically materialize into a lack of support, as many other factors described earlier, such as behavior and interpersonal skills, can play an even more dominant role.

However, one factor is certain to sway public opinion, and it is self-diagnosed by SOF themselves. When asked about what they believed to be the military's biggest hurdle to overcome in the arena of humanitarian and development assistance, one military respondent shared without hesitancy, "We as the military already have a loss of credibility, as they are hesitant to work with us because they know it's a one-off thing,"[93] thereby making it difficult to gain their support and trust while carrying out that mission. Once the threat is contained, the relationship with the population is severed. It is because of the short-term deployment cycles, and security-focused objectives that one CA Officer stated, "I would hesitate to call myself a humanitarian."[94] But another believed that in Tajikistan, the one-off distribution of winter jackets for local village children was purely a humanitarian deed by SOF, and felt that the unit had truly gained the support of the people, judging by how locals welcomed them each subsequent time.[95]

Where possible, SOF referred to leveraging USAID to improve its image vis-à-vis local populations. This effort, based on the earlier mentioned perceptions of locals, *did* make a difference as it helped *soften* SOF's optics. But maintaining long-term relationships with civilians is not the business of the military and this inevitably leads to civilians being reluctant to trust someone attempting to exercise influence in their own communities, who will likely be gone abruptly and soon. The transactional approach to engaging with local communities has another layer. In observing the provision of medical services by the military to local communities in the Eastern Democratic Republic of Congo, one NGO respondent noted that:

> For the military to remain medically ready and to meet the training mission as an integrated part of their response to humanitarian assistance, they have to have a certain number of hours of practice as a qualification for their credentials, so they need to systematically rotate. So, the local population thinks that the US military is just coming in and practicing on them.[96]

The concerns of short-lived interactions are not only between SOF and populations. As discussed at length in chapter 4, they are also between SOF and NGOs.

Scales reminds us of the reality that the level of the relationship with locals is dependent on how the military behaves. Donini agrees that association with an organization or international contingent is less relevant to forming good relationships, and "whoever provides visible assistance is viewed positively."[97] But it is not necessarily the good or service that military or development actors provide. One Department of State respondent described how soldiers taking a hike with local kids near the city mountains "meant more to them than a new building or clean toilets ever could."[98] Another CA interviewee shared, "We raised 600 dollars to buy backpacks. The kids were using old shopping bags to carry books. They loved the donation, but they mostly loved our time."[99] This is logical. Earlier, the analysis described how it was the military's short-term deployment cycles, and as a result *absence* from the communities, which was their ultimate shortfall.

Lastly, when taking into consideration the military and NGOs' similar functions, abilities, as well as deficiencies in the gray space, who is better perceived by communities and why? Taking account of their similarities, is there a differentiation or concern in the eyes of local communities about *who* provides the assistance?

When speaking about peacekeeping operations, Holshek argues that local populations often do not differentiate between military and humanitarian personnel carrying out humanitarian activities.[100] In his observation about Afghanistan, the majority of which was not considered as a gray space later in the conflict, because it was highly kinetic, and the military were recognizable due to wearing uniforms, Donini states that "ordinary Afghans do not have the ability to distinguish between foreigners other than between the military and the civilians."[101] When it comes to the less intense gray space, one NGO interviewee puts it bluntly:

> Most of the locals don't really have a clue as to who we are. In their eyes, we are just foreigners. This separation between agencies, donors, NGOs, private security, military, it's all in our eyes, not theirs. Unless it's a combat zone with an actual military intervention and it's all out visible in the community.[102]

This is most relevant for the gray space. Unlike in high-intensity conflict, where foreigners are often secluded from the population, the gray space allows more access for all actors. Here, the military are not always obviously dressed in uniform. This is not to say that soldiers in uniform can blend in with civilians. Rather, in the gray space, which is not ridden with conflict, who provides what assistance and whether they are uniformed is less relevant.

Furthermore, consultation on recipients' needs is challenging, but not impossible or always unsuccessful. Local perceptions of aid in crisis settings are difficult to measure and assess, and vary between contexts. Much of this depends on the scale of the operation, the number of actors, and the amount of resources on the ground. For example, most recently in Ukraine, personnel on the ground shared how for the most part Ukrainian refugees are finding their own way to Europe. Still, understanding their experiences, and their immediate needs, so that NGOs can improve the aid they offer, in a setting of a full-on war and with conditions changing every day, is a challenge. Feedback and input are critical for assessing operations, and those fleeing are "not just literally sitting there ready to answer your questions."[103] The gray space is subjected to less movement and less drastic restrictions than what is experienced in high-intensity conflict zones, where international militaries and aid agencies limit themselves to heavily fortified enclaves.

Lastly, Ankersen asked whether aid looks different when not delivered from the barrel of a gun. But Donini argues that in places like Afghanistan, recipients were not concerned about whether aid came from "a military truck or under the auspices of a principled NGO," and that what is provided took precedence over who provided it.[104] In the Philippines, Burkina Faso, Colombia, Lebanon, and many of the other places where interviewees had served, the military respondents had no evidence of their assistance in communities being rejected by locals simply because they wore a uniform. Conversely, there was no evidence to confirm that assistance by local communities was accepted solely on the basis that it came from a development actor. What this shows is that when services are absent, their provision, rather than who supplies them, takes priority. This is a reality that those on the ground know all too well. In certain instances, NGOs have essentially replaced the role of governments, such as the case with MSF, which has been running long-term healthcare through nearly 80 percent of its programming.[105]

Chapter 3 argued that considering the fluidity of the gray space and involvement of other actors in it, namely private security companies, NGOs are not the altruistic do-gooders working in the interest of communities as they may wish to be perceived. Donini argues that NGOs label themselves in whichever convenient way that suits the context or audience or donors who hold the purse strings to their funding. The military, too, call their projects humanitarian, when in fact they are security cooperation initiatives.

In examining these two entities—SOF and NGOs—several observations are in order. The U.S. military, no matter its mandates and involvement, shapes its narrative among the local community merely with its physical presence. As is discussed later, they often score higher in public opinion than the HN military. For CA who cut across the mandates of various contexts, sometimes dressed in civilian clothing instead of a uniform, the optics override the mandate. In remote areas, which in the gray space are vulnerable to weak governance and are rife with insecurity, rural populations may never or very rarely see a diplomat or an NGO worker who is based in the capital, but they will frequently see a soldier. This soldier may be from a particular specialty, rank, or background. He or she could be an SF soldier, or a CA specialist, who engages not only with the populace but also with the HN military who are part of the populace.

Ultimately what becomes clear is that, from the point of view of populations, perceptions are dichotomous in the gray space and are driven by individual-specific values, realities, and beliefs, as well as by the provision of services. Across the series of contexts—peacekeeping, peacebuilding, counterinsurgency, natural disasters, and complex emergencies—the challenges in the military-NGO relationship persist, but the military-population and NGO-population relationships are variable. What is evident is that in the gray space, locals are less concerned about who provides them assistance, and more about having agency in the process, and feeling respected. Despite the discussion in chapter 3 that NGOs struggle with consulting recipient populations, compared to the military, NGOs do better at consultative mechanisms, because of their emphasis on transferring over from stable development contexts into fragile settings. With the military, consulting populations and giving them agency is often improvised, short-lived, and heavily dependent on interpersonal skills. For the military, there is no scientific mechanism for employing assessment processes, or adapting them from one type of setting to another. As a result, the very access to local populations in the gray space allows these entities to converge. Contrastingly, these actors' divergence is not due to what we would expect—the hard power of the military versus the soft power of the NGOs. The military's sheer and consistent presence is often their most powerful influence. For NGOs, they diverge from the gray space, due to the expectation that as non-security actors they are more permanent and consequently more efficient in what they provide to local communities. Unlike the military, in speaking with local populations, and drawing on existing evidence, there is little evidence to show that NGOs' sheer presence provides reassurance to local communities. Due to their diversity, discussed in chapter 3, some NGOs have de facto replaced government services. For others, their ad hoc approach to assessment and programming places them in the same category as the military—non-permanent and self-serving.

POPULATIONS AND THE HOST NATION MILITARY

The significant link between U.S. SOF, and their main interlocutor—the HN military, was addressed in chapter 2. Depending on the context, unlike the frequently accepted view in the West where the military are perceived as protectors of society, in fragile and low-intensity-driven settings of the gray space the military can be seen as either friendly protectors or as dangerous perpetrators. When it comes to the gray space, "the boundaries between categories like military/civilian, coercion/persuasion, victim/perpetrator, public authority/private protector, licit/illicit [are] porous and constantly shifting."[106] For example, Mali's military is still committing war crimes.[107] In Nigeria, scholars have argued that the lack of professionalism of the Nigerian military vis-à-vis their relationship with civilians, is the reason for populations' negative perceptions of the force, motivating these same local citizens to form their own security apparatus.[108] One local community respondent in the Philippines shared, "In Sulu the community is afraid of the military."[109] According to another local respondent, "populations feel intimidated by the people in uniform."[110] An

NGO respondent gave reasoning that, if the HN military is not always paid on time, "they go around looting and pillaging."[111] This is in addition to HN forces being accused of human rights violations[112] or other crimes against the very people they should protect.[113]

In occurrences where the HN military is perceived negatively or not accepted by the local population, the relationship between U.S. SOF, the HN military partner, and the community takes another twist. SOF can play the role of an equalizer. The sheer presence of SOF can be their most valuable commodity, and one that carries across to their relationship with the HN partner. As a result, negative perceptions of the HN military can be improved by SOF's presence. In Colombia, for example, the U.S. military takes a mentorship role, and is not in charge, as the Colombian military is mostly responsible for engaging with populations and NGOs. While SOF's primary interlocutor *is* the HN military, negative perception by the local population, one would assume, would extend on to SOF too. But the opposite is true. As one military respondent noted, in some instances "the locals prefer to see the US than their own military, and people generally feel comfortable when the Americans show up. Everyone tends to behave themselves."[114] In Niger, for example, the U.S. military is viewed more favorably than its HN partner military.[115] And in certain instances, this contrast can be observed vis-à-vis the United States' Allies, where one respondent from DOS noted about their experience in Niger, "the US is still much more popular than the French."[116]

Contrastingly, there are areas where the local military is well established and effective. With Acción Integral functioning as part of the Colombian military, the interaction with populations is much more developed and U.S. SOF are less directly involved. For example, under Plan Colombia—the U.S. economic and security assistance plan to help counternarcotics, launched in the year 2000, the United States provides the funding, but Acción Integral carries out the work on the ground. If the HN military is fully stood up, operational and efficient, and the SOF relationship vis-à-vis the HN partner is strong, as discussed in chapter 2, SOF would then coordinate with NGOs through its local counterpart. One respondent shared how in some instances the partnership between SOF and the HN military partner CA arm is so strong, "We as the U.S. are shadow humanitarians" to the local force who provide the humanitarian assistance to the populace.[117] This funder-implementor partnership for HN and SOF is comparable to the donor-NGO relationship discussed at length in chapter 3. What is different, however, is that unlike some donors who are not the direct implementers of projects, at times SOF are directly involved in carrying out such projects on the ground, or as is the case in Colombia, funding them, but still shadowing the HN military.

Chapter 2 discussed how sometimes there are challenges and points of disconnection between the HN military and SOF as trainer and mentor. Chapter 5 argued that there are contradicting views on SOF's ability to exercise cultural awareness, and empathy vis-à-vis NGOs. Unlike U.S. SOF, who are outsiders, the partner force is on its home turf, and is part of the general population. In other words, the HN partner *is* the populace. As such, in instances where the HN military is perceived well by some locals, the HN partner wants to ensure that this positive perception transfers on to their U.S. SOF training partner, as well. An HN military officer in the Philippines, who is also a member of a local community, described an instance of their interaction with a member of the U.S. SOF team in the local community:

> To try to get him acquainted with the locals, I brought a young US NCO with me to the local market. One of the fishermen said to him "Are you interested in buying some lobsters?", to which the NCO asked about the price. Once the fisherman shared it with him, the NCO said "No, it's too expensive!" So instead, I used my own money to buy the lobster because I didn't want the US military to look bad. They are our partners. It's always about asking how my response would make the other person feel?[118]

In sum, in their engagement with the HN partner, U.S. SOF are by extension *also* engaging with the local community. In other words, the separation of the local community between civilian and military is only in theory. The same was observed in chapter 3 about the separation between local NGOs and beneficiary communities. Specifically that often the local NGO *is* the community. In the same way that various local community respondents perceive *any* outsiders, military or civilian, as *just* foreigners. In practice, there is often a lack of recognition of the nuances at play. Namely that beyond HN military or local NGOs, or local communities, all these groups are *citizens* of the places where foreigners deploy.

Regardless of the technical training or utility of the military assistance provided to the HN military, as with civic assistance by SOF to local populations, the sociocultural aspect of the U.S. military can carry more weight than the goods or services being delivered. As one former SOF operator noted, the United States needs to develop a better understanding of the people it trains, namely "the [host nation] military, instead of just sending money towards long-term training and equipment programmes."[119]

DO NO HARM

> When it comes to meeting the needs in a local context, we simply don't get it. Because we are afraid to say that we don't get it, we make up for it by doing things so we can pat ourselves on the back and say that we did something.[120]

Much has been said about the U.S. military and development actors being a detriment to the communities in which they intervene. As this analysis has shown, hard and soft power are inextricably linked, but much of what is demonstrated in this analysis is that they should not be thought of in exclusive terms. Military coercion is not always ineffective, and NGO assistance is not guaranteed to be beneficial. Foreign policy, naturally, consists of a mix of coercion and reward. A hard-powered military, whether from the United States or the HN, can be the cause of tens of thousands of civilian deaths, while it can also be a stabilizing presence in an area for decades without ever firing a shot. NGOs and development actors, too, can fail to match commitments with actual disbursements, or abruptly pull funding and shut down programming, causing chaos and panic over the scarcity of resources, or disruption to financial institutions.[121]

Much of the debate has centered around the military's role as a soft-powered development actor, through CERP, leading overwhelmingly to conclusions that the military has no place in conducting development. Earlier, evidence from military interviewees shed light on how development activities were not the appetite of military commanders. OHDACA projects, compared to programs such as CERP, are minuscule, giving even less reason for sophisticated and consistent analysis of SOF as nation builders. But no institutionalized mechanisms for measuring second-order effects on communities exist, even if examples of the military doing more harm than good exist in abundance. As one military respondent noted, because humanitarianism is not the business of the military, the consequences of assistance programs of such scale are less relevant:

> We don't measure this stuff, and we don't care about the populations, because it's not humanitarian to begin with. These projects are designed to give a kinder, gentler face to DoD. So, nobody really cares what the beneficiaries think, and nobody cares if the projects are working or not. These projects are based on the deployment cycle, not on need.[122]

While there are mandates on the protection and the mitigation of harm to civilians,[123] as a result of the impact of the military's hard power,[124] no international robust legal framework or convention exists on the protection of commodities or economic intervention by military actors.[125] As discussed in previous chapters, for all humanitarian, development, and military actors, it is unclear who is accountable if a well dries up or an electric grid breaks down.

In the context of SOF CA, previous chapters discussed how the tools which the military uses to assess the environment—ASCOPE and PMSEII—do not account for the second-order effects on populations. This leaves behind projects which may have not been well-thought-out in terms of how they benefit the community, or whether they can be sustained in the long term. One senior military respondent shared how even if well-intentioned, working in communities may not always have a positive impact. Short-term deployment in these communities exacerbates these challenges, as is one example in Lebanon:

> We helped stand up a municipality building. It was more symbolic than anything. It brought together the Lebanese army and Lebanese government. One project or program can turn the population on its head, in a really positive way. At the same time, if we pull the lever too hard, we establish a new standard, which is beyond the local, or acceptable standard, and we can't maintain it. So, in a way, we overdeliver as a way to compensate for the fact that we won't be able to sustain these projects, because secretly we acknowledge that we will leave someday. So now we have created a problem.[126]

While the OHDACA projects discussed in this analysis may not be the large-ticket items most synonymous with CERP and the big wars in Iraq and Afghanistan, several respondents noted how even in the most benign and well-intentioned attempts to help local communities, harm can be done. One military respondent noted:

> We handed out 30,000 masks to help with COVID. What we didn't realize is that we were putting a bunch of women out of work who were making them out of cloth and selling them to the local community. It totally undermines the local economy.[127]

A CA officer shared an account of standing up a program in the Philippines to teach trades to local men as a way to help them earn a living, and not turn to the insurgency. Once specialized, however, young people could not find jobs in the local community, and so moved to larger cities, creating a brain drain in the village.[128] In recalling one experience in Africa, a CA team member noted that in building classrooms for children in rural villages, the result may be the opposite of what the project intended, "children might be educated while their families need them to work," or even if that is not the case, once they receive their education, they are not able to get jobs with that same education.[129]

Sometimes harm can be done to the community by a simple lack of deconfliction with donor agencies or other NGOs. Chapter 4 discussed how, institutionally, NGOs and the military fail to be aligned, and that any synergies in the civil-military relationship were driven by individuals, not institutions. But interviews with the military demonstrated that sometimes it is the individual who can be the cause of failure of the relationship, or cause harm to the community. One military respondent told of a situation in a fishing village in the Philippines, where CA were asked to help support the local economy by developing local fisheries. A young officer took a proactive approach, and did not conduct the needed due diligence. Along with CA colleagues, the officer chose to work with the only NGO they could find. That particular NGO did not possess knowledge of local artisanal fisheries specific to that community, and the results were devastating. The new variety of fish that the project introduced into the local community's fisheries was invasive and destroyed the established, native varieties already being raised by local farmers. This almost destroyed the local fish farming within the village.[130] What is evident is that in addition to the earlier mentioned *softening up* of SOF due to the optics of their working alongside development actors and NGOs, deconfliction with NGOs, also produces better results. Or, in the least prevents harm.

Other times, when harm is done, it is mostly due to a disconnect *within* the U.S. military or *between* U.S. military branches. One former SOF unit commander described how their small footprint engagement with the locals was overtaken by other U.S. military branches. During their time in the Philippines, in 2007, the U.S. Navy sailed the USS *Peleliu*, filled with doctors and engineers to conduct medical assistance for local communities:

[B]ut the military showed up like a bull in a China shop as it deployed Landing Craft Air Cushions[131] that tore up the beaches. To assist the local population, the US NAVY performed cataract surgery, but cataract surgery needs follow-up, and the small SOF unit now had to provide it, even though we didn't have the capacity to do so. So, this did more harm than good.[132]

Much of chapter 4 discussed the challenge related to the military's short-term deployment cycles, or not spending enough time understanding local communities, both of which are detriments to forming rapport and relationships with local populations. But, according to a military respondent, "hanging around and being among the population is also not a good thing, as it poses a security risk for the community."[133] Contrary to what was described earlier, the simple optics of being seen around the community does not always result in a positive image. Another respondent seconded this perspective in expressing that:

The Colombians can live without us, and they have no issue with us leaving. They are proud people. When it comes to meeting with anybody in government, they like to have us around, they like to show themselves associated with us. But they can live without us.[134]

Whether intended or not, even if they are purely security cooperation projects, the military's involvement in the humanitarian and development space can have negative as well as positive benefits for communities. On the development side, the picture is similarly not so straightforward. Aid can be harmful if it crowds out private investment, or if it creates a series of parallel and non-governmental systems, which seek to replace what governments *should* provide.[135] On the one hand, robust and consistent evidence shows that aid can reduce poverty.[136] Scholars have also argued how interventions and aid can fuel but not resolve conflict.[137] By contrast, aid critics such as Moyo argue that external aid cultivates corruption, dependency, and artificial economies.

Lastly, in the context of crises, where services are disrupted, too much assistance being given too quickly can also cause an imbalance in an already fragile environment. As discussed in earlier chapters, the lack of HN government accountability is one of the major characteristics in fragile spaces, with weak social contracts between populations and institutions. As mentioned in chapter 3, as NGOs seek to work in fragile settings, they often contract PMSCs to help them navigate insecure environments. Having a presence of security actors in what may be sufficiently secure spaces raises the security pressure in local communities. But with all the criticism toward outside entities engaging in fragile states, where little governing exists, the alternatives are limited if a community is to seek and be given help. In these chronically ungoverned and unstable places, NGOs and aid, and even the U.S. military, may be the only available vice to keep the gray space from further debilitating. What would happen in the gray space if it were not for outside actors to help eradicate smallpox, polio, river-blindness, and meningitis, or provide anti-retroviral drugs to reduce the impact of HIV/AIDS?

There has been a widely recognized disconnect and a lack of communication between outside interveners, the military, and development actors. Many scholars also examine the divide between these outside entities and the local populations they serve. Karlborg argues that in Afghanistan, the disconnect between locals and international outside entities was mostly on religious grounds,[138] not on the burdensome layers of the donor-recipient relationship between them. What is more striking is that across the series of contexts— whether it be peacekeeping, peacebuilding, counterinsurgency, natural disasters, and complex emergencies—the challenges in the military-population and the NGO-population relationship are very similar and do persist.

CONCLUSION

The center of gravity—the populations whose very existence necessitates the work of SOF and NGOs—can be the drivers of success or failure of a mission or project. In examining the impacts of these military and development projects, evidence shows that they can be measured quite subjectively based on locals' perceptions. Furthermore, the locals' perceptions of a project's success have less to do with the sophisticated mechanisms used to design it, and more with the practical implications of the commodity or service provided. Perceptions are also heavily driven by both SOF's and NGOs' exhibited interpersonal behaviors, respect for local cultures, and inclusion of recipients in the consultative process. This applies also to the U.S. SOF-HN military relationship when the HN military are unavoidably part of the local community.

When seen as present together with, or working alongside NGOs, there is evidence that SOF are perceived more favorably by local communities. These findings contradict the traditional understanding of *who*—the military or non-security actors, should provide assistance. Instead, it becomes clear that *what* is provided, and *how* it is provided overrides *who*—whether the military or NGOs are better suited as development or humanitarian actors.

Unlike the previous chapters which draw on the military and international NGOs, who have participated in a myriad of global operations, contexts, and experiences, the insight gained in this chapter is the most local, but ironically the least subjective. Unlike the perceptions of deployed military or NGOs from hubs around the world in Geneva, London, North Carolina, or Brussels, the perspectives of local populations are exactly that—local and insular. The prisms through which communities in Mindanao in the Philippines, Riohacha in Colombia, Lewa in Kenya, or Bobo in Burkina Faso view the military and NGOs, are myopic only to the communities who inhabit those places. Yet, the patterns observed are the same—a confessed disconnect between communities, NGOs, and military actors. What becomes clear is that there is no understood or permanent social contract between any of these entities, but an imperfect and constantly evolving relationship. Both NGOs and SOF seek to separate and influence target groups for influence—insurgents versus allies, working with the HN military, but against non-state actors. NGOs, too, may alienate one group over another, as programming may seek to assist women over men, young versus old, Christians over Muslims, for instance. But keeping these separations and expecting positive outcomes for these projects of SOF or NGOs is unrealistic. The populace is integrated into all these layers of a society's fabric, interlinked and inseparable. Trying to separate them to meet *our* agenda, or fit to *our* bureaucratic structures, goes against the spirit of complexity inherent in the gray space.

Nearly three decades ago, Slim argued about the natural convergence of the military and humanitarian organizations in conflict spaces. The gray space only reconfirms that this relationship is becoming more converged, even if not more efficient. Inside of these spaces, populations' perceptions of the military are formed by the behaviors of soldiers, not any less than they are by their technical skill, just as Scales predicts when he talks about the warrior of the twenty-first century. The traditionalists—both scholars and practitioners—would not be opposed to the military carrying out projects to influence populations, even with a few blunders, as long as soldiers do not lose their fighting edge. Indirectly, this is also in line with Taw and Brooks, who take a realistic view of the necessary and functioning intersection of warriors and aid workers, as an unavoidable work in progress. All these scholars speak about how *we* as outsiders should behave, and what *our* role should be. Yet, when it comes to the gray space, the center of gravity gives little importance to *whom* aid comes from. Their perception of outsiders—military or civilian—can sometimes be driven by the utility of such assistance, and it is mostly defined by *how* we as outsiders behave when we operate in their communities.

NOTES

1. The center of gravity may be interpreted in multiple ways in warfare. I use the term "center of gravity" as an interpretation of what Strange and Iron, "Center of Gravity," refer to as being the spirit of the populace. In the context of this argument, the center of gravity is the population.
2. Gilbert, "Money."
3. Donini, "Local Perceptions."
4. McGann and Johnstone, "The Power Shift," 68.
5. *Ibid.*
6. U.S. Department of the Army, "Civil Affairs Planning," 1–10.
7. Dijkzeul and Wakenge, "Doing Good, but Looking Bad?," 1140.
8. Seferis and Harvey, "Accountability," 8.
9. Donini, "Local Perceptions," 167.
10. McNeil, Herzog, Cosic, and PRISM Research, "Citizen Review of Service Delivery," 3.
11. Seybolt, *Humanitarian Military Intervention,* 31.
12. Slim, "Is Humanitarianism being Politicised? A Reply to David Rieff," 1.
13. Smillie, *The Alms Bazaar,* 177.
14. Ryan, "The Military and Reconstruction Operations," 181–90.
15. Hall, "Political and Social Determinants of Disease Eradication."
16. Storeng, Palmer, Daire, and Kloster, "Behind the Scenes," 555–69.
17. R 51.
18. *Ibid.*
19. R 18.
20. Brown and Langer, "Horizontal Inequalities and Conflict," 27–55.
21. Anderson et al., *Time to Listen.*
22. R 28—High Ranking NCO, March 3, 2021.
23. R 44.
24. R 9—Senior Military Officer Respondent, February 12, 2021—Discussing the Philippines.
25. Anderson et al., *Time to Listen,* 24.
26. *Ibid.*
27. R 84—Local citizen Respondent (Policeman), Philippines—September 28, 2021.
28. R 10—Member of the Local Community—February 14, 2021.
29. Sabrow, "Local Perceptions," 163.
30. Platteau, "Monitoring elite."

31. Donini, "Local Perceptions," 166.

32. Collinson and Elhawary, "Humanitarian Space," 22.

33. Madiwale and Virk, "Civil–Military Relations in Natural Disasters."

34. Platteau, "Monitoring Elite."

35. R 67 and Jansen, "Gender and War," 135.

36. Jaspars and Maxwell, "Targeting in Complex Emergencies," 24.
Dijkzeul and Wakenge, "Doing Good," 1140.

37. R 15.

38. Platteau, "Monitoring Elite," 225.

39. R 16.

40. R 10.

41. *Ibid.*

42. Diehl and Major, "Measuring the Impact of US Global Health Engagements," 37–50.

43. Kay, "Indonesian Public Perceptions," 3–64.

44. Egnell, "Civil–Military Coordination for Operational Effectiveness," 249.

45. McCurry, "American Soldier Jailed for Rape in Philippines."

46. Donini, "Local Perceptions," 163.

47. Inigo, "Civil Affairs Team Help Teach."

48. United States Institute of Peace, "The Asia Foundation's 12th Annual Poll of Public Perceptions," Remarks by Panelist Zach Warren, December 8, 2016.

49. R 76—Local Citizen/Senior Military Officer, Philippines, September 14, 2021.

50. Putnam, "Social capital," 2.

51. Bachmann, "Whose Hearts and Minds?," 16.

52. Ruffa and Vennesson, "Fighting and Helping?," 610.

53. R 10.

54. *Ibid.*

55. R 10.

56. R 88—Local Citizen Respondent, Philippines—October 2, 2021.

57. Hart, Review of "My Share of the Task," 85.

58. Brass et al., "NGOs and International Development," 138.

59. Grünewald, Pirotte and Husson, *Beneficiaries or Partners*; Hilhorst, "Victims, Right Holders, Clients or Citizens?"

60. Herbert, "Perception Surveys in Fragile and Conflict-Affected States"; Catapang, Chaisson, Gong, Hecht, Hiller, Houston, and Hsiao, "Lessons for US Doctrine."

61. Smillie, *The Alms Bazaar*.

62. De Waal, *Famine*.

63. Pettit and Beresford, "Emergency," 314.

64. Collinson and Elhawary, "Humanitarian Space."

65. *Ibid.*, 6.

66. Anderson et al., *Time to Listen*, 26.

67. Nouvet, Abu-Sada, de Laat, Wang, and Schwartz, "Opportunities, Limits and Challenges," 358–77.

68. Autesserre, "International Peacebuilding," 125.

69. Yeboah, "Solving Local Problems or Looking Good," 1–17.

70. R 51.

71. Anderson et al., *Time to Listen*, 40.

72. *Ibid.*, 22.

73. Lamb and Mixon, "Rethinking Absorptive Capacity," 5.

74. Anderson et al., *Time to Listen*, 46.

75. *Ibid.*, 40.

76. *Ibid.*, 18.

77. Pottier, "Why Aid Agencies Need," 328.

78. Brown and Grävingholt, "Chapter 1: Security Development and the Securitization of Foreign Aid," 88.

79. Shawcross, *The Quality of Mercy.*

80. *Ibid.*, 164.

81. *Ibid.*

82. *Ibid.*

83. Anderson et al., *Time to Listen*, 46.

84. *Ibid.*, 1.

85. Donini, "Local Perceptions," 158.

86. Davis, Larson, Haldeman, Oguz, and Rana, "Understanding and Influencing Public Support," 79.

87. Philipps and Arango, "Who Signs Up to Fight."

88. R 51.

89. Shapiro and Howell, "What Are Small Wars?"

90. R 57.

91. Sabrow, "Local Perceptions," 161.

92. R 10.

93. R 18.

94. R 39.

95. R 28.

96. R 40.

97. Donini, "Local Perceptions," 165.

98. R 70—Department of State Local Employee, EUCOM Region.

99. R 16 Discussing Deployment in Africa.

100. Holshek, "Humanitarian Civil-Military Coordination."

101. Donini, "Local Perceptions," 168.

102. R 1.

103. Welsh, "How International NGOs Are Setting Up a Ukraine Response from Scratch."

104. Donini, "Local Perceptions," 161.

105. Abu-Sada, "Introduction," 5.

106. Verweijen, "The Ambiguity of Militarization," 346.

107. Lcymaric, "France's Unwinnable Sahel War."

108. Musa and Heinecken, "The Effect of Military (un) Professionalism on Civil-Military Relations," 1–17.

109. R 77—Local Population Respondent, Philippines, October 3, 2021.

110. R 90—Local Population Respondent, October 4, 2021 and R 10.

111. R 51.

112. Human Rights Watch, "Burkina Faso."
     Turse, Mednick, and Sperber, "Exclusive."

113. Amnesty International, "Stars on Their Shoulders. Blood on Their Hands."

114. R 8—Civil Affairs Officer Colombia—February 16, 2021.

115. Litt, "Why Is the United States in Niger, Anyway?"

116. R 33.

117. R 16.

118. R 15—Describing Their Experience in Afghanistan, March 8, 2021.

119. Turse et al., "Exclusive."

120. R 6.

121. Mellen and Ledur, "Afghanistan Faces Widespread Hunger."

122. R 61.

123. See DOD INSTRUCTION 3000.17 CIVILIAN HARM MITIGATION AND RESPONSE https://www.esd.whs.mil/Portals/54/Documents/DD/issuances/dodi/300017p.pdf

124. United Nations Peacekeeping, "Protection of Civilians Mandate."

Valentino, Huth, and Croco, "Covenants without the Sword," 339–77.

125. The closest to a holistic policy is human security, which according to NATO's definition includes the combating and trafficking in human beings, children, and armed conflict, conflict-related sexual violence, protection of civilians, and protection of cultural property. See NATO Human Security https://www.nato.int/cps/en/natohq/topics_181779.htm

126. R 15.

127. R 16. Discussing deployment in Africa.

128. R 9.

129. Scribner, St Benoit, Tabeling, Hazell, Thacker, Brau, Sizemore, Leitch, Kiser, and Strong, "Understanding Civil Affairs Operations," 12.

130. R 9.

131. Landing Craft Air Cushion (LCAC) is an air-cushion vehicle used for landing the US Navy's Assault Craft Units.

132. R 75.

133. R 18.

134. R 13.

135. Gibbs, *First Do No Harm*; Anderson, *Do No Harm*; Donini, "Local Perceptions."

136. Mahembe and Odhiambo, "Does Foreign Aid Reduce Poverty?," 875–93.

137. Hingorani, "The New Deal for Engagement in Fragile States," 87–93.

138. Karlborg, "Enforced Hospitality," 425–48.

Conclusion

The challenge of ameliorating the sources of insecurity—be they economic, social, or physical security in gray spaces—or trying to create conditions for security lies in finding the root causes of problems, not in simply reacting to their symptoms. Historically, multilateral and bilateral aid agencies, along with international NGOs, tended to avoid project financing in these spaces except in the event of large-scale crises and emergencies. By contrast, these spaces, have not only been home to some of Special Operations Forces (SOF's) most lethal missions, but also their soft arm extension. For more than a decade, however, the scale and scope of developmental operations financed by aid donors and NGOs has exploded. Particularly, since the "New Deal" for engagement in fragile states, actors have focused on the roots of instability as well as on an "interconnectedness of the various risks, fragilities, and adaptive capacities," of different actors.[1]

As the constellation of security, social, and economic concerns continues to converge in fragile settings, civilian-military relationships are subject not only to an array of new tensions and challenges, but also opportunities. This is not only due to the commonly accepted difference between military and civilian actors' contrasting values. The difficulties in the relationship are also due to a series of functional, behavioral, and accountability measures. Inquiring into *how* these actors interact in the expansive fragile space, this analysis finds that these traditionally different organizations *converge* or *diverge* based on their differences or similarities, as they adapt themselves to navigate a newfound space accessible to them both. As they navigate the gray space, they converge operationally through a series of push factors, such as funding, optics by the community, and the need to meet populations' needs. Ultimately, the military *can* and *do* "soften up" just as development actors *can* and *do* "harden up." Where these actors cannot meet eye to eye is in their competing organizational cultures, conflicting objectives, and differing operational modalities.

This analysis has argued that despite their objectives being for security purposes, the humanitarian and development assistance SOF provide *can* have positive benefits to the local populations, and such assistance causes a natural convergence between SOF and civic actors in the low-intensity conflict space. In the eyes of the populace in fragile spaces, SOF are better off coordinating, consulting, and de-conflicting their efforts with NGOs. This immediately creates opportunities for better efficiencies between SOF and development actors. The obstacle is that SOF's self-serving approach as an organization causes it to simultaneously diverge away from the same civic actors. Ultimately, the traditionalists, such as Huntington and Gentile, would view this finding as a way to only further support their belief that the military's main job is to meet security objectives. Conversely, progressives such as Sarkesian and Scales would recognize that in threading the gray space, SOF's soft power is a necessity, not a choice. Similarly, NGOs, on their end, are rarely impartial and neutral actors. As they have grown in size and diversified in how they fund their work, they are savvy at navigating conflict spaces across the spectrum. There also seems to be an organically formed and tight-knit network of "military gone NGO" professionals who enrich, strengthen, and ultimately cause SOF and NGOs to converge in the spaces where they operate. This makes the relationship more efficient. While this convergence would not be viewed as fitting to the development debate, namely that the military and development actors belong together, Collier and Sachs would welcome this convergence as a necessary one, as long as the involvement of the external military can break the vicious cycle of insecurity. Also, with veterans from Iraq and Afghanistan joining humanitarian and development efforts as NGO workers, an expansion of available and experienced professionals has the potential to skew the qualified candidate pool and change the nature of the relationship between NGOs and the security forces.

When it comes to how these organizations compare at the ground level, both in terms of individuals and organizations, this analysis finds the contrary of what have been some of our long-held perceptions. Divergent from our general belief that the military outsizes and outspends development actors, at the project level, Department of Defense (DOD) spending on small-scale projects in the gray space is comparable and sometimes dwarfed by its NGO counterparts. This causes these entities to converge in size and scale of their programming. The analysis uncovers how small Civil Affairs (CA) SOF teams and small NGO footprints on the ground are similar in terms of how they budget, organize, and sometimes deploy. This is good news as it creates an impetus for these organizations to have comparable outcomes and more scalable project and recipient relationships. This symbiosis is simply a reflection of what Brooks describes to be the fading boundary between those who carry guns and those who carry stethoscopes. The military will continue to have a role in fragile spaces, as combatants and development actors. Collier would recognize the utility of this convergence as a way to break the cycle of insecurity and poverty. All of this is even more of a reason to find ways for these entities to work more closely and better together.

There is more positive news for the gray space and the evolving civil-military relationship. How well these entities work together is mostly dependent on the personalities of those involved at the ground level, not mandates or organizational arrangements. Scales and Mackinlay would not be surprised by how the behaviors of soldiers define NGOs' perceptions, too, not just those of the populations. McFate's analysis of the psychosocial skills the military needs to possess extends to what NGOs could also improve upon. Additionally, both of these organizations could ramp up their skills when dealing with populations, and each other. Organizations are ultimately human enterprises. What is needed for a productive civil-military relationship already exists. We should leverage it, as lengthy organizational bureaucratic processes or institutional change often prove too slow to react to the vast and changing state of modern conflict.

The last piece of good news for the civil-military relationship is perhaps the most important. When it comes to populations as beneficiaries of the goods and services provided by SOF and NGOs, in the gray space, populations give less importance to *whom* aid comes from, causing these entities to converge. Local communities' concerns with outsiders—military or civilian—are about the utility of the assistance provided, *how* outsiders behave inside their communities, and less on *who* they are. It is time that our organizational beliefs align with the needs and perception lenses of populations in the gray space, especially as they will account for more than a quarter of the world's population in less than seven years from now. If those receiving assistance from outside actors, inside fragile gray spaces, give little importance to *whom* assistance comes from, perhaps it is time for us as outsiders to honestly re-evaluate if the rules by which we operate are relevant to anyone besides ourselves. This will be a reminder that we must adapt to a new reality of modern conflict and not expect that the majority of the world population, who will be residing in these spaces, will adapt to *us*. It is also a reminder that one of the key requirements in achieving favorable receptions among populations is for outside actors to give them agency in the process and greater community ownership. This will give better utilization and longer-term viability to anything which either the military or development actors do. As recipients are not only passive communities, their acceptance of what is being provided can make aid more effective.

RECOMMENDATIONS

This analysis has demonstrated that the impetus for convergence in the operating space typically comes from individual initiative, rather than institutional direction. Taking into account the merit of this work on why civil-military actors should better coordinate in the gray space, the following recommendations offer a series of small and practical steps, which can be applied at the individual level.

Expand sharing of information. SOF CA can work toward establishing open and robust mechanisms for storing and sharing information that can be available to civic actors. Ideally, this should be done through a formal and robust platform. In the absence of such, this can also be done at the individual level. The recent evacuation from Afghanistan, where those helping evacuate Afghans who worked for the Coalition were using WhatsApp Groups, Signal, and Facebook, proved that coordination and exchange of information can work well, even under the most pressing circumstances, and without pre-established and official mechanisms. Where such information exchange mechanisms already exist, SOF CA Teams and NGOs should look to institutionalize them for their successors through Memoranda of Understanding. Ultimately, this will help both entities have more accurate and reliable information about the terrain and help them coordinate and become more effective. As a start, it would be by remembering that nothing that occurs in the gray space should lead any of these organizations—military or NGOs— to believe that they are the only game in town. To ignore the other side or to constantly find reasons for why engagement is *not* possible or necessary, undermines an entire layer of this complex space.

Incorporate actors in joint planning where appropriate. Working on the advice and insights of the civil-military liaison officers within the United States Agency for International Development (USAID), or other donor agencies, and DOD, both of these entities should explore how to carve out space to help one another in their planning processes. How can planning look differently at the local level, and with actors outside of the organization or the interagency? Particularly, the military must weigh the benefits and disadvantages of classifying information. As the gray space converges these actors, there is a riper opportunity to rethink the traditional ways in which information is classified and utilized. In some of the interviews, when asked what the ideal NGO-military relationship would look like, NGOs expressed that they would want to be part of the military planning processes. SOF CA are predominantly working in the unclassified space. Almost all information is open information. Fragile contexts are ripe opportunities for inquiry, unlike high-intensity ones. In an attempt to get away from the lethal, SOF must do a better job at reassuring development actors. The key outcome of including each other in the process would be to allow for mid-course correction, and more accurate programmatic design and outcomes for all parties—humanitarian, development, and security.

Institutionalize a community of practice. In conducting interviews, many of the groups interested in this space and analysis belong only to the military or only to the development side. There is a wealth of interest in creating an official civil-military community. Such is already the Civil Affairs Association on the military side, most of the members within which are United States Government (USG) with former military experience. For NGOs, InterAction serves the purpose of exchanging and collaborating. These groups should consider engaging in a systematic dialogue through an independent party from within USG, which holds credibility with both sides. A community of interest would also be a platform for information exchange aimed at reducing information gaps, working with more current information, and making more accurate assessments for the future. It seems that much of this dialogue has waned with the end of the big wars in Iraq and Afghanistan. Yet, there are so many lessons to be drawn, and plenty of room and need to still apply them.

Measure relationship durability. In a few of the interactions with the military, respondents did identify a positive working relationship with an NGO as an indicator of success in the gray space. Currently, these organizations focus on the quantifiable outputs of their missions. For the military, certain objectives are easy to count—the number of people detained, insurgents targeted or killed. In their role as development actors—how many wells were built, and bridges repaired? The same is true for NGOs, whose success is measured by the number of blankets handed out, or schools built. But there is an obvious need to measure the longevity of the joint relationship. Simple and routine mechanisms can be established for the military to measure how effectively it is engaging with development and civic actors. How frequent are the interactions between security and non-security actors? Are they positive/negative? Why? Do they add value? Who shows up to the meeting? The civil-military relationship is a test of both of these actors' abilities to engage with someone unlike themselves. If the military does a poor job at engaging with NGOs who have a strong understanding of the local context, it would most certainly do a poor job at engaging with populations. A closer relationship would ultimately help for better coordination, which would help information exchange and cost-effective use of resources, avoid redundancy, create more favorable outcomes, and harmonize efforts.

Create practical skills through training and learning. Much of the collaboration and coordination in these actors' learning and engaging together is between DOD and USAID at the strategic and operational levels, and at the level of the interagency. More should be done at the ground level. This should be done preemptively, and not only when an NGO becomes contracted as an implementing partner. DOD can also invite some of the NGOs with whom it deals regularly to its training courses, and as appropriate. DOD's myriad educational institutions, such as the National Defense University, the Naval War College, the Naval Postgraduate School, and DOD's school houses, to mention a few, should invite NGOs to participate in instruction, where possible and applicable. NGOs may also be better positioned to provide mission-critical information on social and cultural conditions in fragile contexts.

Similarly, DOD should try to set conditions within its institutions to entice non-security actors into its activities. For instance, it should continiously seek out opportunities to send its men and women to the various courses offered by both humanitarian and development actors in Geneva, New York, or at any headquarters of major NGOs, but also the field level. Both of these different approaches have become even more accessible post-COVID with online courses becoming increasingly available. This would enable both of these actors to consider how they can replicate these skills in their respective organizations and to develop more robust and flexible tools for assessments of long-term development needs. Existing resources on how to conduct civil-military engagements should be leveraged. Where such resources—trainings, guidelines, manuals, scenarios, to mention a few—are lacking or are outdated, they should be created by bringing the talents and insights of both organizations.

Identify strategic areas of collaboration. Finding areas of collaboration would ultimately increase coordination, avoid overlap, and decrease conflict between military and civilian actors. The military and NGOs may have approaches to engaging with communities in which they operate based on the length of time these entities are in the country and based on their specialties; these differences can be leveraged to identify common areas for collaboration. For example, the military can leverage its capabilities in health security while NGOs can develop innovative mechanisms for medical assistance to vulnerable communities. The response to COVID-19 provides an instructive case in point. The military set up hospitals, provided protective equipment, and conducted research, while the NGOs provided emergency medical assistance to outbreak areas. Because of the military's short-term cycles, they can provide medical care, while NGOs can perform the follow-up. This can also facilitate opportunities for joint planning, as mentioned above.

This is not to imply that the military should take the proper place of bilateral, multilateral, and non-governmental actors in the development and humanitarian space. Nor does it dismiss the utilization of current civil-military coordination guidelines or mechanisms, such as through United Nations Office for the Coordination of Humanitarian Affairs, where and to the extent to which they apply. Most importantly, neither foreign military nor outside development actors should drive the agenda, replace local solutions or government structures. As the fragile space expands, so will the need to tackle it in a much more systematic, practical, flexible, and sustainable way. It is unrealistic to think either of these entities—NGOs or SOF CA—can tackle it alone. Both entities have a large pool to draw from, and as a result, more responsibility.

A FINAL NOTE

The last twenty years have been a testing laboratory for the civil-military relationship. What we have seen is that the space between war and peace is not an empty one, but a rich tapestry of civilians, combatants, humanitarians, soldiers, and private or public entities, internationals and locals, operating for the short and long run. Much of our energy has been spent on placing these entities into their institutional boxes, debating giving or denying them access, dividing and conquering where they should operate, and most importantly, *how*. But with or without such a debate, these entities have already carved out a role for themselves in the non-linear gray space. This will continue to be the case, as "US military forces will be continually engaged in some dynamic combination of combat, security, engagement, and relief and reconstruction."[2] The most noticeable and urgent need for this is happening right now with the chronic impact of climate change.

SOF and NGOs should seize this opportunity and work toward the establishment of a closer relationship, as working separately, they will undermine each other. They have what it takes to be effective partners in this gray space. With this synergy comes a responsibility. For SOF, they have an obligation to reassure their civic counterparts that they can be trustworthy partners and can establish new areas for collaboration without treating everything and everyone as an asset in chasing down terrorists. SOF *must* go back to their roots, stop killing their way to victory, and prove that they *can* transform their wholesale hard killing power into a retail soft power beyond what they are already doing. They can re-learn, return, and re-engage away from their lethality, to what was once their core craft of working with and among populations and other civic actors. This is especially if they are serious about preventing sources of insecurity, which span beyond just security and into the socioeconomic layers of a society. It is exactly because of this blend of sources of insecurity that NGOs and development actors, too, have a responsibility. On their end, development actors have the institutional know-how on what, other than security, causes fragility from a socioeconomic angle. An effort should be made to educate everyone else that is in this space, as NGOs have much to teach security actors in this process.

One in four people in the world will be a customer of development and security actors in fragile settings. These spaces will not be conventional or large in magnitude. They will be minuscule, omnipresent, and chronic. Operating in a conventional military context for security forces, and conventional development contexts for NGOs, will become the exception, not the rule. It is because of these realities that both sides must seize the moment of the challenges they *both* face, and find more and better ways to start coming to the table less coincidently and more deliberately. What has drawn these two together is that both SOF and NGOs know that viewing the world only through one prism—security or development is not how the needs of populations in this expansive and complex space can be met. They also know that dividing the world between them is not how their relationship can flourish. As warriors, development actors, and humanitarians in a space which is constantly shifting between war and peace, these actors should embrace the unavoidable fading of the barrier between them.

NOTES

1. Ingram and Papoulidis, "Rethinking How to Reduce State Fragility."
2. Muggah, "Chapter Two: Stabilising," 44.

Appendix 1

Methodology

INTERVIEWS

Because of limited access to the field due to COVID restrictions, the majority of data gathering was carried out remotely. Remote data gathering included phone interviews, video, email correspondence, and a survey. This allowed for greater access to military participants, less access to NGOs, and limited access to populations. The survey provided data from a community in the Philippines. A total of eighty-seven individuals took part in this study. These individuals were selected from my own professional experience and networks in the field. The lack of in-person interviewing did not compromise the quality of the data in any way.[1] The responses from groups engaged to collect primary data are as follows:

- 42 U.S. military respondents to include civil affairs, psychological operations, and special forces.
- 1 host nation military respondent.
- 28 NGO respondents. These include local and international NGOs, including, but not limited to, implementing partners of USAID, as well as USAID and OTI staff. Respondents also included international multilateral organizations, U.S. diplomats serving in the Department of State.
- 16 population respondents.

Both primary and secondary interview data have been used throughout the analysis. The military included conversations with a mix of tactical, operational, and strategic-level professionals. On the NGO side, respondents represented international and local NGOs, donor agencies, and international organizations that employ NGOs or INGOs as implementing partners. In chapter 6—The Center of Gravity—which discusses the military and NGO perception of populations, secondary data dominates. This is in addition to primary data gained from several interviewees and surveys. Population data also included speaking to NGO workers and host nation military in their capacity as citizens of their community, which benefits from military and NGO projects. What imbalance exists between these groups and the approach taken is due to limited physical access in traveling to the field. The open-ended qualitative questions posed to interviewees are presented in table A.1 as follows:

Table A.1 Semi-Structured Interview Framing

Recipients	Military Personnel	NGO Personnel
Theme 1: Consultation between entities/groups		
Does the military consult with you/listen to your needs? How do they do/not do that? When and how often?	Do you consult with/listen to local communities? How do you prioritize humanitarian projects?	Does the military consult with you? Do they understand your role? Do they coordinate with you? Why? Why not? How? Do you proactively coordinate with them? Why? Why not? How?
Theme 2: Cross-perceptions		
What do you understand about the role of the military? What is their main purpose here? Please explain. What do you understand about the role of the NGO? What is their main purpose here? Please explain.	What do you understand about the role of the local community? Do you believe that you understand their needs? Why/why not?	What do you understand to be the role of the local community? What do you understand to be the role of the military? What is their main purpose? Please explain.
Theme 3: Project follow-up and end-use		
Are the projects provided by the military of utility to you? Why? Why not?	How do you measure whether the projects provided by you to the local community are of utility to them? Who do you speak with? When? How often?	Are the projects the military provides to locals of utility to them? Why? Why not? How do you know? How do they compare to your projects? How do you measure that? How do they compare to projects you have delivered based on coordination with the military?

(continued)

Table A.1   Semi-Structured Interview Framing (Continued)

Recipients	Military Personnel	NGO Personnel
Theme 4: Behavior, attributes, and credibility		
If the U.S. military promised to provide your community with a public good or service in the future, would this promise be credible? Please describe why/why not.	If you committed to providing a public good or service to the community, how do you believe that it would be received? What leads you to your answer?	If you committed to providing a public good or service to the community, how do you believe that it would be received? What leads you to your answer? If the military committed to providing a public good or service, together with you, to the community, how do you believe that this coordination would be received by the community? What leads you to your answer?

Source: Author.

NOTE

1. Novick, "Is There a Bias against Telephone Interviews," 391–98.

Appendix 2

Typology of Civilian and Military Entities' Attributes

A typology of relevant SOF/military vs. NGO attributes. When examined more closely, these entities possess many different but also similar characteristics (table A.2 on the next page).

Table A.2 General SOF and NGO Operational Attributes

	SOF	NGO
Objectives	• Security	• Development/Humanitarian assistance
Constraints	• Possible hostility by the population	• Accepted by the population
	• Full access	• Some limit to access
	• Host militaries as counterparts	• Donors and host nation government
Modalities of field operation	• Lethal/hard-power oriented	• Non-lethal/soft-power oriented
	• Partial/non-neutral	• Sometimes impartial/neutral
	• Training	• Broader scope
	• Small footprint	• Variable footprint
	• Plans short-term and reactively	• Plans long-term and proactively
	• Short deployments	• Can respond short-term, reactive to immediate needs
		• Permanence
Organizational characteristics	• Specialized/generalist	• Multi-sector
	• Hierarchical (flat at field level)	• Flat
	• Autonomous	• Entrepreneurial
	• Relationships with multiple actors	• Relationship with few actors
	• Vertical accountability	• Horizontal accountability
	• Does not adapt to receive resources	• Adapts to receive resources
Programmatic Characteristics	• Reinforced by an organizational hub	• No organizational hub
	• Exclusively small in scale	• Variable scale
	• Little monitoring and evaluation of activities	• Significant monitoring and evaluation of activities
Communication with actors	• Classified or restricted	• Open (depending on context)
	• Some consultation with populations	• Varying degrees of consultation with populations
Assessing local needs	• No in-depth assessment to identify entry points	• Needs in-depth assessment to identify entry points
	• Low knowledge of the intricacies of the local community	• High knowledge of the intricacies of the local community

Source: Author.

Bibliography

Aall, Pamela, and Dan Snodderly. "Introduction." In *Responding to Violent Conflicts and Humanitarian Crises*. Eds., Pamela Aall and Dan Snodderly, 13. Cham: Palgrave Macmillan, 2021.

Aall, Pamela and Jeffrey W. Helsing. "Non-Governmental Organizations." In *Responding to Violent Conflicts and Humanitarian Crises*. Eds., Pamela Aall and Dan Snodderly, 53–87. Cham: Palgrave Macmillan, 2021.

Abiew, Francis Kofi. "From Civil Strife to Civic Society: NGO-Military Cooperation in Peace Operations." *Occasional Paper* 39 (2003): 11.

Abiew, Francis K., and Tom Keating. "NGOs and UN Peacekeeping Operations: Strange Bedfellows." *International Peacekeeping*. 6, no. 2 (2007): 89–111.

Abu-Sada, Caroline. "Introduction." In *Dilemmas, Challenges, and Ethics of Humanitarian Action: Reflections on Médecins Sans Frontières' Perception Project*. Ed., Caroline Abu-Sada. McGill-Queen's University Press, 2012.

Aikins, Matthieu. "Last Tango in Kabul." *Rolling Stone Magazine*. August 18, 2014. https://www.rollingstone.com/politics/politics-news/last-tango-in-kabul-2-228927/.

Aldis, William. "Health security as a public health concept: a critical analysis." *Health Policy and Planning*. 23, no. 6 (2008): 369–375.

Allen, Nathanael L. "Leader development in dynamic and hazardous environments: Company commander learning in combat. Doctoral Dissertation. The George Washington University, 2006. https://www.proquest.com/pagepdf/305331952?accountid=36339.

Amnesty International. "Stars on their shoulders. Blood on their hands: War crimes committed by the Nigerian military." Amnesty International, 2015. https://www.amnesty.org/en/wp-content/uploads/2021/05/AFR4416572015ENGLISH.pdf.

Anderson, Mary B. *Do No Harm: How Aid can Support Peace - or War*. Boulder, CO: Lynne Rienner Publishers, 1999.

Anderson, Mary B., Dayna Brown and Isabella Jean. *Time to Listen: Hearing People on the Receiving End of International Aid*. Cambridge, MA: CDA Collaborative Learning Projects, 2012.

Angba, A.O., P. Ekuri, and I. A. Akpabio. "Performance of Non Governmental Organizations' Workers in Rural Development in Cross River State, Nigeria." *Journal of International Social Research*. 1, no. 2 (2008): 35–46.

Anheier, Helmut K. *Nonprofit Organizations: Theory, Management, Policy*. London: Routledge, 2014.

Ankersen, Christopher. *The Politics of Civil-Military Cooperation: Canada in Bosnia, Kosovo, and Afghanistan*. Springer, 2014.

Armed Forces Staff College. "Anthony Zinni. Operations Other Than War." *YouTube* video, 1:17:59. 1993. https://www.youtube.com/watch?v=kd_k90iL9q4.

Autesserre, Séverine. "International Peacebuilding and Local Success: Assumptions and Effectiveness." *International Studies Review.* 19, no. 1 (2017): 114–32.

Bachmann, Jan. "Whose Hearts and Minds? A Gift Perspective on the US Military's Aid Projects in Eastern Africa." *Political Geography.* 61 (2017): 11–18.

Bachmann, Jan. "Kick Down the Door, Clean up the Mess, and Rebuild the House–The Africa Command and Transformation of the US Military." *Geopolitics.* 15, no. 3 (2010): 564–85.

Baker, Jon. "Quick Impact Projects: Towards a Whole of Government Approach." *Paterson Review.* 8 (2007): 1–21.

Baldursdóttir, Sigríður, Geir Gunnlaugsson, and Jónína Einarsdóttir. "Donor Dilemmas in a Fragile State: NGO-ization of Community Healthcare in Guinea-Bissau." *Development Studies Research.* 5, no. sup1 (2018): S27–S39.

Banfield, Garric M., and Jonathan G. Bleakley. "The role of civil affairs in unconventional warfare." Master's Thesis. Naval Postgraduate School Monterey, CA Defense Analysis Dept, 2012. https://apps.dtic.mil/sti/pdfs/ADA573583.pdf.

Bell, Sam R., Amanda Murdie, Patricia Blocksome, and Kevin Brown. "Force Multipliers: Conditional Effectiveness of Military and INGO Human Security Interventions." *Journal of Human Rights.* 12, no. 4 (2013): 397–422.

Bibb, Andrew. "Destruction, Creation, and Engagement." *Civil Affairs Association Eunomia Journal.* (2020). https://www.civilaffairsassoc.org/post/destruction-creation-and-engagement (online journal).

Bjork, Kjell, and Richard Jones. "Overcoming Dilemmas Created by the 21st Century Mercenaries: Conceptualising the Use of Private Security Companies in Iraq." *Third World Quarterly.* 26, no. 4–5 (2005): 777–96.

Bourdeaux, Margaret Ellis, Lynn Lawry, Eugene V. Bonventre, and Frederick M. Burkle. "Involvement of the US Department of Defense in Civilian Assistance, Part I: A Quantitative Description of the Projects Funded by the Overseas Humanitarian, Disaster, and Civic Aid Program." *Disaster Medicine and Public Health Preparedness.* 4, no. 1 (2010): 66–73.

Brainard, Lael, Derek Chollet, and Vinca LaFleur. "Chapter 1: The Tangled Web: The Poverty-Insecurity Nexus." In *Too Poor for Peace? Global Poverty, Conflict, and Security in the 21st Century.* Eds., Lael Brainard and Derek Chollet. Brookings Institution Press, 2007.

Brass, Jennifer N., Wesley Longhofer, Rachel S. Robinson, and Allison Schnable. "NGOs and International Development: A Review of Thirty-Five Years of Scholarship." *World Development.* 112 (2018): 136–49.

Breede, Christian H. "Special (Peace) Operations: Optimizing SOF for UN Missions." *International Journal.* 73, no. 2 (2018): 221–40.

Bremer, Catherine, and Andrew Cawthorne. "Haiti Says 200,000 may be Dead, Violence Breaks Out." *Reuters.* January 14, 2010. https://www.reuters.com/article/us-quake-haiti/haiti-says-200000-may-be-dead-violence-breaks-out-idUSTRE60B5IZ20100115.

Brennan, John, Steve Marks, and Ed Croot. "The Turmoil of Identity Crisis: Special Forces Organizational Culture." *A Better Peace: the War Room Podcast,* August 4, 2020. https://podcasts.apple.com/ke/podcast/a-better-peace-the-war-room-podcast/id1368621724.

Brewer, R. Christion. "US Army Civil Affairs and the Fate of Reserve Special Operations Forces in Support of Current and Future Operations." Academic Research Project. Army War College Carlisle Barracks, PA, 2004. https://apps.dtic.mil/sti/pdfs/ADA423315.pdf.

Brière, Sophie, Denis Proulx, Olga Navaro Flores, and Mélissa Laporte. "Competencies of Project Managers in International NGOs: Perceptions of Practitioners." *International Journal of Project Management.* 33, no. 1 (2015): 116–25.

Brinkerhoff, Derick W. "Developing Capacity in Fragile States." *Public Administration and Development: The International Journal of Management Research and Practice.* 30, no. 1 (2010): 66–78.

Brinkerhoff, John R. "Waging the War and Winning the Peace: Civil Affairs in the War with Iraq." Andrulis Research Corporation, Arlington, VA: US Army Reserve, 1991. https://apps.dtic.mil/sti/pdfs/ADA288659.pdf.

Brooke, James. "VIGILANCE AND MEMORY: KANDAHAR; Pentagon Tells Troops in Afghanistan: Shape Up and Dress Right." *The New York Times.* Sept. 12, 2002. https://www.nytimes.com/2002/09/12/us/vigilance-memory-kandahar-pentagon-tells-troops-afghanistan-shape-up-dress-right.html.

Brooks, Rosa. *How Everything Became War and the Military Became Everything.* New York: Simon & Schuster, 2016.

Brown, Graham K., and Arnim Langer. "Horizontal Inequalities and Conflict: A Critical Review and Research Agenda." *Conflict, Security & Development.* 10, no. 1 (2010): 27–55.

Brown, L. David, and David C. Korten. "Understanding Voluntary Organizations: Guidelines for Donors." Policy Research Working Paper Series No. 258. The World Bank, 1989. https://ideas.repec.org/p/wbk/wbrwps/258.html.

Brown, Stephen, and Jörn Grävingholt. "Chapter 1: Security Development and the Securitization of Foreign Aid: Trends, Explanations and Prospects." In *The Securitization of Foreign Aid.* Eds., Stephen Brown and Jörn Grävingholt, 237–55. London: Palgrave Macmillan, 2015.

Brown, Stephen, Jörn Grävingholt, and Rosalind Raddatz. "Chapter 11: Trends, Explanations, and Prospects." In *The Securitization of Foreign Aid.* Eds., Stephen Brown and Jörn Grävingholt, 237–55. London: Palgrave Macmillan, 2015.

Bruce B. Bingham, Daniel L. Rubini and Michael J. Cleary, "US Army Civil Affairs: The Army's ounce of Prevention." The Institute of Land Warfare, The Land Warfare Papers, 41, 2003. https://www.ausa.org/sites/default/files/LWP-41-US-Army-Civil-Affairs-The-Armys-Ounce-of-Prevention.pdf.

Burduja, Radu. "Use of Special Operations Forces in United Nations Missions: A Method to Resolve Complexity." Master's Thesis US Army School for Advanced Military Studies Fort Leavenworth United States, 2015. https://apps.dtic.mil/sti/citations/AD1001250.

Burke, Kevin. "Civil Reconnaissance: Separating the Insurgent from the Population." Master's Thesis. Naval Postgraduate School, Monterey CA, 2007. https://apps.dtic.mil/sti/pdfs/ADA475781.pdf.

Büthe, Tim, Solomon Major, and André de Mello e Souza. "The Politics of Private Foreign aid: Humanitarian Principles, Economic Development Objectives, and Organizational Interests in NGO Private Aid Allocation." *International Organization.* 66, no. 4 (2012): 571–607.

Cancian, Mark F. "US Military Forces in FY 2021: The Last Year of Growth?." Center for Strategic and International Studies Report, 2021.

Catapang, Gabriel, Stephen Chaisson, Rebecca Gong, Joanna Hecht, Shannon Hiller, John Houston, Amanda Hsiao. "Lessons for US Doctrine: Challenges in Stabilization Operations." Graduate Policy Workshop Report. Princeton: Woodrow Wilson School of Public & International Affairs, 2015. https://wws.princeton.edu/sites/default/files/content/Stabilization Workshop Report FINAL 2015.pdf.

Cecchine, Gary, Forrest E. Morgan, Michael A. Wermuth, Timothy Jackson, Agnes Gereben Schaefer, and Matthew Stafford. *The U.S. Military Response to the 2010 Haiti Earthquake: Considerations for Army Leaders.* Santa Monica, CA: RAND Corporation, 2013. https://www.rand.org/pubs/research_reports/RR304.html.

Center for Strategic and international Studies Report, 2021. https://csis-website-prod.s3.amazonaws.com/s3fs-public/publication/210107_Cancian_FY2021_Other.pdf.

Cheadle, Samuel P. "Private Military Contractor Liability under the Worldwide Personal Protective Services II Contract." *Public Contract Law Journal.* 38/3 (2009): 690.

Church of Jesus Christ of Latter-day Saint. "2020 Annual Report." https://www.latterdaysaintcharities.org/annual-reports/2020?lang=eng.

Civil Affairs Association. "2020 Civil Affairs Symposium Report." December 23, 2020. https://ca-roundtable.heysummit.com.

Civil Affairs Association. "2021 Civil Affairs Symposium Report." December 30, 2021. https://fb9cc97d-daff-4fca-bc96-2d807a0888c6.filesusr.com/ugd/efc179_0c2444b267764cb6a520de0 5213f65ce.pdf.

Civil Affairs Association. "Civil Affairs Association Roundtable 2022." April 5, 2022.

Collier, Paul. *The Bottom Billion: Why the Poorest Countries are Failing and What Can Be Done About it.* New York: Oxford University Press, 2008.

Collinson, Sarah and Samir Elhawary. "Humanitarian Space: A Review of Trends and Issues." Humanitarian Policy Group. Report 32, 2012. https://cdn.odi.org/media/documents/7643.pdf.

Cornell Law School. "10 U.S. Code § 333 - Foreign Security Forces: Authority to Build Capacity." Legal Information Institute, 2016. https://www.law.cornell.edu/uscode/text/10/333.

Croot, Edward C. "There is an Identity Crisis in Special Forces. Who are the Green Berets Supposed to Be?." Fellows Strategy Research Project Thesis. Army War College, Carlisle, PA, 2020. https://warroom.armywarcollege.edu/wp-content/uploads/FSRP-AY20-USAWC-Fellow-COL-Ed-Croot-14-April-20.pdf.

Curtis E. LeMay Center for Doctrine and Development Education. *Introduction to Foreign Internal Defense.* Air Force Doctrine Publication (AFDP) 3-22. United States Air Force, 2020. https://www.doctrine.af.mil/Portals/61/documents/AFDP_3-22/3-22-D01-FID-Introduction.pdf.

D'Alelio, Drew. "US Aid to Fragile States: Where Does the Money Go?" *Center for Global Development,* June 11, 2018. https://www.cgdev.org/blog/us-aid-fragile-states-where-does-money-go.

Davis, Paul K., Eric V. Larson, Zachary Haldeman, Mustafa Oguz, and Yashodhara Rana. "Understanding and Influencing Public Support for Insurgency and Terrorism." RAND National Defense Research Institute, SANTA MONICA CA, 2012. https://apps.dtic.mil/sti/citations/ADA562875.

De Waal, Alex. *Famine That Kills.* Oxford University Press, 2005.

Defense Security Cooperation Agency. "Chapter 12 – Overseas Humanitarian, Disaster, and Civic Aid (OHDACA)." https://samm.dsca.mil/chapter/chapter-12#C12.1 (last accessed May 23, 2022).

Defense Security Cooperation Agency. *Evaluation of Department of Defense (DoD) Programs and Activities funded with the Overseas Humanitarian. Disaster, and Civic Aid (OHDACA) Appropriation.* Defense Security Cooperation Agency: 2020. (Unpublished in possession of author).

Defense Security Cooperation Agency. *Overseas Humanitarian, Disaster, and Civic Aid.* Fiscal Year (FY) 2021 Budget Estimates. Washington DC: Defense Security Cooperation Agency, 2020. https://comptroller.defense.gov/Portals/45/Documents/defbudget/fy2021/budget_justification/pdfs/01_Operation_and_Maintenance/O_M_VOL_1_PART_2/OHDACA_OCO_OP-5.pdf.

Defense Security Cooperation Agency. *President's Budget 2019 Defense Security Cooperation Agency.* Exhibit R-2, RDT&E Budget Item Justification. Washington DC: Defense Security Cooperation Agency, 2018. https://apps.dtic.mil/descriptivesum/Y2019/Other/DSCA/stamped/U_0605147T_7_PB_2019.pdf.

Defense Security Cooperation Agency. *Strategic Plan 2025: Security Through Global Partnerships.* Washington DC: Defense Security Cooperation Agency, 2021. https://www.dsca.mil/sites/default/files/2021-05/dsca_strategic_plan_2025.pdf.

Defense Visual Information Distribution Service - https://www.dvidshub.net/search?filter[type]=image.

Defense Visual Information Distribution Service. "MEDFLAG - Medical Assistance Project by USAFRICOM Combined Joint Task Force – Horn of Africa." Photograph by Lesley Waters. August 7, 2009. https://www.dvidshub.net/image/195444/medflag-09.

Defense Visual Information Distribution Service. "Military Veterinarians Fosters Connection Between U.S., Beninese People." June 11, 2009. https://www.dvidshub.net/image/179302/military-veterinarians-fosters-connection-between-us-beninese-people (accessed on December 2021).

Delcoure, Dustin E. "The Smooth Operator: Understanding Cross-Cultural Interpersonal Skills in Special Operations." Master's Thesis. Naval Postgraduate School Monterey, CA, 2014. https://apps.dtic.mil/sti/pdfs/ADA621011.pdf.

Department of Defense Joint Chiefs of Staff. *Department of Defense Dictionary of Military and Associated Terms.* Joint Publication 1-02. Washington DC: Joint Chiefs of Staff, 2016. https://www.jcs.mil/Portals/36/Documents/Doctrine/pubs/dictionary.pdf.

Department of Defense Security Cooperation Agency. *Overseas Humanitarian, Disaster, and Civic Aid (OHDACA)*. Fiscal Year 2022 President's Budget. Washington DC: Department of Defense, 2021. https://comptroller.defense.gov/Portals/45/Documents/defbudget/fy2022/budget_justification/pdfs/01_Operation_and_Maintenance/O_M_VOL_1_PART_2/OHDACA_OP-5.pdf.

Department of Defense. *Joint Operations*. Joint Publication 3-0. Washington DC: Joint Chiefs of Staff, August 11, 2011.

Desai, Raj M., and Homi Kharas. "What Motivates Private Foreign Aid? Evidence from Internet-based Microlending." *International Studies Quarterly*. 62, no. 3 (2018): 505–19.

Diehl, Glen B. and Solomon Major. "Measuring the Impact of US Global Health Engagements: An Econometric Approach." *Military Operations Research*. 21, no. 3 (2016): 37–50.

Dijkzeul, Dennis and Iguma Claude Wakenge. "Doing Good, but Looking Bad? Local Perceptions of Two Humanitarian Organisations in Eastern Democratic Republic of the Congo." *Disasters*. 34, no. 4, (2010): 1139–70.

DiMaggio, Paul J. and Walter W. Powell. "The Iron Cage Revisited: Institutional Isomorphism and Collective Rationality in Organizational Fields." *American Sociological Review*. 48, 2 (1983): 147–60.

Doctors Without Borders. "Ways to Give." https://www.doctorswithoutborders.org (last accessed January, 2, 2022).

Donini, Antonio. "Local Perceptions of Assistance to Afghanistan." *International Peacekeeping*. 14 no. 1 (2007).

Donovan II, R. J. "Medical Stability Operations: An Emerging Military Health Skill Set." (Presentation to the 2011 Military Health System Conference, January 24-27, National Harbor, Maryland, January 25, 2011.) https://apps.dtic.mil/sti/citations/ADA556389.

Drifmeyer, Jeff, and Craig Llewellyn. "Overview of Overseas Humanitarian, Disaster, and Civic Aid Programs." *Military Medicine*. 168, no. 12 (2003): 975–80.

Duffield, Mark. *Global Governance and the New Wars: The Merging of Development and Security*. London: Zed Books, 2014.

Eaglen, Mackenzie. "Putting Combatant Commanders on a Demand Signal Diet." *War on the Rocks*. November 9, 2020. https://warontherocks.com/2020/11/putting-combatant-commanders-on-a-demand-signal-diet/.

Ebrahim, Alnoor. "Accountability in Practice: Mechanisms for NGOs." *World Development*. 31, no. 5 (2003): 813–29.

Egnell, Robert. "Explaining US and British Performance in Complex Expeditionary Operations: The Civil-Military Dimension." *Journal of Strategic Studie*. 29, no. 6 (2006): 1041–75.

Egnell, Robert. "Civil-Military Aspects of Effectiveness in Peace Support Operations." Swedish Defense Research Agency, Defense Analysis: Stockholm, 2008.

Egnell, Robert. "Civil–Military Coordination for Operational Effectiveness: Towards a Measured Approach." *Small Wars & Insurgencies*. 24, no. 3 (2013): 237–56.

Enstad, Kjetil, and Paula Holmes-Eber. *Warriors Or Peacekeepers?: Building Military Cultural Competence*. Springer International Publishing AG, 2020.

Epstein, Aaron. "American Veterans, Medical Professionals Train Ukrainians in Combat Care." *Fox News*, March 29, 2022. https://video.foxnews.com/v/6302191615001#sp=show-clips.

Farina, Emily K., Lauren A. Thompson, Joseph J. Knapik, Stefan M. Pasiakos, James P. McClung, and Harris R. Lieberman. "Physical Performance, Demographic, Psychological, and Physiological Predictors of Success in the US Army Special Forces Assessment and Selection Course." *Physiology & Behavior*. 210 (2019): 112647.

Farmer, Steven M., and Donald B. Fedor. "Volunteer Participation and Withdrawal." *Nonprofit Management and Leadership*. 9, no. 4 (1999): 349–68.

Farrell III, William H. "No Shirt, No Shoes, No Status: Uniforms, Distinction, and Special Operations in International Armed Conflict." *Military Law Review*. 178 (2003): 94.

Fawaz,Mona. "Hezbollah as Urban Planner? Questions to and from Planning Theory." *Planning Theory* 8, no. 4 (2009): 323–34.

Fehrenbach, Heide, and Davide Rodogno. "A Horrific Photo of a Drowned Syrian Child: Humanitarian Photography and NGO Media Strategies in Historical Perspective." *International Review of the Red Cross.* 97, no. 900 (2015): 1121–55.

Fischl, Jack. "Almost 82 Percent of Social Workers are Female, and This is Hurting Men." *PolicyMic .com.* March 25, 2013. https://www.mic.com/articles/30974/almost-82-percent-of-social-workers -are-female-and-this-is-hurting-men#:~:text=Women%20constitute%2081.6%25%20of%20social ,in%20the%20next%20couple%20decades.

Flanigan, Shawn Teresa. "Nonprofit Service Provision by Insurgent Organizations: The Cases of Hizballah and the Tamil Tigers." *Studies in Conflict & Terrorism.* 31, no. 6 (2008): 499–519.

Flavin, William. "Civil Military Operations: Afghanistan. Observations on Civil Military Operations during the First Year of Operation Enduring Freedom." Research Project. Peacekeeping and Stability Operations Institute, ARMY War College Carlisle Barracks, PA, 2004. https://apps.dtic.mil /sti/pdfs/ADA593506.pdf.

Fowler, Alan. "Chapter 6: Development NGOs." In *The Oxford Handbook of Civil Society.* Ed., Michael Edwards, 42–54. Oxford University Press, 2011.

Fox, Sarah, Sophie Witter, Emily Wylde, Eric Mafuta, and Tomas Lievens. "Paying Health Workers for Performance in a Fragmented, Fragile State: Reflections from Katanga Province, Democratic Republic of Congo." *Health Policy and Planning.* 29, no. 1 (2014): 96–105.

Francis, Diana. "Culture, Power Asymmetries and Gender in Conflict Transformation." In *Transforming Ethnopolitical Conflict: The Berghof Handbook.* Eds., Austin, Alex, Martina Fischer, and Norbert Ropers, Springer Science & Business Media, 2013.

Franke, Volker. "The Peacebuilding Dilemma: Civil-Military Cooperation in Stability Operations." *International Journal of Peace Studies.* 11, no. 2 (2006): 5–25.

Freire, Maria Raquel, and Paula Duarte Lopes. "Peacebuilding in Timor-Leste: Finding a Way Between External Intervention and Local Dynamics." *International Peacekeeping.* 20, no. 2 (2013): 204–18.

Fyvie, Claire, and Alastair Ager. "NGOs and Innovation: Organizational Characteristics and Constraints in Development Assistance Work in The Gambia." *World Development* 27. no. 8 (1999): 1383–95.

Galula, David. *Counterinsurgency Warfare: Theory and Practice.* London and Dunmow: Pall Mall Press, 1964.

Gentile, Gian P. "A (slightly) Better War: A Narrative and Its Defects." *World Affairs.* 171, no. 1 (2008): 57–64.

Gentile, Gian. "The U.S. Army must Remain Prepared for Battle." *The Washington Post.* April 17, 2014. https://www.washingtonpost.com/opinions/gian-gentile-the-us-army-must-remain-prepared -for-battle/2014/04/17/78b2fc8c-b6c3-11e3-8cc3-d4bf596577eb_story.html.

Gibbs, David N. *First Do No Harm: Humanitarian Intervention and the Destruction of Yugoslavia.* Nashville: Vanderbilt University Press, 2009.

Gibson-Fall, Fawzia. "Military Responses to COVID-19, Emerging Trends in Global Civil-Military Engagements." *Review of International Studies.* 47, no. 2 (2021): 155–70.

Gilbert, Emily. "Money as a 'weapons system' and the entrepreneurial way of war." *Critical Military Studies.* 1, no. 3 (2015): 202–19.

Gisselquist, Rachel M. "Aid and Institution-Building in Fragile States: What Do We Know? What can Comparative Analysis Add?." *The ANNALS of the American Academy of Political and Social Science.* 656, no. 1 (2014): 6–21.

Glenn, Russell W. "Band of Brothers or Dysfunctional Family? A Military Perspective on Coalition Challenges During Stability Operations." Santa Monica, CA: RAND National Defense Research Institute, 2011. https://www.rand.org/pubs/monographs/MG903.html.

Gourevitch, Peter A., and David A. Lake. "Beyond Virtue: Evaluating and Enhancing the Credibility of Non-Governmental Organizations." In *The Credibility of Transnational NGOs: When Virtue is not Enough.* Eds., Peter A. Gourevitch, David A. Lake, and Janice Gross Stein. Cambridge, UK: Cambridge University Press, 2012.

Gowrinathan, Nimmi, and Kate Cronin-Furman. *The Forever Victims? Tamil Women in Post-War Sri Lanka.* New York, NY: Colin Powell School for Civic and Global Leadership

Gradishar, Kali. "Civil Affairs Teams Ensure Local Population Needs Met." *12th Air Force (Air Forces Southern).* June 18, 2014. https://www.12af.acc.af.mil/News/Article-Display/Article/667687/civil-affairs-teams-ensure-local-population-needs-met/.

Greene, Talya, Joshua Buckman, Christopher Dandeker, and Neil Greenberg. "The Impact of Culture Clash on Deployed Troops." *Military Medicine.* 175, no. 12 (2010): 958–63.

Grünewald, François, Claire Pirotte, and Bernard Husson. *Beneficiaries or Partners: The Role of Local Populations in Humanitarian Action.* Groupe URD, 2005.

Guttieri, Karen. "Humanitarian Space in Insecure Environments: A Shifting Paradigm." *Strategic Insights.* 4, no. 11 (2005).

Hall, Robert. "Political and Social Determinants of Disease Eradication." In *Disease Eradication in the 21st Century: Implications for Global Health.* Eds., Stephen L. Cochi and Walter R. Dowdle, 47–61. The MIT Press, 2011.

Hanhauser IV, George J. "Comprehensive Civil Information Management: How to Provide It." Master's Thesis. Army War College, Carlisle Barracks, PA, 2012. https://apps.dtic.mil/sti/pdfs/ADA563216.pdf.

Hart, Gary. Review of "My Share of the Task: A Memoir by Stanley McChrystal." *The National Interest,* March/April, no. 124 (2013): 81–88.

Hassan, Muhammad Mubbashar, Sajid Bashir, and Syed Moqaddas Abbas. "The Impact of Project Managers' Personality on Project Success in NGOs: The Mediating Role of Transformational Leadership." *Project Management Journal.* 48, no. 2 (2017): 74–87.

Hathaway, Oona A., Tobias Kuehne, Randi Michel, and Nicole Ng. "Congressional Oversight of Modern Warfare: History, Pathologies, and Proposals for Reform." *William & Mary Law Review.* 63 (2021): 137.

Hellinger, Daniel. "Humanitarian Action, NGOs and the Privatization of the Military." *Refugee Survey Quarterly.* 23, no. 4 (2004): 192–220.

Herbert, Siân. "Perception Surveys in Fragile and Conflict-Affected States." Governance and Social Development Resource Center, 2013. http://www.gsdrc.org/docs/open/hdq910.pdf.

Hilhorst, Dorothea. "Victims, Right Holders, Clients or Citizens? The Recipient Side of the Tsunami." In *The Netherlands Yearbook on International Cooperation.* Ed., Paul Hoebink.

Hilhorst, Dorothea, Ian Christoplos, Gemma Van, and Der Haar. "Reconstruction 'From Below': A New Magic Bullet or Shooting from the Hip?" *Third World Quarterly.* 31, no. 7 (2010). 1107–24.

Hinds, Travis, Thomas Ott, Michael Regan, Armando Pena, and Russell Schott. "Civil Affairs Veterinary and Agricultural Assessment, Analysis, and Planning Methodology." Group Research Project - Center for Nation Reconstruction and Capacity Development. United States Military Academy, West Point, New York, 2013. https://www.westpoint.edu/sites/default/files/inline-images/centers_research/national_reconstruction_capactity_development/pdf%20tech%20reports/CA%2520Final%2520Report.pdf.

Hingorani, Yannick. "The New Deal for Engagement in Fragile States: Where are We Now?" *Journal of Peacebuilding & Development.* 10, no. 2 (2015): 87–93.

Holshek, Christopher. "Humanitarian Civil-Military Coordination: Looking Beyond the 'Latest and Greatest'". In *History and Hope.* Ed., Kevin H. Cahill, 270–86. New York: Fordham University Press, 2013.

Holsti, Ole R. "Chapter 1: Of Chasms and Convergences: Attitudes and Beliefs of Civilian Elites at the Start of a New Millenium." In *Soldiers and Civilians: The Civil-Military Gap and American National Security.* Eds., Peter D. Feaver and Richard H. Kohn, 15–100. Cambridge, MA: MIT Press, 2001.

Holton, Tara L., Angela R. Febbraro, Emily-Ana Filardo, Marissa Barnes, Brenda Fraser, and Rachel Spiece. "The Relationship Between Non-Governmental Organizations and the Canadian Forces: A Pilot Study." Technical report. DEFENCE RESEARCH AND DEVELOPMENT, TORONTO CANADA, 2010. https://cradpdf.drdc-rddc.gc.ca/PDFS/unc216/p535308_A1b.pdf.

Human Data Exchange. "All Organisations." https://data.humdata.org/organization. (last accessed February 5, 2022).

Human Rights Watch. "Burkina Faso: Residents' Accounts Point to Mass Executions." July 8, 2020. https://www.hrw.org/news/2020/07/08/burkina-faso-residents-accounts-point-mass-executions#.

Huntington, Samuel. "New Contingencies, Old Roles." *Joint Force Quarterly*. no 2. (1993): 38–43.

Impl.Project. "Our Team." https://implproject.org/team/. (last accessed October 2, 2021).

Ingram, George and Jonathan Papoulidis. "Rethinking How to Reduce State Fragility." *Brookings*, March 29, 2017. https://www.brookings.edu/blog/up-front/2017/03/29/rethinking-how-to-reduce -state-fragility/.

Inigo, Jessica. "Civil Affairs Team Help Teach Senegalese Soldiers to Rely on Themselves." *US Africa Command, Public Affairs,* March 3, 2014. https://www.africom.mil/article/11813/senegal -ca-7-2014.

International Federation of Red Cross and Red Crescent. "Code of Conduct for the International Red Cross and Red Crescent Movement and NGOs in Disaster Relief." https://media.ifrc.org/ifrc/who -we-are/the-movement/code-of-conduct/ (last accessed June 23, 2021).

Jacobs, Jeffrey. "The Army's Civil Affairs Problems." *Real Clear Defense.* October 03, 2017. https:// www.realcleardefense.com/articles/2017/10/03/the_armys_civil_affairs_problems_112420.html #comments-container.

Jaff, Dilshad, Lewis Margolis, and Edward Reeder. "Civil–Military Interactions During Non-Conflict Humanitarian Crises: A Time to Assess the Relationship." *Defence Studies.* (2022): 1–16.

Jansen, Golie G. "Gender and War: The Effects of Armed Conflict on Women's Health and Mental Health." *Affilia.* 21, no. 2 (2006): 134–45.

Jaspars, Susanne and Daniel Maxwell. *Targeting in Complex Emergencies: Somalia Country Case Study.* Tufts University, MA, USA: Feinstein International Center, 2008.

Jenkins, Scott. "Operation Allies Welcome – Operation Allies Refuge." *USMC News.* September 27, 2021. https://www.quantico.marines.mil/News/Article/2789312/operation-allies-welcome-opera- tion-allies-refuge/.

Jeong, Ho- Won. *Peacebuilding in Postconflict Societies: Strategy & Process.* Boulder, CO: Lynne Rienner, 2005.

Joachim, Jutta, and Andrea Schneiker. "New Humanitarians? Frame Appropriation Through Private Military and Security Companies." *Millennium.* 40, no. 2 (2012): 365–388.

Joint Chiefs of Staff, "J 1 – Personnel, J2 – intelligence, J3 – Operations, J4 – Logistics, J5 – Plan- ning, J6 – Communications." - https://www.jcs.mil/Doctrine/Joint-Doctine-Pubs/ (last accessed April 1, 2022).

Junger, Sebastian. "How PTSD became a problem far beyond the battlefield." *Vanity Fair.* June 2015. https://www.vanityfair.com/news/2015/05/ptsd-war-home-sebastian-junger.

Kamenka, Eugene. "Gemeinschaft and Gesellschaft." *Political Science.* 17, no. 1 (1965): 3–12.

Karlborg, Lisa. "Enforced Hospitality: Local Perceptions of the Legitimacy of International Forces in Afghanistan." *Civil Wars.* 16, no. 4 (2014): 425–48.

Kassem, Susann. "22: Peacekeeping, Development, and Counterinsurgency: The United Nations Interim Force in Lebanon and Quick Impact Projects." In *Land of Blue Helmets.* Eds., Karim Makdisi, and Vijay Prashad. California: University of California Press, 2016.

Kay, Lena. "Indonesian Public Perceptions of the US and Their Implications for US Foreign Policy." *Issues and Insight.* 5 (2005): 3–64.

Keating, Vincent C., and Erla Thrandardottir. "NGOs, Trust, and the Accountability Agenda." *The British Journal of Politics and International Relations.* 19, no. 1 (2017): 134–51.

Khodyakov, Dmitry. "Trust as a Process: A Three-Dimensional Approach." *Sociology* 41, no. 1 (2008): 115–132. https://doi.org/10.1177/0038038507072285

Kilcullen, David. *The Accidental Guerilla: Fighting Small Wars in the Midst of a Big One.* London: Hurst and Company, 2009.

King, Elisabeth, and John C. Mutter. "Violent Conflicts and Natural Disasters: The Growing Case for Cross-Disciplinary Dialogue." *Third World Quarterly.* 35, no. 7 (2014): 1239–55.

Kingsley, Maria. "Ungoverned Space? Examining the FARC's Interactions with Local Populations in Northern Ecuador." *Small Wars & Insurgencies.* 25, no. 5–6 (2014): 1017–38.

Kober, Avi. "Low-Intensity Conflicts: Why the Gap Between Theory and Practise?." *Defense & Security Analysis.* 18, no. 1 (2002): 15–38.

Koffi, James Robert C. "Effects of DoD Engagements in Collaborative Humanitarian Assistance." Master's Thesis. Naval Postgraduate School, Monterey, CA, 2013. https://apps.dtic.mil/sti/pdfs/ADA589688.pdf.

Krulak, Charles C. "The Strategic Corporal: Leadership in the Three Block War: Operation Absolute Agility." *Marines Magazine.* January 1999. https://apps.dtic.mil/dtic/tr/fulltext/u2/a399413.pdf.

Lamb, Christopher J., and Evan Munsing. "Secret Weapon: High-Value Target Teams as an Organizational Innovation." National Defense University Institute for Strategic Studies, 2011. https://apps.dtic.mil/sti/pdfs/ADA540046.pdf.

Lamb, Robert D., and Kathryn Mixon. "Rethinking Absorptive Capacity: A New Framework, Applied to Afghanistan's Police Training Program." Center for Strategic and International Studies. Washington DC: Rowman & Littlefield, 2013. https://csis-website-prod.s3.amazonaws.com/s3fs-public/legacy_files/files/publication/130617_Lamb_RethinkingAbsorptiveCap_WEB.pdf.

Laurence, Janice H. "Military Leadership and the Complexity of Combat and Culture." *Military Psychology.* 23, no. 5 (2011): 489–501.

Lawry, Lynn. "Guide to Nongovernmental Organizations for the Military: A Primer for the Military About Private, Voluntary, and Nongovernmental Organizations Operating in Humanitarian Emergencies Globally." The Center for Disaster and Humanitarian Assistance Medicine (CDHAM) and US Department of Defense, Washington DC: 2009. https://fas.org/irp/doddir/dod/ngo-guide.pdf.

Leymarie, Philippe. "France's Unwinnable Sahel War." *Le Monde Diplomatique.* March 2021. https://mondediplo.com/2021/03/05mali.

Litt, David. "Why Is the United States in Niger, Anyway?." *Foreign Policy.* October 25, 2017. https://foreignpolicy.com/2017/10/25/why-is-the-united-states-in-niger-anyway/.

Lomoriello, Robert Schiano and Rachel Scott, "Chapter 4: What official development assistance went to fragile contexts?," in *States of Fragility*, 2018. Organisation for Economic Co-operation and Development, 2018.

Losey, Stephen. "After War Zone Scandals, Special Operators Are Curbing Deployments and Investing in Ethics Training." *Military Times.* 12 April 2021. https://www.military.com/daily-news/2021/04/12/after-war-zone-scandals-special-operators-are-curbing-deployments-and-investing-ethics-training.html.

Lythgoe, Trent. "Our Risk-Averse Army: How We Got Here and How to Overcome It." *Modern War Institute.* May 8, 2019. https://mwi.usma.edu/risk-averse-army-got-overcome/.

Mac Ginty, Robert. "Against Stabilization." *Stability: International Journal of Security and Development.* 1, no. 1 (2012).

MacDougall, Colin and Frances Baum. "The Devil's Advocate: A Strategy to Avoid Groupthink and Stimulate Discussion in Focus Groups." *Qualitative Health Research.* 7, no. 4 (1997): 532–541.

Mackinlay, John. "Co-operating in the Conflict Zone." NATO, 2002. https://www.nato.int/acad/fellow/99-01/mackinlay.pdf.

Madiwale, Ajay, and Kudrat Virk. "Civil–Military Relations in Natural Disasters: A Case Study of the 2010 Pakistan Floods." *International Review of the Red Cross.* 93, no. 884 (2011): 1085–1105.

Mahembe, Edmore, and Nicholas Mbaya Odhiambo. "Does Foreign Aid Reduce Poverty? A Dynamic Panel Data Analysis for Sub-Saharan African Countries." *The Journal of Economic Inequality.* 19, no. 4 (2021): 875–93.

Malcy, Kayla. "Publicly Available Information on the Private Military and NGO Relationship: A Case Study." Academic Thesis. University of Colorado, Boulder, 2018. https://scholar.colorado.edu/downloads/xk81jk990.

Marshall, Jeffery H., and David Suárez. "The Flow of Management Practices: An Analysis of NGO Monitoring and Evaluation Dynamics." *Nonprofit and Voluntary Sector Quarterly.* 43, no. 6 (2014): 1033–51.

Matelski, Thomas R. "Developing Security Force Assistance: Lessons from Foreign Internal Defense." Academic Thesis., School of Advanced Military Studies United States Army Command and General Staff College Fort Leavenworth, KS, 2008. https://apps.dtic.mil/sti/pdfs/ADA495486.pdf.

Mathieu, Fabien, and Nick Dearden. "Corporate Mercenaries: The Threat of Private Military & Security Companies." *Review of African Political Economy.* 34, no. 114 (2007): 744–55.

McCauley, Daniel. "Failing With Single-Point Solutions: Systems Thinking For National Security." *Small Wars Journal.* (2015).

McElligott, John E. "Leveraging Returned Peace Corps Volunteers." *Civil Affairs Association.* April 5, 2020. https://www.civilaffairsassoc.org/post/leveraging-returned-peace-corps-volunteers.

McFate, Montgomery. "Anthropology and Counterinsurgency: The Strange Story of Their Curious Relationship." *Military Review.* 85, no 2, (2005).

McGann, James, and Mary Johnstone. "The Power Shift and the NGO Credibility Crisis." *International Journal for Not-for-Profit Law.* 8 (2005).

McNeil, Mary, Andre Herzog, Sladjana Cosic, and PRISM Research. "Citizen Review of Service Delivery and Local Governance in Bosnia and Herzegovina." World Bank Governance Working Paper Series, 2009. https://assets.publishing.service.gov.uk/media/57a08b3de5274a27b2000a45/BIHWeb.pdf.

Mears, Emily Speers. "Private Military and Security Companies and Humanitarian Action." Professional Development Brief. Security Management Initiative, Geneva: 2009.

Mednick, Sam. "In Burkina Faso, US Troops Train Local Soldiers." *Pulitzer Center Mail & Guardian,* August 11, 2020. https://pulitzercenter.org/stories/burkina-faso-us-troops-train-local-soldiers.

Mellen, Ruby and Julia Ledur. "Afghanistan Faces Widespread Hunger Amid Worsening Humanitarian Crisis." *The Washington Post.* January 24, 2022. https://www.washingtonpost.com/world/2022/01/24/afghanistan-humanitarian-crisis-hunger/.

Miller, Laura L. "From Adversaries to Allies: Relief Workers' Attitudes Toward the US Military." *Qualitative Sociology.* 22, no. 3 (1999): 181–97.

Mizruchi, Mark S., and Lisa C. Fein. "The Social Construction of Organizational Knowledge: A Study of the Uses of Coercive, Mimetic, and Normative Isomorphism." *Administrative Science Quarterly.* 44, no. 4 (1999): 653–83.

Moyo, Dambisa. *Dead Aid: Why Aid is Not Working and How There is a Better Way for Africa.* New York: Farrar, Straus and Girous, 2009.

Muggah, Robert. "Chapter Two: Stabilising Fragile States and the Humanitarian Space." *Adelphi Series.* 50, no. 412–413 (2010): 33–52.

Murray, Williamson. "Does Military Culture Matter?." *Orbis.* 43, no. 1 (1999): 27–42.

Musa, Sallek Yaks, and Lindy Heinecken. "The Effect of Military (un) Professionalism on Civil-Military Relations and Security in Nigeria." *African Security Review.* (2022): 1–17.

Nagl, John A. *Learning to Eat Soup with a Knife: Counterinsurgency Lessons from Malaya and Vietnam.* Chicago, IL: University of Chicago Press, 2002.

Neuhaus, Susan J. "Chapter 9: Medical Aspects of Civil–Military Operations: The Challenges of Military Health Support to Civilian Populations on Operations." In *Civil-Military Cooperation in Post-Conflict Operations.* Ed., Christopher Ankersen, 219–242. London: Routledge, 2007.

Newbrander, William, Ronald Waldman, and Megan Shepherd-Banigan. "Rebuilding and Strengthening Health Systems and Providing Basic Health Services in Fragile States." *Disasters.* 35, no. 4 (2011): 639–60.

Newman, Patricia. *Army Special Forces: Elite Operations.* Minneapolis, MN: Lerner Publications Company, 2013.

Norwood. "Russian Hybrid Warfare Sparks New US Jedburgh Unit." SOFREP Military Grade Content, August 25, 2016. https://sofrep.com/news/americas-short-attention-span-double-edged-sword/.

Nouvet, Elysée, Caroline Abu-Sada, Sonya de Laat, Christine Wang, and Lisa Schwartz. "Opportunities, Limits and Challenges of Perceptions Studies for Humanitarian Contexts." *Canadian Journal of Development Studies.* 37, no. 3 (2016): 358–77.

Novick, Gina. "Is There a Bias Against Telephone Interviews in Qualitative Research?" *Research in Nursing & Health.* 31, no. 4 (2008): 391–98.

Nussbaum, Tobias, Eugenia Zorbas, and Michael Koros. "A New Deal for Engagement in Fragile States." *Conflict, Security & Development.* 12, no. 5 (2012): 559–87.

Oda, Yasuko. "Speed and Sustainability Reviewing the Long-Term Outcomes of UNHCR's Quick Impact Projects in Mozambique." United Nations High Commissioner for Refugees, Policy Development and Evaluation Services. 2011. https://www.unhcr.org/4e9829d09.pdf.

Organisation for Economic Co-operation and Development. *OECD Development Co-operation Peer Reviews: United States 2016.* Paris: OECD Publishing, 2016. doi: 10.1787/9789264266971-en.

Organisation for Economic Co-operation and Development. *States of Fragility 2018: Highlights.* OECD Publishing, 2018.

Østensen, Åse Gilje. "In the Business of Peace: The Political Influence of Private Military and Security Companies on UN Peacekeeping." *International Peacekeeping.* 20, no. 1 (2013): 33–47.

Otto, Gustav A. "The End of Operational Phases at Last." *InterAgency Journal.* 8, no. 3 (2017).

Overstreet, Lucas. "Building the Special Operations Force enterprise through Partnerships." *US Army.* March 1, 2012. https://www.army.mil/article/74620/building_the_special_operations_force_enterprise_through_partnerships.

PeaceCorps. "Peace Corps Announces Top States and Metropolitan Areas," December 7, 2009. https://www.peacecorps.gov/news/library/peace-corps-announces-top-states-and-metropolitan-areas-2/.

Petrik, Jaroslav. "Chapter 8: Provincial Reconstruction Teams in Afghanistan: Securitizing Aid through Developmentalizing the Military." In *The Securitization of Foreign Aid.* Eds., Stephen Brown and Jörn Grävingholt, 163–187. London: Palgrave Macmillan, 2015.

Pettit, Stephen J., and Anthony KC Beresford. "Emergency Relief Logistics: An Evaluation of Military, Non-Military and Composite Response Models." *International Journal of Logistics: Research and Applications.* 8, no. 4 (2005): 313–31.

Philipps, Dave, and Tim Arango. "Who Signs Up to Fight? Makeup of U.S. Recruits Shows Glaring Disparity." *The New York Times.* January 14, 2020. https://www.nytimes.com/2020/01/10/us/military-enlistment.html.

Pike, Thomas. "Beyond PMESII: Advancing JIPOE for Integrated Campaigning." *NSI - Future of Global Competition & Conflict Speaker Series,* October 3, 2019. https://nsiteam.com/beyond-pmesii-advancing-jipoe-for-integrated-campaigning/.

Platteau, Jean-Philippe. "Monitoring Elite Capture in Community-Driven Development." *Development and Change.* 35, no. 2 (2004): 223–46.

Pottier, Johan. "Why Aid Agencies Need Better Understanding of the Communities They Assist: The Experience of Food Aid in Rwandan Refugee Camps." *Disasters* 20, no. 4 (1996): 324–337.

Putnam, Robert. "Social Capital: Measurement and Consequences." Unpublished White Paper, OECD, 2001. https://www.oecd.org/innovation/research/1825848.pdf.

Roads for Life. "Tactical Casualty Combat Care." https://www.roadsforlife.org/courses/tccc (last accessed October 2, 2021).

Ruffa, Chiara, and Pascal Vennesson. "Fighting and Helping? A Historical-Institutionalist Explanation of NGO-Military Relations." *Security Studies.* 23, no 3 (2014): 582–620.

Ruffa, Chiara. "Military Cultures and Force Employment in Peace Operations." *Security Studies.* 26, no. 3 (2017): 391–22.

Ryan, Mick. "The Military and Reconstruction Operations." *Australian Journal of Multi-Disciplinary Engineering.* 6, no. 2 (2007): 181–90.

Rysaback-Smith, Heather. "History and Principles of Humanitarian Action." *Turkish Journal of Emergency Medicine.* 15 (2015): 5–7.

Sabrow, Sophia. "Local Perceptions of the Legitimacy of Peace Operations by the UN, Regional Organizations and Individual States–A Case Study of the Mali Conflict." *International Peacekeeping.* 24, no. 1 (2017): 159–86.

Sachs, Jeffrey D. *The End of Poverty: Economic Possibilities for our Time.* New York: Penguin Books, 2006.

Samaritan's Purse International Relief. "Careers for U.S. Military Veterans." https://www.samaritanspurse.org/our-ministry/u-s-military-veterans/. (last accessed July 1, 2021).

Sarkesian, Sam and Robert Connor Jr. *The US Military Profession into the Twenty-First Century: War, Peace and Politics.* Routledge, 1999.

Sarkesian, Sam C. *Beyond the Battlefield: The New Military Professionalism.* Permagon Press, 1981.

Savell, Stephanie and Rachel McMahon. "Numbers and Per Capita Distribution of Troops Serving in the U.S. Post-9/11 Wars in 2019, By State." Costs of War. Watson Institute of International and Public Affairs, Brown University, 2019. https://watson.brown.edu/costsofwar/files/cow/imce/costs/social/Troop%20Numbers%20By%20State_Costs%20of%20War_FINAL.pdf.

Scales, Robert. "Clausewitz and World War IV." *Military Psychology. 21,* suppl. 1 (2009): 23–35.

Scheidt, Kenneth W. "NGOs in the Operational Theater: What Commanders Need to Understand and How to Work Together," Research Project. Naval War College, Joint Military Operations Department, Newport, RI, 2005. https://apps.dtic.mil/sti/pdfs/ADA463870.pdf.

Schopp, Julien. "Guidelines for NGO Coordination with military Actors During Humanitarian Crisis." *Interaction.* July 13, 2018. https://www.interaction.org/blog/guidelines-for-ngo-coordination-with-military-actors-during-humanitarian-crises/.

Scribner, David R., Tracy St Benoit, Jason B. Tabeling, Riannon M. Hazell, Tony Thacker, Peter Brau, Michael Sizemore, Thomas Leitch, Brian Kiser, and Timothy Strong. "Understanding Civil Affairs Operations: A Qualitative Exploration of Self-Reported Civil Affairs Operational Experiences." ARL-TR-8534. Technical Report. US Army Research Laboratory, September, 2018. https://apps.dtic.mil/sti/pdfs/AD1061341.pdf.

Seferis, Louisa and Paul Harvey. "Accountability in Crises: Connecting Evidence from Humanitarian and Social Protection Approaches to Social Assistance." BASIC Research Working Paper 13. Brighton: Institute of Development Studies, 2022.

Seybolt, Taylor B. "The Myth of Neutrality." *Peace Review.* 8, no. 4 (1996): 521–27.

Seybolt, Taylor B. *Humanitarian Military Intervention: The Conditions for Success and Failure.* USA: Oxford University Press, 2007.

Shamir, Eitan, and Eyal Ben-Ari. "The Rise of Special Operations Forces: Generalized Specialization, Boundary Spanning and Military Autonomy." *Journal of Strategic Studies.* 41, no. 3 (2018): 335–71.

Shapiro, Jake and Pat Howell. "What are Small Wars?" *Irregular Warfare Podcast,* May 21, 2020. https://esoc.princeton.edu/publications/irregular-warfare-podcast-what-are-small-wars.

Shawcross, William. *The Quality of Mercy.* New York: Simon & Schuster, 1984.

Shilling, Adam. "Development Activities Locator and Assessment Method (DALAM)." CAA-2012049. Center for Army Analysis, BELVOIR VA, 2013. https://apps.dtic.mil/sti/pdfs/ADA589884.pdf.

Siegel, Adam B. "Civil-Military Marriage Counseling: Can this Union Be Saved?." *Special Warfare.* 15, no. 4 (2002): 28–34.

Simons, Anna. "Chapter 6: The Military Advisor as Warrior-King and Other "Going Native" Temptations." In *Anthropology and the United States Military: Coming of Age in the Twenty-first Century.* Eds., Pamela Frese and Margaret Harrell. New York: Palgrave Macmillan, 2003.

Singer, Peter W. "Corporate Warriors: The Rise of the Privatized Military Industry and Its Ramifications for International Security." *International Security.* 26, no. 3 (2002): 186–20.

Singer, Peter W. "Strange Brew: Private Military Contractors and Humanitarians." In *Disaster and the Politics of Intervention.* Ed., Andrew Lakoff. New York: Columbia University Press, 2010.

Sisk, Kurt. "House Divided: The Splitting of Active Duty Civil Affairs Forces." Master's Thesis. Naval Postgraduate School, Monterey, CA, 2009. https://apps.dtic.mil/sti/pdfs/ADA514382.pdf.

Slim, Hugo. "Is Humanitarianism Being Politicised? A Reply to David Rieff." In *The Dutch Red Cross Symposium on Ethics in Aid*. 2003. http://reliefweb.int/sites/reliefweb.int/files/resources/D660A0743B431902C1257225003842B3-HDC-Oct2003.pdf.

Slim, Hugo. "The Stretcher and the Drum: Civil-Military Relations in Peace Support Operations." *International Peacekeeping*. 3, no. 2 (1996): 123–40.

Smillie, Ian. *The Alms Bazaar: Altruism Under Fire; Non-Profit Organizations and International Development*. Ottawa: International Development Research Center, 1995.

Sphere. "Antonio Donini, Senior Researcher, Tufts University." *YouTube* video, 7:37. July 10, 2014. https://www.youtube.com/watch?v=GTidzB6ZrRE&t=2s.

Spirit of America Jobs. "Spirit of America Is Hiring." https://spiritofamerica.org/jobs (last accessed September 12, 2021).

Spirit of America. "2019 Annual Report for Spirit of America." https://issuu.com/spiritamerica/docs/spirit_of_america_annual_report_2019?fr=sYjEzZjE3NTM3NTI.

Spirit of America. "Board and Advisors." https://spiritofamerica.org/about/board-and-advisors. (last accessed September 12, 2021).

Statista. "U.S. military spending from 2000 to 2020." November 10, 2021. https://www.statista.com/statistics/272473/us-military-spending-from-2000-to-2012/ (last accessed March 3, 2022).

Stavridis, James, and Evelyn N. Farkas. "The 21st Century Force Multiplier: Public–Private Collaboration." *The Washington Quarterly*. 35, no. 2 (2012): 7–20.

Stephenson, Carolyn. "Nongovernmental Organizations." Beyond intractability Knowledge Base, January 2005. https://www.beyondintractability.org/essay/role_ngo.

Stewart, Patrick and Kaysie Brown. "The Pentagon and Global Development: Making Sense of the DoD Expanding Role." Working Paper Number 131, Center for Global Development, 2007. https://papers.ssrn.com/sol3/papers.cfm?abstract_id=1101526.

Stone, Nomi. "Imperial Mimesis: Enacting and Policing Empathy in US Military Training." *American Ethnologist*. 45, no. 4 (2018): 533–45.

Storeng, Katerini T., Jennifer Palmer, Judith Daire, and Maren O. Kloster. "Behind the Scenes: International NGOs' Influence on Reproductive Health Policy in Malawi and South Sudan." *Global Public Health*. 14, no. 4 (2019): 555–69.

Stortz, Sharon, K., Lisa M. Foglia, Andrew S. Thagard, Barton Staat, and Monica A. Lutgendorf, "Comparing Compensation of US Military Physicians and Civilian Physicians in Residency Training and Beyond." *Cureus* 13, no. 1 (2021).

Strange, Joseph L. and Richard Iron. "Center of Gravity - What Clausewitz Really Meant." *Joint Force Quarterly* 35, (Summer 2003): 20–27.

Suri, Jeremy. "History is Clear. America's Military is Way Too Big." *The New York Times*. August 30, 2021. https://www.nytimes.com/2021/08/30/opinion/american-military-afghanistan.html.

Suri, Jeremy. "History is Clear. America's Military is Way Too Big." *The New York Times*. August 30, 2021. https://www.nytimes.com/2021/08/30/opinion/american-military-afghanistan.html.

Tan, Michelle. "Report: General's Killer Fired 30 Rounds." *Army Times*. December 4, 2014. https://www.armytimes.com/news/pentagon-congress/2014/12/04/report-general-s-killer-fired-30-rounds/.

Taw, Jennifer Morrison. "Stability and Support Operations: History and Debates." *Studies in Conflict and Terrorism*. 33, no. 5 (2010): 387–407.

Team Rubicon Global. "Team Rubicon Global gives military veterans around the world the opportunity to continue to serve." https://teamrubiconusa.org/capabilities-services/. (last accessed December 3, 2021).

Thaler, David E., Michael J. McNerney, Beth Grill, Jefferson P. Marquis, and Amanda Kadlec. *From Patchwork to Framework: A Review of Title 10 Authorities for Security Cooperation*. Santa Monica, CA: RAND Corporation, 2016.

Thijssen, Peter. "From Mechanical to Organic Solidarity, and Back: With Honneth Beyond Durkeim." *European Journal of Social Theory* 15, no. 4 (2012): 454–70.

Tkach, Benjamin, and Joe Phillips. "UN Organizational and Financial Incentives to Employ Private Military and Security Companies in Peacekeeping Operations." *International Peacekeeping.* 27, no. 1 (2020): 102–23.

Tkach, Benjamin. "Private Military and Security Companies, Contract Structure, Market Competition, and Violence in Iraq." *Conflict Management and Peace Science.* 36, no. 3 (2019): 291–311.

Toennies, Ferdinand. *Community and Society.* East Lansing: Michigan State University Press, 1957.

Trent, John E. *The Need for Rethinking the United Nations.* London: Routledge, 2013.

Trevino, Alice, Jessica Greathouse, Jordan Siefkes, and James Ting. "Leveraging Our War-Fighting Capabilities through the Lens of Operational Contract Support." *Air & Space Power Journal.* 33, no 3, (2019): 4–14.

Turse, Nick, Sam Mednick and Amanda Sperber. "Exclusive: Inside the Secret World of US Commandos in Africa." *Pulitzer Center, Mail and Guardian.* August 11, 2020. https://pulitzercenter.org/stories/exclusive-inside-secret-world-us-commandos-africa.

Turse, Nick. "American Special Ops Forces Have Deployed to 70 Percent of the World's Countries in 2017: And we're only halfway through the year." *The Nation.* June 26, 2017. https://www.thenation.com/article/archive/american-special-ops-forces-have-deployed-to-70-percent-of-the-worlds-countries-in-2017/.

United Nations Development Programme. *Human Development Report, 1994.* Oxford: Oxford University Press, 1994.

United Nations Office for the Coordination of Humanitarian Affairs. *Civil-Military Guidelines Reference for Complex Emergencies.* Inter-Agency Standing Committee. New York: United Nations, 2008. https://reliefweb.int/sites/reliefweb.int/files/resources/E87ABE5C1E4B9D1485257405007643D9-Full_Report.pdf.

United Nations Peacekeeping. "Protection of Civilians Mandate." https://peacekeeping.un.org/en/protection-of-civilians-mandate. (last accessed May 5, 2022).

United Nations. "Sustainable Development Goals 2019." https://sustainabledevelopment.un.org/sdg16. (last accessed April 29, 2022).

United Nations. "International Convention against the Recruitment, Use, Financing and Training of Mercenaries." General Assembly Resolution 44/34. UN, New York, 4 December 1989. https://legal.un.org/avl/ha/icruftm/icruftm.html.

United States Air Force. *Irregular Warfare.* Air Force Doctrine Publication (AFDP) 3-2. Curtis E. LeMay Center for Doctrine and Development Education, 2019. https://www.doctrine.af.mil/Portals/61/documents/AFDP_3-2/3-2-AFDP-IRREGULAR-WARFARE.pdf.

United States Department of Defense Joint Chiefs of Staff. *Joint Doctrine for Military Operations Other Than War.* Joint Pub 3-07. Washington DC: Joint Chiefs of Staff, 1995. https://www.bits.de/NRANEU/others/jp-doctrine/jp3_07.pdf.

United States Department of State. *Stabilization Assistance Review - Framework for Maximizing the Effectiveness of U.S. Government Efforts to Stabilize Conflict Affected Areas.* Washington DC: US Department of State, 2018. https://www.state.gov/wp-content/uploads/2019/06/SAR-Final.pdf.

United States Department of the Army. *Multi-Service Techniques for Civil Affairs Support to Foreign Humanitarian Assistance.* ATP 3-57.20/MCRP 3-33.1C. Washington DC: Headquarters Department of the Army/United States Marine Corps, 2013. https://armypubs.army.mil/epubs/DR_pubs/DR_a/pdf/web/atp3_57x20.pdf.

United States Institute of Peace. *Guidelines for Relations Between U.S. Armed Forces and Non-Governmental Organizations in Hostile or Potentially Hostile Environments.* Washington DC: United States Institute of Peace, 2007. https://www.usip.org/publications/2007/07/guidelines-relations-between-us-armed-forces-and-nghos-hostile-or-potentially.

United States Marine Corps. "PMESII and ASCOPE Matrices Templates." https://www.trngcmd.marines.mil/Portals/207/Docs/wtbn/MCCMOS/Planning%20Templates%20Oct%202017.pdf?ver=2017-10-19-131249-187.

United States Marine Corps. *Small Wars Manual*. Department of the NAVY Headquarters United States Marine Corps. FMFRP 12-15. Washington DC: Department of the Navy, 1990.

UNSW Canberra. "Operating with the Military an NGO Perspective - Ms Beth Eggleston." *YouTube* video, 26:17. June 18, 2017. https://www.youtube.com/watch?v=xNY0riPKDZ8.

US Agency for International Development. "Project Monitor and Evaluation Plan." https://www.usaid.gov/project-starter/program-cycle/project-monitor-evaluation-plan.

US Agency for International Development. *Fiscal year (FY) 2019 Development and Humanitarian Assistance Budget*. Washington DC: US Agency for International Development, 2019. https://www.usaid.gov/sites/default/files/documents/1869/USAID_FY2019_Budget_Fact-sheet.pdf.

US Agency for International Development. *Joint Humanitarian Operations Course (JHOC), Civil-Military Roles in International Disaster Response*. Washington DC: Office of US Foreign Disaster Response, 2015. https://pdf.usaid.gov/pdf_docs/pbaaf965.pdf.

US Congress. House Armed Services: Committee, Subcommittee on Emerging Threats and Capabilities. *Statement of Joseph L. Votel, U.S Army Commander, United States Special Operations Command*. 114th Congress, March 18, 2015. https://docs.house.gov/meetings/AS/AS26/20150318/103157/HMTG-114-AS26-Wstate-VotelUSAJ-20150318.pdf.

US Department of Defense Joint Chiefs of Staff. *Operational contract support*. Joint Publication 4-10. Washington DC: Department of Defense Joint Chiefs, 2019. https://www.jcs.mil/Portals/36/Documents/Doctrine/pubs/jp4_10.pdf.

US Department of Defense Joint Chiefs of Staff. *Peace Operations*. Joint Publication 3-07.3. Washington DC: Joint Chiefs of Staff, 2018. https://publicintelligence.net/jcs-peace-operations/.

US Department of Defense. *Assessment, Monitoring, and Evaluation Policy for the Security Cooperation Enterprise*. DOD INSTRUCTION 5132.14. Washington DC: Office of the Undersecretary of Defense for Policy, 2017. https://open.defense.gov/portals/23/documents/foreignasst/dodi_513214_on_am&e.pdf.

US Department of Defense. *Civil-Miliary Operations*. Joint Publication 3-57. Washington DC: 2018. https://www.jcs.mil/Portals/36/Documents/Doctrine/pubs/jp3_57.pdf.

US Department of State. "Non-Governmental Organizations (NGOs) in the United States." Fact Sheet. Bureau of Democracy, Human Rights and Labor, January 20, 2021. https://www.state.gov/non-governmental-organizations-ngos-in-the-united-states/.

US Department of State. *Department of State, Foreign Operations and Related Programs*. Fiscal Year 2022 Congressional Budget Justification. Washington DC: Department of State, 2022. https://www.usaid.gov/sites/default/files/documents/FY_2022_State_USAID_Congressional_Budget_Justification.pdf.

US Department of State. *United States Strategy to Prevent Conflict and Promote Stability*. Washington DC: Bureau of Conflict and Stabilization Operations, US Department of State, 2022. https://www.state.gov/united-states-strategy-to-prevent-conflict-and-promote-stability/#introduction.

US Department of the Army. *Civil Affairs General Concepts*. GTA 41-01-001. Washington DC: Department of the Army Headquarters, 2019. https://armypubs.army.mil/epubs/DR_pubs/DR_a/pdf/web/ARN16411_GTA%2041-01-001_FINAL.pdf.

US Department of the Army. *Civil Affairs Operations*. Army FM 41 – 10. Washington DC: Department of the Army Headquarters, 2000. https://www.globalsecurity.org/military/library/policy/army/fm/41-10_2000/appg.htm.

US Department of the Army. *Civil Affairs Planning*. ATP 3-57.60. Washington DC: Department of the Army Headquarters, 2014. https://irp.fas.org/doddir/army/atp3-57-60.pdf.

US Department of the Army. *Civil Affairs Tactics, Techniques, and Procedures*. FM 3-05.401/MCRP 3-33.1A. Washington DC: Department of the Army Headquarters, 2003. https://irp.fas.org/doddir/army/fm3-05-401.pdf.

US Embassy Sofia. "Renovation of Yan Bibiyan Kindergarten in Haskovo." 27 October, 2020. https://bg.usembassy.gov/bg/renovation-of-yan-bibiyan-kindergarten-in-haskovo-bg/.

US Government Accountability Office. *Humanitarian and Development Assistance: Project Evaluations and Better Information Sharing Needed to Manage the Military's Efforts.* GAO-12-359. Washington DC: 2012. https://www.gao.gov/assets/gao-12-359.pdf.

US Government Accountability Office. Special Operations Forces: Opportunities Exist to Improve Transparency of Funding and Assess Potential to Lessen Some Deployments. GAO-15-571 Washington, DC, 2015. http://www.gao.gov/products/GAO-15-571.

US Library of Congress. Congressional Research Service. Defense Primer: Special Operations Forces, by Barbara Salazar Torreon and Andrew Feickert. IF10545. 2024. https://crsreports.congress.gov/product/pdf/IF/IF10545

US Library of Congress. Congressional Research Service. U.S. Special Operations Forces (SOF): Background for Congress. Andrew Feickert. RS21048. 2024. https://crsreports.congress.gov/product/pdf/RS/RS21048

US Library of Congress. Congressional Research Service. *International Crises and Disasters: U.S. Humanitarian Assistance Response Mechanisms,* by Rhoda Margesson. RL33769. 2020. https://crsreports.congress.gov/product/pdf/RL/RL33769.

US Library of Congress. Congressional Research Service. *Japan 2011 Earthquake: U.S. Department of Defense (DOD) Response,* by Andrew Feickert and Emma Chanlett-Avery. R41690. 2011. https://sgp.fas.org/crs/row/R41690.pdf.

Valentino, Benjamin, Paul Huth, and Sarah Croco. "Covenants without the Sword: International Law and the Protection of Civilians in Times of War." *World Politics.* 58, no. 3 (2006): 339–77.

Vergano, Dan. "Mudslide Buries More Than 350 in Afghan Village." *National Geographic.* May 3, 2014. https://www.nationalgeographic.com/science/article/140502-afghanistan-landslide-deaths-united-nations.

Verweijen, Judith. "The Ambiguity of Militarization: The Complex Interaction between the Congolese Armed Forces and Civilians in the Kivu provinces, Eastern DR Congo." Doctoral Dissertation. Utrecht University, 2015. https://dspace.library.uu.nl/handle/1874/325581.

Vogelsang, Robert. "Special Operations Forces Veterinary Personnel." *US Army Medical Department Journal* (2007): 69–71.

Votel, Joseph L., Charles T. Cleveland, Charles T. Connett, and Will Irwin. "Unconventional Warfare in the Gray Zone." *Joint Forces Quarterly.* 80, no. 1 (2016): 101–9.

Walker, Peter. "Conclusion: the Shape of Things to Come – an Essay on Humanitarian Challenges." In *Dilemmas, Challenges, and Ethics of Humanitarian Action: Reflections on Médecins Sans Frontières' Perception Project.* Ed., Caroline Abu-Sada. McGill-Queen's University Press, 2012.

West, Simon, Edward Canfor-Dumas, Ronald Bell, and David Combs. "Understand to Prevent: The Military Contribution to the Prevention of Violent Conflict." A Multinational Capability Development Campaign project report for the UK Ministry of Defense: 2014. https://assets.publishing.service.gov.uk/government/uploads/system/uploads/attachment_data/file/518617/20150430-U2P_Main_Web_B5.pdf.

Whalley, Lucy A., Judith M. Vendrzyk, and George W. Calfas. *Improving US Army Civil Affairs Assessment: A Consideration of Social Power, Construction Engineering Research Laboratory.* Champaign, IL: The U.S. Army Engineer Research and Development Center (ERDC), 2017.

White Paper. *Colin Powell School for Civic and Global Leadership.* New York: The City College of New York, 2015

Wilson, David and Gareth E Conway. "The Tactical Conflict Assessment Framework: A Short-Lived Panacea." *The RUSI Journal.* 154, no. 1, (2009): 10–15.

Wilson, James Q. *Bureaucracy: What Government Agencies Do And Why They Do It.* New York: Basic Books, 1991.

Winslow, Donna. "Misplaced Loyalties: The Role of Military Culture in the Breakdown of Discipline in Peace Operations." *Canadian Review of Sociology.* 35, no. 3 (1998): 345–367.

Winslow, Donna. "Strange Bedfellows: NGOS and the Military in Humanitarian Crises." *International Journal of Peace Studies.* 7, no. 2 (2002): 35–55.

World Association of Non-Governmental Organizations (WANGO). "Worldwide NGO Directory." https://www.wango.org/resources.aspx?section=ngodir (last accessed May 25, 2022).

World Bank. "FY22 List of Fragile and Conflict-affected Situations." https://thedocs.worldbank .org/en/doc/bb52765f38156924d682486726f422d4-0090082021/original/FCSList-FY22.pdf_(last accessed May 1, 2022).

World Bank. *World Development Report, 2011: Conflict, Security, and Development*. Washington DC: The World Bank, 2011.

World Health Organization. "Gender and Health Workforce Statistics." *Spotlight on Statistics*. Issue 2, February 2008. https://www.who.int/hrh/statistics/spotlight_2.pdf.

Yair Ansbacher, and Ron Schleifer. "The Three Ages of Modern Western Special Operations Forces." *Comparative Strategy*. 41, no. 1 (2022): 32–45.

Yeboah, Sampson Addo. "Solving Local Problems or Looking Good: An Ethnography of the Field Practices of Foreign Sponsored NGOs in Rural African Communities." *The European Journal of Development Research* (2021): 1–17.

Index

Note: Page numbers in *italics* refer to figures and tables. Page numbers followed by "n" refer to notes

About the Author

Dr. Stanislava P. Mladenova is a Global Fellow at Brown University's Center for Human Rights and Humanitarian Studies. Her work has brought her to Africa, Central and South Asia, South America, and the Balkans. She has held positions at various institutions, including the United States Institute of Peace, and has worked in West Africa to establish a dialogue between security actors and local communities. As a Political Advisor for NATO in Afghanistan, she helped shape policy on economic issues, governance, corruption, disaster management, humanitarian assistance, and preventing the recruitment of child soldiers. Her research at the Department of War Studies at King's College London focused on the functional relationship between military and civilian entities in settings affected by low-intensity conflict and state fragility. Stanislava is a former fellow of the Irregular Warfare Initiative at West Point.

(Photo by McLaughlin Photography)

206